Praise for
Grace Without God

"What an important book. I inhaled every word. Every person struggling to live a meaningful life will find wisdom and sustenance in *Grace Without God*."

—Mary Johnson, author of *An Unquenchable Thirst*

"Whether you are atheist, spiritual-but-not-religious, an occasional meditator, or a confused seeker, *Grace Without God* will help answer life's big questions."

—Laura Fraser, bestselling author of *An Italian Affair*

"With insight and sensitivity, Ozment presents a compelling, informative, and inspirational account of emergent secular culture. Highly recommended for those who no longer believe or congregate, but yearn to live a meaningful life all the same."

—Phil Zuckerman, author of *Living the Secular Life*

"*Grace Without God* fundamentally changed the way I will raise my children." —Steven D. Levitt, bestselling coauthor of *Freakonomics*

"In her deeply personal quest, Ozment has created an important book for our time." —Ethan Watters, author of *Crazy Like Us*

"Profound, moving, and uplifting, *Grace Without God* is destined to become a classic in the genre."

—Julien Musolino, author of *The Soul Fallacy*

"A deep, satisfying read."

—Julia Scheeres, bestselling author of *Jesus Land*

"There's nothing like putting yourself in the hands of a writer who rewards that decision on every page. Katherine Ozment is such a writer, and *Grace Without God* is just that good."

—Dale McGowan, author of *Parenting Beyond Belief*

"It's not a spoiler to say that Katherine Ozment goes looking for grace only to discover she's had it all along. I felt proud to belong to her tribe—human and godless both."

—Catherine Newman, author of *Catastrophic Happiness*

"*Grace Without God* is a pilgrimage. Katherine Ozment is one of millions who have left traditional religion only to find that not only is something missing in their lives, but also that they long to give their children the meaning, sense of belonging, and spiritual depth of religion. In *Grace Without God,* we are invited to travel with her as she searches religion, philosophy, and social science for tools to construct meaning in our time.

—Peter Morales, President, Unitarian Universalist Association

"This well-crafted, accessible exploration of a pressing topic, full of hard questions and astute observations, can serve as a springboard for discussion by parents—and others—who wonder whether people 'need God to be good.'" —*Publishers Weekly,* starred review

"Ozment offers her own version of do-it-yourself religion, encouraging everyone to wonder, to seek knowledge, and to connect to a larger purpose. *Grace Without God* is thoughtful and insightful."

—June Sawyers, *Booklist*

"An informative and relatable discussion on the changing landscape of religion, society, and identity." —*Library Journal*

"An astute journalist, Ozment deftly explores whether meaningful ritual can offer an adequate substitute for organized religion. Her candor, open-mindedness, and reflection provide solace to the reader struggling with similar issues in their own lives, respectfully honoring the ghost of religion rather than writing it off." —*Humanist*

GRACE *Without* GOD

GRACE
Without
GOD

THE SEARCH FOR MEANING, PURPOSE, AND BELONGING IN A SECULAR AGE

KATHERINE OZMENT

Nancy – may your path be filled with grace! Warmly – Kat Ozment

HARPER PERENNIAL

NEW YORK • LONDON • TORONTO • SYDNEY • NEW DELHI • AUCKLAND

A hardcover of this book was published in 2016 by HarperCollins Publishers.

The names of some of the individuals featured throughout this book have been changed to protect their privacy, and the chronology of a few events has been changed for the sake of narrative flow.

HarperCollins books may be purchased for educational, business, or sales promotional use. For information, please e-mail the Special Markets Department at SPsales@harpercollins.com.

FIRST HARPER PERENNIAL EDITION PUBLISHED IN 2017.

Designed by Bonni Leon-Berman

The Library of Congress has catalogued the hardcover edition as follows:

Names: Ozment, Katherine, author.
Title: Grace Without God : the search for meaning, purpose, and belonging in a secular age / Katherine Ozment, Harper Wave.
Description: FIRST EDITION. | New York, NY : HarperCollins Publishers, 2016. | Includes bibliographical references and index.
Identifiers: LCCN 2016004086 (print) | LCCN 2016012166 (ebook) | ISBN 9780062305114 (hardcover) | ISBN 9780062305152 (eBook)
Subjects: LCSH: Religion. | United States--Religion. | Spiritual biography. | Spirituality. | Spiritual life.
Classification: LCC BL48 .O96 2016 (print) | LCC BL48 (ebook) | DDC 200.973—dc23
LC record available at http://lccn.loc.gov/2016004086

ISBN 978-0-06230513-8 (pbk.)

17 18 19 20 21 OV/LSC 10 9 8 7 6 5 4 3 2 1

For Michael,

who opened the door.

And William,

Jessica, and Anne,

who lit the way.

IN THE LIBRARY

There's a book called
"A Dictionary of Angels."
No one has opened it in fifty years,
I know, because when I did,
The covers creaked, the pages
Crumbled. There I discovered

The angels were once as plentiful
As species of flies.
The sky at dusk
Used to be thick with them.
You had to wave both arms
Just to keep them away.

Now the sun is shining
Through the tall windows.
The library is a quiet place.
Angels and gods huddled
In dark unopened books.
The great secret lies
On some shelf Miss Jones
Passes every day on her rounds.

She's very tall, so she keeps
Her head tipped as if listening.
The books are whispering.
I hear nothing, but she does.

—Charles Simic, *The Book of Gods and Devils*

CONTENTS

GRACE *Without* GOD

PROLOGUE

"We're Nothing"

One night four years ago, I heard a strange noise outside the window of our brick row-house near Boston. We lived across the street from a Greek Orthodox church, a squat stone structure with a domed roof topped by a cross. Just as I was about to go to bed, I heard the sound of muffled patting, like hundreds of shuffling feet, growing closer.

"Mama!" my son, who was nine, called. "Come look."

I joined him by the window, and together we watched members of the church—elderly, middle-aged, twenty-somethings, teenagers, and children—walk en masse up the street, which was closed off to accommodate their passage. They walked silently, each holding a candle, led by a priest in a long robe. Just behind the priest, several men carried an ornate bier covered in fresh flowers and bearing a small doll wrapped in white cloth. As my son and I watched, the procession stopped in front of our house. Little boys pulled at too-tight ties, girls swayed in long skirts, and husbands and wives pressed close to each other in the cool night air.

"What are they doing?" my son asked.

"It's a ritual," I said, thinking it must be their Good Friday.

"Why don't we do that?" he asked.

"Because we're not Greek Orthodox," I said.

"Then what are we?"

I thought of the candy and trinkets I bought for him and his two younger sisters for Easter every year, the overfilled baskets I placed in their rooms as they slept, and the indoor Easter-egg hunts I put together. The only things my children knew about the most sacred holiday in Christianity were colorful plastic eggs and foil-wrapped chocolate bunnies. Even that doll wrapped in white cloth outside—the symbolic baby Jesus—was a mystery to them.

The priest, in his dark robe and traditional flat-topped hat, read a passage aloud in Greek, and the crowd sang a verse in response. After several more exchanges, he turned to the church and walked toward it. The congregants followed him down the street and into the building, like a river narrowing through a lock.

Turning from the window after the street had emptied, my son persisted: "So, what are we?"

I looked at him and felt my face flush. I wrestled with how to answer him, but then blurted out words I'd soon regret.

"We're nothing," I said.

I knew right away that this was a terrible thing to say. And I sensed that I had let him down, not just in that moment but also in a larger, more important way. My inability to find the words to describe us reflected the fact that my husband and I had never created a cohesive narrative for the life we had chosen to live—a narrative that would tie us to a like-minded group via a clear moral framework, meaningful rituals, and a deep sense of belonging. The moment at the window was the culmination of so many other small moments, times when I felt at a loss to describe who we were, what we believed, and where we fit. My son had asked the simplest of questions—*What are we?*—and I couldn't answer him. Why was that?

I WAS RAISED Presbyterian but drifted from religion before my son was born. I'd grown up reciting the Lord's Prayer and singing hymns on Sundays. I'd snacked on cookies and apple juice in church basements after services, attended Sunday school, and read long passages of the Bible for religion classes in high school. Though I didn't recall all the details of those religious stories, I knew on a visceral level, and know even still, the poetry of a biblical verse, the moral core of a religious parable, and the heft of a minister's sermon. Christianity was such an ever-present and unremarkable part of my upbringing that it was like water I didn't know I was swimming in. Yet I no longer practiced religion, and it never came up in my daily life. At some point, I quit calling myself a Christian altogether. What I didn't know was when or why I stopped.

My husband, Michael, had been raised Jewish, but he'd also left religion. Like me, he couldn't pinpoint when or how it happened, though he suspects it was the first weekend after his bar mitzvah, when, freed from the bonds of Saturday morning Hebrew school, he chose to play basketball with his friends instead of going to temple.

We were bringing up our three children without any connection to the kinds of spiritual traditions, beliefs, and community with which we had been raised. But we had let our religious practices and beliefs fall away without ever considering the costs. Did our children need the kind of spiritual ritual and tribe my son and I had observed outside our window? What were the ramifications of our choice to raise them without any faith and accompanying traditions? It seemed irresponsible of us not to know.

....

AFTER I ANSWERED, my son didn't verbally respond to what I'd said. He just cocked his head slightly to one side, like a small, curious bird. Before I could ask what he thought, he told me goodnight and walked upstairs to bed. But I couldn't let go so easily. I stood at the window a bit longer, watching the policemen remove the wooden barricades that had been used to close off the street. I decided then and there that I would seek a better answer for my son, for myself, and for my family.

Lowering the blind, I turned away from the scene outside and surveyed the room before me. Strewn in all directions were art projects, sports balls, books, backpacks, and newspapers. Somewhere in that cluttered mishmash—somewhere in the very lives that we were living—were values, rituals, and sources of meaning worth naming. I knew that we were *something*, but what? And that is how this book began—as one woman's search for a better answer to her son's big question.

As soon as I started researching this question, I learned that my family wasn't the only one struggling to define itself. All over the country a similar story of leaving organized religion was unfolding. People from every faith, racial background, ethnic group, education level, and income bracket were turning away from their religious traditions. Never before had so many Americans stopped aligning themselves with their parents' and grandparents' religious communities, practices, and beliefs so quickly. It turned out that my son's question was one that researchers, philosophers, and secular families across the United States and around the world were all struggling to answer.

The first step in my several years of research for this book was to turn back to religion. I sang sacred harp music with a room full of divinity school students, sat in stillness for Taizé night song in a church tucked in the hills of Northern California, attended CCD class in a Catholic school cafeteria, and took part in a walking meditation at a Buddhist temple in San Diego. I interviewed religious leaders and followers to find out what religion meant to them and how religious beliefs and practices enhanced their lives.

Then I delved into American nonreligious life to see how people were meeting the needs once satisfied by the one-stop shop of religion. I discovered that secular and humanist groups—aka "godless congregations"—are proliferating, binding the nonreligious together in values-based community. And I researched well-established "religious lite" options, such as Unitarian Universalism, Humanistic Judaism, and Ethical Culture. How were these congregations different from the newer, so-called atheist churches? Was a more eclectic religious experience better than no religion at all?

As I traveled to religious and nonreligious gatherings, interviewed academics, community leaders, and parents, and observed my family and others, I was trying to answer a single question—the one I think my son was really asking: Could my family and I find valid alternatives to all the good that religion gives? My journey took me to a nature-based coming-of-age program that stands in for the traditional bar mitzvah or confirmation; to mountaintops, where my children and I felt, if not the presence of God, at least a powerful sense of wonder; and to a secular Buddhist retreat in New Mexico where spirituality means sitting still and breathing.

Everywhere I went, I was on the lookout for scams and charlatans. With a marketplace increasingly geared toward making money from individual spiritual angst, the offerings are vast and unregulated. I wanted to know where the authentic experiences—and the good people—lay. Time and again, I met people like myself, who'd been raised with religion and long since walked away. I found in many of them the deep kindness, strong values, and commitment to charity so often attributed to the best of the religious. And I felt something I never thought I would—that I was part of an entity larger than myself, a swelling secular movement searching for its path.

I don't pretend to be a religious scholar. I am, rather, a curious seeker who took a deep dive into a huge and fascinating topic and came out changed. While it could take lifetimes to understand the history of religion and the role it plays in the world, it seems that there are several main areas in which religion has served human needs: identity and belonging, rituals, shared stories, moral authority, and belief in God and the afterlife. I address all of these themes in this book. Because I am most familiar with mainstream Judeo-Christian culture, it is from that vantage point that I organized and pursued my quest. I hope that even for those who come from different backgrounds, there is something of value in reading about the journey of a fellow traveler.

This book is not a theological treatise, a historical text, or a defense of atheism, agnosticism, or secular humanism. It is not a handbook for how to live. It is, at heart, a letter to my children and every future generation of Americans trying to understand their place in the world. It tells the story of a crucial turning point, when the ancient frameworks that had long grounded us started to give way—and we sought to create something new in their place. After a lifetime of pondering these questions, and three years of interviewing and crisscrossing the country, I didn't find a single, easy answer to my son's question. Instead, I found many communities that heartened me, met many people who inspired me, and learned that we are all seeking meaning in our own ways.

It's not always comfortable to ask hard questions. This journey has taken my family and me to some unexpected places. It is in those unexpected places where the true search for meaning goes on. I hope you'll come along with me, to find it for yourself.

LOSING IT

CHAPTER 1

Losing My Religion

It is only when we forget all our learning
that we begin to know.

—Henry David Thoreau, Journal, 4 October 1859

When my grandfather Edgar died at the age of fifty-two after a brief treatment for leukemia, my grandmother spent a long night driving the 375 miles home to Arkansas from the hospital in Temple, Texas, with her eldest son. She was known to everyone—including her grandchildren—as "Susie," and she was the most religious person I ever knew. Susie had deep brown eyes and a pouf of white hair that circled her high, wide forehead like a cloud. She was smart and funny and independent, a columnist for the town paper, a writer of short stories and poetry, and the first woman to run for public office in Arkansas, where she lived her entire life. But it was her devout faith that most defined her. She played piano and served as an elder in the First Presbyterian Church in downtown Camden, Arkansas, a city of eleven thousand not far from the Texas border. She said grace before meals and read the Bible before bed. For a time she even worked as a missionary, traveling to British Guiana with her Bible, her sketchbook, and her straw hat. She and Edgar raised their four children to attend church every Sunday, and then some.

It was past midnight when she crossed the Arkansas border, and she drove the final stretch home with dread. Her teenage children would be sleeping in the quiet house, and she felt a growing unease about reentering her darkened home without Edgar. As she turned her Chevrolet onto her tree-lined street, she noticed something strange. All the windows of her house were lit and there were people standing out in the yard and on the street. She thought she was imagining them, but, pulling up to the house, she saw scores of people she knew—from church and town—standing outside in the middle of the night as if attending a Sunday church potluck. Up the front steps and winding through the rooms of her house, people were gathered to welcome her and ease her grief. I can only imagine the feeling of comfort she had when she saw them all. Later, she said of the experience: "It was the moment I knew what it meant to be a survivor."

In dark moments, I sometimes worry about what would happen to my children and me if we were in a similar situation. What belief system would ground us? What spiritual guide would give us answers? Who would come to comfort us, and how long would they stay? At the outset of my questioning, I wanted to know when my family began to lose its ties to religion. How, in the space of two generations, did we go from my grandmother's experience of religious identity and support to my standing alone at a window telling my son we were "nothing"?

....

MY MOTHER GREW up going to Sunday school and hosting Bible study one night a week. She even attended the conservative Christian Bob Jones University for a year before transferring to the University of Arkansas. My father, also from Arkansas, was raised Methodist; he hadn't spent as much time in church growing up as my mother had, but he understood religion's importance to our collective history and attended divinity school after college.

By the time I came around in the late 1960s, however, my parents' ties to religion had loosened. They'd left Arkansas, and my father had completed divinity school to become a religious historian. Months after I was born, he took his first job, as an assistant professor at Yale, where he started the career that would make him an expert on Martin Luther and the Protestant Reformation. (He once told me I was named after Martin Luther's wife, Katherine von Bora, a Catholic nun who is said to have escaped her convent in a fish barrel so she could marry Luther.)

My parents would take my two brothers and me to church every now and then, usually on Christmas and Easter, but the counterculture had taken hold, and attendance at mainline Protestant churches by families like mine was starting to dwindle. At home I sometimes peeked at the colored drawings of Jesus, Noah, or Moses in the children's Bible on the shelf in our front hallway. (Susie had probably given it to us.) But during my early childhood, no one read those Bible stories to us. We didn't attend church every Sunday or say a blessing before meals. Still, I had a vague sense that there was someone called God in a place called heaven and that he was watching us. One night, when I confessed to my brother Matt, seven years older than me, that I was scared of the dark, he told me to place my hands together, squeeze my eyes closed, and say, "Now I lay me down to sleep, pray my Lord my soul to keep. If I should die before I wake, pray my Lord my soul to take." For years, I would say the prayer each night, imagining someone or something—I couldn't quite picture what—watching over us.

Across the street, I witnessed a more rigorous practice of religion as my Italian-Catholic friends and their families piled into their station wagons every Sunday morning and drove up the steep, rough hill we dubbed "Bumpety" to attend Mass. They would return for a few hours, then disappear again, this time to their grandparents' houses for Sunday dinner: spaghetti, meatballs, and homemade sauce that had simmered all day on the stove. I knew this because sometimes they would invite me to come with them, and I would get a glimpse of what a big extended *famiglia* looked like.

On Wednesdays after school these same friends attended CCD, the Confraternity of Christian Doctrine classes meant to instill Catholic teachings and beliefs, and our neighborhood streets would empty of the shouts and laughter of kids playing kickball or four square or tag. I would sit inside, watching *General Hospital* or reading *The Chronicles of Narnia*. Even then I had the sense that religion bonded those families together more tightly than our family was bonded. It organized and gave meaning to their Sundays, Wednesdays, and possibly even their entire lives. I envied my friends their clear identity—it seemed like they were *something*, and religion was a crucial part of it. My family's identity seemed to be forming around the lack of that something.

MY CATHOLIC FRIENDS and their families weren't the only devout practitioners of religion I knew. Every summer, after several scorching days in the car, we would reach Camden to visit our religious aunts, uncles, and cousins—and of course Susie. About two hours southwest of Little Rock on Rural Route 1, Susie's oversized mailbox would heave into view. We'd drive up her long, circular driveway, paved with smooth, butterscotch-colored stones that crunched under our tires, and exit the hot car into the slightly sour smelling air that blew in from the paper mill across town.

Susie was always waiting just inside the screen door of her porch, wearing a patterned polyester housedress. My brothers and I would bound through the door with our Yankee accents and shaggy hair, racing past the fresh-cut roses in their porcelain vases to jump on the canopy bed and sneak slim green bottles of Coca-Cola from the kitchen pantry. Visiting Susie was a plunge into southern culture. We ate fried food. We spent hot afternoons in rocking chairs on the wide front porch watching green lizards dart over railings and 18-wheelers speed toward Texas along the highway at the bottom of the wide, sloping front yard. We tramped through woods careful to avoid rattlesnakes and played Marco Polo in our cousins' pool.

We also prayed more than we ever did back home. For my brothers and me, going to Arkansas was a plunge into an exotic religious zone. Above the fireplace in Susie's living room was an oil painting of Mary and the baby Jesus that was so realistic, and so compelling, that when I was young I thought it was my mother and oldest brother. Before every meal—even breakfast—we would hold hands and listen as Susie thanked our Heavenly Father for the food we were about to eat. Sometimes she would ask him to help the struggling people she knew, each of whom she listed by name. I remember the firm grip of her fingers pressing into mine as she said the blessing. Six or seven years old, I would close my eyes and try to envision the God Susie talked about so much, but I wasn't sure what I was supposed to see. Was God an old man up in the clouds, or that young, longhaired guy in the robe and sandals on the cover of the children's Bible we didn't read very often back home? If God was a "he," why couldn't we see or hear him? Usually I gave up just as Susie said "Amen" and we stabbed our forks into steaming plates of fried eggs, bacon, and grits.

On one visit to Arkansas, Susie asked me what my favorite Bible stories were. I started to answer her but realized I didn't know any.

She pressed her lips together, disappointed. How could I know so little?

Even then I felt at a distance from "real" religion. I associated faith in God, church, and prayer with the well-kept homes and polished manners of my southern cousins, who lived just down the hill from Susie, or with my Catholic friends who were always driving off to Mass, Sunday dinners, and CCD classes. There seemed a togetherness about the religious families I knew, a sense of unity. My brothers and I were different. We were as wild as the brambles between Susie's house and our cousins' swimming pool. There was a reckless danger in the way we lived, along with a sweet freedom.

WHEN I WAS eight years old, my parents called my brothers and me into the living room for an unprecedented "family meeting" to announce that they were separating. I ran to my room, buried my head in my pillow, and cried. It was 1976, and though our parents were the first in our neighborhood to divorce, we were at the leading edge of a national trend that would remake the American family. We went from being a single unit coalescing under one roof to a collection of disjointed pieces flung in different directions. The result was a custody agreement that stipulated my shuttling between two homes, taking a twenty-minute car ride in my father's orange Subaru to New Haven and back each weekend. My brothers were teenagers, with parties and football games to attend on weekends, so more often than not they chose to stay home with our mother. But I learned to straddle the two worlds, and when it came to religion, they soon diverged.

My mother took a job as a secretary and started meditating after work each day, retreating to her basement office to burn incense and sit for twenty minutes during which we had to take the phone off the hook so it wouldn't ring and disturb her. Like many other Americans, she was experimenting with Eastern forms of spirituality, including transcendental meditation, yoga, and EST. She was more likely to spend Sunday mornings listening to James Taylor LPs on her headphones (which looked like two halves of a brown coconut), knotting her macramé wall hangings, or planting Johnny-jump-ups in her garden than packing us all off to church.

If we worshipped anything in our chaotic household it was our creativity. Instead of going to church, we spent our time creating the art projects that sprawled across our dining room table, tending the fat tomatoes and thick zucchini in our vegetable garden, or making soap from bacon fat, and candles from colored wax that we melted and laid in bright stripes across the bottom halves of milk cartons cut in two. Authority came not from a preacher or sacred text but from our own instincts. We kids were left to our own devices most days, which was great when it came to running through the woods out behind our house, but not as much fun when it came to making our own dinner.

My father's house was a different world. Soon after my parents' divorce, he married a woman he'd met at work. She was more religious than our family had ever been, and I started to attend services at the Episcopal Church on the New Haven Green with them on weekend visits. Though my voice warbled over the hymns, never hitting the right notes, the sweet songs of the boys' choir mesmerized me. I'd sit in the pew listening to the alternating roar and lull of the organ music and gazing at the colorful stained-glass windows depicting biblical stories. For communion, I'd kneel on the maroon velvet cushion at the front of the church as the minister swished toward me in his white robe, the heels of his shoes clicking on the hard floor and echoing up to the rafters. When he placed the wafer onto my outstretched palm, I pressed it to my tongue. I drank the wine, a symbol of the blood of Christ, God's sacrifice to humanity, and walked back to the pews. I still couldn't see the God we were all praying to, but I was calmed and comforted by the idea that we were not alone.

A FEW YEARS after my parents' divorce, my relationship to religion took another twist. My mother decided to move back to the South, and I went with her. My brothers were off to college by then, so it was just the two of us starting out in a new place: Little Rock, Arkansas. Seeking a fresh start, my mother signed us up to be members of a large, modern Presbyterian church just off the highway and enrolled me in an Episcopal school downtown where we wore uniforms and attended chapel every Friday morning. After those weekend jaunts to the Episcopal church in New Haven, my daily life was suddenly filled with religion.

In school one day, a new friend told me she was going on an overnight religious retreat and asked if I wanted to come along. That Friday after dinner, my mother dropped me off at Christ the King Church, where two dozen seventh- and eighth-graders spent the weekend watching movies with religious themes (including one about a woman with no arms whose faith sustained her), playing games, and breaking into groups to talk about the Bible. Though I felt like an outsider for having so much less knowledge about Christianity than the other kids, the retreat (the first of many I would attend) was structured in a way that my own home was not, and I liked that. We talked about values such as charity and selflessness—things my mother and I didn't discuss outright.

Once in high school, I started to see religion in a different light. I attended an all-girls Catholic school, where the sense of an "us"—indicating that there must be a "them"—became more apparent to me. Mass was held once a month in the gym and the nuns played guitar onstage as we sang contemporary Catholic liturgical songs. But when it came time to take communion, non-Catholics like me couldn't participate. Instead, we sat on the bleachers and watched the other girls take their turns. It was my first lesson in the way religious tribes, through their beliefs and rituals, exclude others.

During religion class, we were taught that premarital sex was a sin. Rumors flew when a girl in the junior class left the school abruptly, allegedly because she was pregnant. For all the camaraderie that came easily among my high school friends and me, I felt a background air of judgment and the ever-present threat of being shunned. Not being a member of the school's official tribe, I didn't feel I truly belonged.

I left Arkansas in the middle of my junior year, escaping the increasing tension between my mother and my brother Matt, who had flunked out of college and moved in with us. I moved north to live with my father, who by then was living in Massachusetts with my stepmother and their two daughters. On my first day at my new school, instead of asking me what church I belonged to, everyone wanted to know what sports I played. I sat with the school guidance counselor in her office to go over my transcript. She was trying to figure out how to transfer the credits from my Catholic high school. Her pen was making its way down the page when it stopped on "Religion 9A," "Religion 9B," and so on.

"Wow," she said, "that's a lot of religion."

Her eyebrows knit together for a moment as she stared at the page, unsure how to translate those classes into credits. Then they relaxed, and with a curt professionalism, she said, "We'll just call them 'History.' "

And just as easily as religion had appeared in my life, it vanished. Two years later, I went on to attend Harvard. There, during the first week of orientation, I stopped by a table draped with the banner of a young Christian group on campus and talked with the two women sitting behind it. I took their brochure and gave them my phone number, but when I returned to my dorm room, my roommates laughed off my interest. I started to think I was crazy for even considering it. Over the next few weeks, one of the women from the group left several messages about upcoming Christian youth group meetings on our answering machine, but I never called her back.

My vague belief in God remained but had no practice-based tether. I sometimes imagined the presence of an invisible guiding force to which I couldn't put a shape. But without religious rituals or community to reinforce it, even that fell away as I left college and started my first job. I stopped thinking about religion altogether. God was no longer part of the air that I breathed.

The man I would end up marrying had likewise drifted from his faith when I met him. Michael was finishing his PhD in economics, and I was an editor at *National Geographic*. He was Jewish by culture only. When we married, the only religious aspect of our wedding was our huppah, the open-walled canopy used in Jewish weddings as a symbol of the new couple welcoming friends and family into their lives. My mother consulted books on Judaica that she checked out from the public library and painstakingly assembled the huppah from scraps of fabric sent by each of our guests, piecing them together in the style of a southern crazy quilt and embroidering each seam with gold thread.

Our spiritual-but-not-religious ceremony, including readings and songs from First Corinthians, the Apache Nation, and the Talking Heads, may have seemed strange to some of our older guests (not to mention my Southern Baptist cousins), but it resembled the weddings of many of our friends: a mix of old and new that was an attempt to create a more authentic expression of what the couple held dear than a traditional religious wedding ceremony. We never thought about what we were leaving behind.

We figured that when we eventually had children we'd raise them in a colorful blend of religious pluralism—a little Zen Buddhism here, a visit to a Quaker meeting there, a smattering of secularized Christian and Jewish holidays throughout the year from which they would learn the basics of their heritage. When people asked if we were going to raise our kids Jewish or Christian, we'd tell them "both," or "neither," or "something." We just didn't know what that something would be.

But once our son was born, followed by our two daughters, we forgot our lofty intentions. We held no bris or baptisms. We neglected to sign up for Hebrew school or seek a friendly nondenominational parish. We skipped most religious rituals all together, unless you count tearing through holiday wrapping on Christmas morning as a sacred ceremony. Rather than blending into one seamless tapestry, like our beautiful crazy-quilt huppah, our different religious traditions seemed to cancel each other out.

Though many members of our families are religious, no one commented on our child-rearing practices. Michael's parents had passed away, and if my parents were upset when the invitation for a baptism never came, they didn't tell us. As long as we were raising kind, happy kids, who could complain? All the same, the loss of that religious structure and identity sometimes nagged at us. Michael and I worried we might one day regret not giving our children a religious moral grounding, timeworn rituals, and a community to catch them when they fell. That worry crystallized when my son asked me what we were. I felt a new urgency to find an answer.

Were our children Christians or Jews or something else altogether? We—and they—hardly knew. Before our younger daughter was born, our son and older daughter had been in a church only once, for a relative's wedding. Ensconced in the back pews of a New England Congregational church on the town green, complete with white steeple, they grew so irritable—the pews were too hard, the service was boring, the church was too hot—that Michael and I spent the hour glaring at them, swiping hymnals from their sweaty palms so they wouldn't tear the pages, and silently urging them to sit still with sharp, behind-the-pew hand gestures.

They were uncomfortable, certainly. But their physical discomfort stemmed from another kind of unease. They had no idea what to do with themselves in church because they had no idea, in any larger sense, of what it meant to be there. The symbolic space of the church rang hollow for them. That's because church is not just a physical space; it is also a metaphor for spiritual ideas and beliefs that they had never learned.

Watching our children whining and writhing in pain in the pews, I realized they were acting like outraged consumers. Religion offers gratification in exchange for humility, worship, and contemplation, and they were accustomed to gratification on demand. I didn't necessarily want our children to be religious, but I wanted them to have the sense of bowing before something greater than themselves. I just didn't know what that something was—or how to find it. But I would soon learn that I was not the only one searching for an answer.

CHAPTER 2

How Did We Get Here?

Men and women of many villages and regions were thrown together even in the same "ghetto," and before long the new conditions of American life confronted the immigrant with . . . the problem of self-identification and self-location, the problem expressed in the question, "What am I?"

—*Will Herberg, PROTESTANT, CATHOLIC, JEW: AN ESSAY IN AMERICAN RELIGIOUS SOCIOLOGY*

Michael and I were hardly alone in no longer being religious. Among the people we knew, it almost felt like a characteristic of our generation, and I often met people in a similar position to ours. On one blustery evening in November 2012, Michael and I hosted an election-night party. Our house was filled with neighbors, friends, and coworkers, and our dining room table was covered with "foods from the swing states," including Florida oranges and homemade chocolate-and-peanut-butter buckeyes to represent Ohio. As the votes were tallied across a national map on our television screen, the topic of the Red State/Blue State divide came up, and I mentioned casually to a friend that Michael and I were typical Blue Staters in that we'd dropped the whole religion ball, not just for ourselves but also for our kids. I expected my friend to laugh off my concern. We were in Massachusetts, after all.

Instead, she perked right up, saying, "I worry about the same thing." She was a lapsed Catholic from Colombia, and she pulled her husband, a gangly midwestern ex-Lutheran, over to discuss how unsettled they were about raising their two young sons without a trace of religion. Even so, as nonbelievers from two different religious heritages, they couldn't get themselves to go to church. Soon, a small circle gathered around us, and, for the rest of the night, adults of all religious backgrounds spilled their stories of angst and confusion about leaving their ancestral traditions behind.

On the one hand, we agreed, religion offered so much: belonging, community, history, ritual, and prepackaged beliefs that gave meaning and purpose to life. On the other, too often the staunchly religious promulgated outmoded ideas about gender and sexual orientation, encouraged an "us-against-them" tribalism, and held congregants to stringent rites and dogma. Church leaders were known to do immoral things, worshippers didn't always embody the good that they professed, and religion had become highly politicized—and, in the case of 9/11, weaponized. Because of all this, none of the people I spoke with that night, all of whom had been raised with at least some religion, were practicing any as adults. Meanwhile, our kids were upstairs tearing apart the playroom, as oblivious to our concerns as they were to the Torah and the Ten Commandments.

Was my circle of friends unusual, or part of a larger trend of losing the religion that had been passed down through previous generations? One morning, as I was reading the newspaper, a headline grabbed my attention. That fall of 2012, researchers from the Pew Foundation published startling statistics: Approximately one-fifth of Americans no longer identified as religious. The study's authors called these people "Nones" because they checked the box that read, essentially, "none of the above" when asked what religion they were affiliated with. Nearly 50 million Americans identified themselves as religiously unaffiliated, and 88 percent of that group said they had no interest in joining a religious institution, ever. For the first time, my not being part of something felt like being part of something big. (In the fall of 2015, the Pew Foundation released new statistics showing the numbers of Nones had risen even higher: Nearly one-fourth of Americans categorized themselves as nonreligious.)

Turn on the news or listen to politicians on the campaign trail, and it can seem that the United States is becoming more religious, not less. But behind those headlines and beyond politically expedient proclamations of faith, the story religious statisticians are starting to tell is a story of the weakening of all measures of religious belief, behavior, and belonging through the generations. Journey down the rabbit hole of the demographics of religion, and the evidence keeps piling up. Fewer people describe themselves as religious, and those who do have weaker ties to their faith. Of course this isn't true for every individual or family, but scholars of religion say that even people who describe themselves as religious are likely to have a lower commitment to their faith than their parents and grandparents, making the United States appear more religious than it actually is. Some researchers describe this as a kind of "slippery pole," where individuals have gradually entered adulthood at lower levels of religious commitment through recent generations. Cultural changes such as those in the 1960s then made it okay for newer generations to slip off the pole altogether.

Indeed, fewer and fewer Americans attend religious services regularly, even to keep up appearances. The percentage of people who never attend religious services rose from 13 percent in 1990 to 22 percent in 2008. This change reflects a societal shift: Going to church is no longer important, even as an empty ritual because it's expected in your family or community. People let go of the religious identity first, then the churchgoing behavior.

Though the vast majority of Americans believe in God, that number is dipping too. In the 1950s, 99 percent of Americans professed belief in God, but by 2011 that number had dropped to 91 percent, and possible answers included belief in a "higher power" as well as an occasional belief in God. These findings reflect the growing preference for a more diffuse spirituality over traditional religion, which in turn reflects Americans' increasing distaste for institutions of any kind.

Beneath the widening umbrella of Nones are also people who leave religion because of traumatic experiences, be it sexual abuse by a priest, an unacceptable authoritarian family situation dictated by church norms, or a feeling of being brainwashed and needing to escape. Those who leave religion as a kind of fleeing for their sanity, if not their lives, are a vocal, and often articulate, minority.

Where once being an "atheist" was a badge of shame to be kept under wraps, even that is changing. President Obama regularly gives a nod to nonbelievers when he addresses the diversity of faith (including a lack thereof) in his audiences, a courtesy no other president has extended. And recent surveys show a slow uptick in the "acceptability" of being an atheist among Americans. Many people welcome such changes, particularly the acceptance of atheism as part of our multicolored social fabric. But other people have a sense that we're losing something important.

NONES, EXPLAINED

Most of the people I knew left religion without much thought, as if removing an itchy sweater. Curious to know why this was happening, I began to do more research and came across a book called *American*

Grace: How Religion Divides and Unites Us by Robert Putnam and David Campbell. The book looks at the religious attitudes of Americans, including the rising numbers of the Nones. I knew Putnam had written *Bowling Alone: The Collapse and Revival of American Community,* about the way Americans had left civic and community groups such as bowling leagues, Elks Clubs, and the League of Women Voters. In *American Grace,* he was focusing on religion, and on people like my family and friends who were leaving various faiths in droves.

Putnam is a professor at Harvard, not far from where we lived in Central Square, so I e-mailed him to ask, among other questions, if he thought my kids were missing something by not being raised within a religious community. He answered right back and suggested a meeting.

A week later at Darwin's café in Harvard Square, Putnam appeared, red-faced from his morning exercise, and ordered a coffee with two shots of espresso. He tossed his brown hat on the small round table and began peppering me with questions: Where did you grow up? How were you raised? With every question I sensed he was slotting me into a data set, while at the same time trying to understand the complex tangle of factors leading me to where I sat. He was curious about my background because, apparently, I was an example of the bigger picture.

I told him about my seventies-style upbringing: latchkey child of divorced parents, both of whom had been raised religiously in the South—my mother Presbyterian, my father Methodist. My brothers and I had been in and out of churches when we were young, religion always present but never consistent. I asked Putnam if my experience of losing my religion, and my friends losing theirs, was becoming more common. He nodded vigorously. My generation, he said—people who came of age in the late 1970s and early 1980s—was at the leading edge of this mass disaffiliation.

"In historical terms, this is a huge increase, an unbelievable increase," Putnam said. "It's more than any change we've ever seen in religiosity because it's happening very quickly. It's impossible to exaggerate what a historical change this is."

This enormous cultural shift—disaffiliation from religion—that has been happening in this country has taken even political scientists like Putnam by surprise. For as long as researchers have been conducting studies on American demographics, Putnam said, they have included a question about a person's religious affiliation. "There's always been a set of people who have responded to that question as 'I am actually none of the above, I'm nothing,'" he said. For decades, that figure hovered around 7 percent—until 1990, at which point it began to rise sharply. That's about the time children of baby boomers, like me, began to declare what religion they were.

"If you look at the chart, it looks like a hockey stick," he said, holding his arm up at an angle slightly wider than 90 degrees to show the line. "It was flat, flat, flat, and then it starts sharply rising with exactly your age."

Today, one-third of adults under the age of thirty are religiously unaffiliated. While 5 percent of baby boomers were raised without any religious affiliation, 13 percent of Millennials were raised that way. One of the most important predictors of religious affiliation later in life is religious affiliation in childhood, meaning secular America is almost guaranteed to expand.

To reinforce what a dramatic change this is, Putnam explained that secularization in Europe has been going on at a slow and steady "drip, drip, drip" over a century and a half—while in recent years, Americans have been leaving religion at a rate he estimates as ten times higher. But why such a sudden turn away from religion for so many?

Putnam said that while the decline of participation in religion in America has more than one cause, one of the most commonly cited culprits is the social temblor that was the 1960s, when rejecting religion was part of the widespread movement of cultural liberation in America that spread across race, gender, and sexuality. The baby boomers, then entering adolescence, began to explore alternative spiritualities, and also began to cobble together their own individual "religions" based on elements from different traditions, both religious and nonreligious. I thought of the period when my mother spent her Sundays meditating and gardening rather than going to church.

The effect of the counterculture on religion went beyond that wave of people leaving their faiths and cultivating New Age–style spiritualities. All this upheaval had a countereffect, a surge of more conservative Christians reacting against what they took to be the loose values of the hippies. Later, conservative Christians flocked to political groups like the Moral Majority, formed by Jerry Falwell in 1979 as a "pro-family" lobby group for evangelical Christians. (The Moral Majority eventually produced the religious right.) This braiding of religion and politics was off-putting to many who believed strongly that the two realms should remain separate, and it is one of the leading causes put forth by social scientists like Putnam to explain the rise of the Nones.

"Just as the religious right was reacting against the sixties, your generation was reacting against Jerry Falwell," Putnam said. "It's as if this generation said, 'If religion is just about homophobia and abortion, and if to be religious means to be Republican, I'm out of here. That's not me.' "

HALF-IN, HALF-OUT

Religious disaffiliation isn't as simple as an on-off switch, though. Many of us live in a liminal state, between the religious life we knew and the new life we are creating. Though we no longer overtly practice religion, our faith traditions are often loosely threaded through our lives in subtle ways, in the half-remembered notes of a hymn or words of a prayer, or in the occasional practice of religious rituals—Passover Seder or Easter services—as if religion were the good family china to be used only on special occasions, then placed back behind glass doors. It's there, in the form of nostalgia and special customs, but not in our everyday routine. Religion is still part of our lives, but in less important and less frequent ways.

"Most Nones are not children of atheists themselves," Putnam told me. "They're children of people who are semiobservant Methodists or Episcopalians or Catholics or whatever. They're people who know a lot of the culture of religion, which is a lot of the culture of America. Quotations from the Bible and so on are part of their mental equipment. So it's not like they were raised as complete atheists [who] don't have a clue about religion." (In fact, self-identified atheists make up just a little over a tenth of the overall None pie.) And yet, we are a unique generation in that we are not raising our kids to know much of it at all.

It used to be that marriage and becoming a parent were life events that sent people back into the pews. Putnam explained that individual religiosity once had a predictable life cycle. People would move away from their faith in their teens and twenties but come back around once they married, which was an occasion to rejoin religious practice. After that, they initiated their children into their faith. Not anymore. These days, Putnam said, once people lose their religion, they're unlikely to get it back.

I asked Putnam about his own religious background. He told me he was like a lot of people his age in that after marriage to someone of another faith, his religious ties weakened; in fact, when he married his wife, he converted from his Methodist faith to Judaism. He now has grandkids who have been bar and bat mitzvahed. But this path—a couple choosing one of two faiths to belong to—is not as common as it once was. Now when two people of different backgrounds marry, they either stick to their separate faiths or choose nothing at all.

With today's age of first marriage at an all-time high of twenty-seven for women and twenty-nine for men, Americans tie the knot after they're already embedded in work and other communities. Religion does not call young marrieds back to the fold as it once did. Marrying someone of another faith also dilutes a person or family's religiosity. More than one-third of Americans are married to someone of a different religion, and that rate is climbing steadily. If you include Catholic-Protestant unions, marriages of mainline Protestants to evangelical Christians, and unions of seculars and the religious, that number grows even higher. Thirty-five percent of marriages in the first decade of this century were interfaith unions. That's up from nearly 20 percent before 1960. And children raised in interfaith households are more likely to lose touch with religion altogether.

By Putnam's lights, I was a case study for all these factors in losing religion, from my age to my divorced, quasi-counterculture parents to my interfaith marriage. As with so many people, my loss of religion wasn't particularly deliberate or considered. Partly because I grew up with religion, as so many people of my generation did, I always assumed it would be part of my life.

Since the 1960s, the change has been unfolding: Younger generations are less religious than the ones that came before them. "This trend has the potential for completely transforming American society," Putnam said, as he finished his coffee and picked up his hat. He paused, as if to let his words sink in. "It has the potential for just eliminating religion."

Was that the goal? Maybe for some, but I knew that many of the religiously unaffiliated did not view religion frivolously. Faith has meant a great deal to us, and the sense of loss is real, even if we don't always talk about it. For many of us, losing religion happens so subtly that it's barely noticeable at first. Even so, it still comes with costs. For those of us who've let go of religion over decades, or are witnessing that loss within our own family lines, these changes reveal themselves unpredictably, sometimes subtly, often painfully.

....

ERIN O'CONNOR STILL calls herself a Catholic, but what that means to her has changed over her lifetime, and the label means even less to her children, and especially her grandchildren. Erin is in her late fifties and works as a community organizer in Oakland, California. I met her in a writing class in San Francisco.

When she was growing up in California's Sacramento Valley in the 1940s and '50s, Erin, her parents, and her seven siblings would pile into the station wagon every Sunday and attend a lengthy High Mass in Latin. Even if the service was sometimes boring and impossible to decipher, Erin was fascinated by the incense, gilt-edged missals, and incomprehensible words. At the Catholic school she attended, the nuns who taught classes were dressed in black habits from head to toe and held oversized rosaries that included small skull replicas. These symbols enthralled Erin; she saw the nuns as keepers of deep and mysterious knowledge. "Their lives were like these unplumbable depths of . . . I don't know what," she told me when I called her later on the phone. "But it was endlessly fascinating."

In Erin's teen years, that fascination turned to interest in liberation theology and the community organizing run by the church. In fact, it was her engagement with the church-based Latin American Mission program that set her on her life path to do community service work. "I realized that the church could take a stand," she said. But as the church started to change, she felt less connected to it. Around the time she married and started a family, she noticed the church's stance on abortion and the ordination of women taking precedence with church leaders over service and charity. The Catholic Church was becoming more politicized and less about helping those in need.

"I was set adrift as a Catholic," she said. "I continued to practice and would find kindred spirits, but it wasn't the same. It wasn't the feeling that this is a church that matters and is relevant. Rather, it was 'I feel compelled to be here as part of this church, but it's not at this point at all representing what I believe in anymore.' "

Through the years she has experimented with smaller evangelical groups that meet in people's homes, and with her neighborhood parish, largely made up of the Latino immigrant and Vietnamese refugee community. But Erin says that nothing quite fits anymore. After a lifetime of Catholicism, she now calls herself a casual Massgoer. For her children, the drift is even more pronounced. Her three grown daughters have all left the church. In high school one of them protested her confirmation, saying the church was too sexist. None of her children wanted to be married in the Catholic Church because of the religion's refusal to marry gays. She has grandchildren who don't go to church at all. They are, essentially, Nones. As a mother and grandmother, she feels helpless as she watches the traditions of her faith vanish through the generations.

Erin also worries about what effect the loss of religion will have in the community service world in which she works. She has witnessed how instrumental religious groups are in her city. "Faith keeps people in it," she said. "It gives people resilience for the kind of struggle that it is to bring about social justice. Our job is to keep showing up and to not give up and to have a willing disposition, but then to trust that other people are doing the same and that God's grace is at work."

When I asked her what God's grace meant to her, she explained that she believes that we were all created for love by a higher being—or God—and that that higher being lives within us. These beliefs give her a sense of deep meaning, which sustains her through the struggles we all inevitably face. "When you encounter difficulties in life," she said, "it's great to have that kind of a spiritual grounding that enables you to make sense out of what happens. Everybody has suffering in their life, but how do you make meaning of suffering?"

She worries her grandchildren will not have access to that grace, as symbolized in the cross. To her, the horizontal arm of the cross represents connection to others in present time and place, but it is the vertical arm that tethers us, first to the past, and then to the hereafter, or God. A life of meaning according to this concept requires both types of connection. But the power symbolized in the cross is fading for Erin. She has seen it in the changes in the church, in her community service work, and now in her own family's detachment from religion. Even though she is a lifelong Catholic, she says she no longer has a true religious home for herself. When I asked her what concerns her most about all the changes she's seen in her community, in her work, and in her own family, she said, "I'm afraid it will all die with me."

CHAPTER 3

Religion Tries to Stay Relevant

We want to bring our whole selves
through the church doors,
without leaving our hearts and minds behind,
without wearing a mask.

—*Rachel Held Evans,*
Searching for Sunday: Loving, Leaving,
and Finding the Church

When I visited Glide Memorial Church on a warm Sunday morning in August, a line of people was already wrapped around the building in the heart of San Francisco's Tenderloin neighborhood, a pocket of the city that has defied gentrification with its constant presence of prostitutes, drug dealers, and homeless people on its streets. Ushers in fluorescent-colored vests ensured that the line moved smoothly into the building and up the stairs, greeting each of us with a big smile and a warm "We're glad you're here!" Inside, in a city known for its diversity, but where there are invisible color lines in neighborhoods that no one talks about, the Glide crowd really was a mixture of races, ages, ethnic and economic backgrounds, and sexual orientation.

"We welcome everyone," read the motto printed on the cardboard fan a woman handed me as I took my seat in the packed sanctuary. "We value our differences. We respect others." I sat next to a couple speaking French and saw that the woman was holding a guidebook to the city. I looked around and took in the rest of the packed, diverse crowd. A man who appeared homeless stumbled down the aisle to take his seat, draped in an American flag and wearing beat-up silver high-tops. A young mother and father sat in front of me, their tow-headed son standing between them so he could see. No one seemed to care what anyone was wearing: Some people were dressed up in full church finery; others wore jeans and T-shirts.

It was what wasn't there that seemed most telling. There was no cross hanging over any altar. There were no hymnals or Bibles in little wooden racks along the backs of the pews. As the morning unfolded, it became clear that no minister in a robe would preside over services, and we would not be taking communion.

Glide is a different kind of church than any I'd ever been to. It puts on a rollicking, gospel-infused, incredibly diverse Sunday morning service that is all heart and no dogma. And it draws huge, regular crowds. But is it a church or something else altogether?

Glide has been called a church of radical acceptance, a spiritual movement, and a San Francisco tourist attraction. It wasn't always this way. How today's Glide came to be is testament to the way some religious institutions evolve to meet the social forces of our modern, scientific, and individualistic age. Successful religions have always been living faiths; they evolve with the times, maintaining their historic richness while adapting to remain relevant. In *After*

Virtue: A Study in Moral Theory, the Scottish philosopher Alasdair MacIntyre described living traditions as being in ongoing dialogue with the past. When traditions simply repeat the past, they die. But if they engage with the past, they remain alive. There's a difference between a rooted, living tradition and a stuck, dead one. And at no other time in our country's history has it been more important for religious organizations to discern how best to remain among the living. Many churches and synagogues today are struggling to survive, but Glide understood the challenge—and responded to it—decades ago.

In 1930, Lizzie Glide, a philanthropist whose cattleman husband left a fortune after his death, opened the Glide Memorial United Methodist Church in his memory. By the early 1960s the mostly white, conservative congregation had dwindled dramatically, and the church was in danger of folding altogether. That's when the church leaders began to embrace the very people who felt most alienated from its mainstream pews.

A charismatic Cecil Williams, one of the first five African American graduates of the Perkins School of Theology at Southern Methodist University in 1955, took over as pastor and decided to return Glide to the true spirit of Christianity—welcoming anyone of any race, sexual orientation, ethnicity, and economic circumstances. In a move counter to the usual religious exclusion of difference and dissent, Williams oversaw a radical expansion of the congregation to include blacks, gays, hippies, drug addicts, and the mentally ill. Williams sought to get to the simple truth of the Christian message, which is that we should embrace first and foremost the poorest, most frail, and most struggling among us. His message resonated, and Glide exploded in popularity. He invited Angela Davis and the Black Panthers to speak, and he welcomed Billy Graham and the socialite crowd to come to services. In 1967, Williams removed the cross from the sanctuary because, he said, it symbolized death, and Glide should celebrate the living. By peeling away the outward signs of religion, Glide found its soul—and the church grew to become a congregation of ten thousand people.

On the day I visited, the pews were filled up to the balcony. The minister who preached that morning spoke of the Black Lives Matter movement, saying, "I know something about anger because I am a black man living in America." He asked us all to stand up, raise our hands in solidarity with innocent black males who had died at the hands of police, and say, "Don't Shoot." After several repetitions, he led us in a "Black Lives Matter" chant. On a screen behind him, faces of those who had died played in rotation.

The talk was the epitome of how Glide seeks to make itself relevant. The minister pointed out that religion and spirituality are not always synonymous and that Glide is what Jesus himself had in mind. Glide's mission to create a just society and alleviate suffering spawned a dizzying array of programs, now numbering eighty-seven, making Glide the largest provider of social services in the city of San Francisco. Glide offers a program that provides three free meals a day and serves three thousand people in need. It also offers rent assistance, childcare, mental and primary health care, women's programs, after-school activities, computer classes, crisis interventions, literacy classes, and drug and alcohol recovery programs. These programs reflect the core of Christian teaching. As one minister said that day, "When life's path is too much, you don't have to walk alone."

One member of Glide, an African American man wearing khakis and a black leather jacket, stood up to tell his story of arriving in San Francisco at nineteen as a closeted gay man from a difficult family. He'd been addicted to meth, jailed three times, and diagnosed with full-blown AIDS in 1990. At the time of his diagnosis, he'd been given five to six months to live, he said, holding out his hands to applause for having beaten those odds. He received free meals from Glide and the support he needed to kick his addiction and improve his health. "Glide does the work the church should do," he said. "This is how church should look."

Not to mention how a church should sound. Glide may be just as famous for its gospel music as it is for its good works. A forty-person choir, dressed in plain clothes and accompanied by an eight-man jazz band, performed nearly continuously during the service, electrifying the crowd.

As fun and inspiring as it was to be there, I couldn't figure out exactly what "there" was. At Glide, in the interest of making the church relevant, religion itself had morphed so much that it didn't feel exactly like religion anymore. When the minister asked how many in the audience were members of Glide, only about thirty hands among the hundreds went up. The rest seemed to be curious onlookers like me. In fact, the couple beside me with the tourist guide to San Francisco stood up halfway through and left. Several others did the same at different points during the service.

Without strict rituals to abide by, there seemed a porousness that was both necessary for the community to continue, but also threatening to the church as an institution. Clearly Glide provides crucial services to the wider community. But as a religious experience, I couldn't locate its unifying center. It was life-giving and sustaining for thousands of people, but without the symbols, rituals, and teachings from scripture, it was hard—for me, at least—to grab hold of.

As waves of people leave the pews, churches and synagogues are struggling to survive by answering the needs of those who want to modernize, to strip religion to its essence. But in doing so, they may lose what makes religion distinct. It's a catch-22: The very aspects that turn people off from organized religion are what set it apart. The ancient rituals and customs and teachings don't sit well with many today, but it's the very ancientness of those things that makes religion special in the first place. Religions have to wrestle with the dilemma of meeting modern culture where it lives without losing itself in the process. Leaders must adapt old meanings to meet new questions. The challenge becomes how far you can go in the direction of change without losing the things that make religious experience unique. These are not new concerns, but they are exacerbated by the times in which we live. Houses of worship are trying to meet modern needs and desires to keep people coming through the door, leading to a wave of change within religious organizations themselves.

Some try doing what Glide has done—returning to the roots of community outreach and caring for the poorest among us, while offering music and programs that lure in other members. Then there are the colossal megachurches, which are like shopping malls for the soul, holding services with praise music in enormous sanctuaries and often including gymnasiums, schools, divorce centers, aerobics studios, computer centers, arcades, banquet halls, and even restaurants.

Smaller, scrappier churches attempt to cast wide appeal by turning to clever logistics: At Christ Episcopal Church in Slidell, Louisiana, church leaders offer two two-hour periods on Ash Wednesday during which congregants can receive ashes at a drive-through. Synagogues offer drop-off Hebrew school for parents who don't want to attend services themselves. In Buffalo, New York, a group called Mass Mob chooses an old, struggling Catholic church each week and, through social media, encourages people to congregate there for worship, temporarily filling what would otherwise be an empty sanctuary. And for a time at Christ Lutheran Church in Scituate, Massachusetts, you could use the church parking lot on Saturdays to participate in your own personal drive-through prayer.

SCARY TIMES

"These are kind of scary times," Graham Robinson, a Presbyterian minister in Aston, Pennsylvania, told me. When I reached him, Robinson said he had recently left a dwindling church whose main members were all in their eighties and nineties. He'd moved his family to a small mission church, where he preaches on Sundays and directs the grief care and support group. From his autobiography on the church website, you can see he's making an effort to have broad appeal: "As for my political beliefs: Jim's Steaks are better than Pat's or Gino's, Chip Kelly [the Philadelphia Eagles coach] should run for Governor, and I can't help myself from rooting for the 76ers." I met Robinson through a friend, and he offered to talk to me about what he sees happening in his world of Presbyterian churches.

Robinson doesn't think the way to attract more congregants is by offering more bells and whistles—the sorts of megachurch grand theatrics that he sees as basically old religion dressed up in a rock 'n' roll costume. He told me about the emergent church model, where groups reimagine Christian practice to create experiences that are more at the heart of Jesus's actual teachings. "Emergent Christianity" is a phrase that describes a number of attempts by churches to move beyond the hierarchical minister-preaching-to-the-congregation model of churchgoing, encouraging more of a conversation with congregants, and opening the pews to a wider diversity of people. Emergent churches often describe themselves as postmodern and believe in deconstructing traditional Christian forms and practices.

The emergent church honors individual spiritual experience, a development that reflects the impulse of the Protestant Reformation itself. In *Emergence Christianity: What It Is, Where It Is Going, and Why It Matters*, Phyllis Tickle explains that every five hundred years, religion goes through a major upheaval, and each upheaval is in response to whatever or whoever holds religious power at the time. Before the Protestant Reformation, the Catholic Church had the most power. Protestants reacted by saying that authority doesn't come from the pope; authority comes from the word. "That turns everything loose," Robinson said, "because the word can be born in a variety of places, inspire people in different ways, and mean so many things." No longer is the institution the only source of knowledge and interpretation; individuals play a greater role, creating their own models. Emergent churches have been known to replace what we think of as the traditional Sunday program with sacred jazz services, elaborate light shows, or open mic nights. Whether such alternatives will work to keep Protestant churches vibrant is still a question.

Robinson says he has noticed a dramatic drop-off in the past twenty years in the amount of time and energy people are willing to commit to building up a church community. His own small mission church is wrestling to survive, using its interpretation of the emergent church model to work with secular groups that provide important services. For example, his church partners with the state government, which has a program to provide early learning centers for families in need. The church hosts a center on its grounds and works with the organizers to reach community members who may need its services.

Even as his church struggles to stake out this new ground, Robinson remains hopeful. He told me that he continues to see "beautiful, small signs of spiritual inquiry, thirst, mission, and interest."

But are such signs enough? The data on religious participation show such efforts may not be helping much. Though Muslim and Hindu populations in the United States are expected to grow from their small starting point, all other religious denominations are declining. In 1975, 7.5 million people reported having left the religion after being raised Catholic; that number is now 28.9 million. In Evangelical Lutheran churches across the country, the average weekly worship attendance dropped 26 percent from 2003 to 2011. Episcopalians closed 45 parishes in 2013 and have stopped trying to plant new ones. While it can be hard to collect data on changes in Judaism because people disagree on the definition of what a Jew is (Is it a culture or religion? Does it have to be both?), recent surveys suggest that 22 percent of Jewish American adults have no religion, a dramatic increase over the past decade. And among Catholics, Baptists, and Presbyterians, the number of child baptisms has dropped rapidly since 1970.

Part of the problem is that religions are like brands, which can become mired in their history. It's hard for people to shake their preconceived notions of them. So, even as religious institutions like Glide, megachurches, and emergent churches strive to evolve, people who were turned off by religion at an earlier time may be hesitant to trust it again. The perception of religion for many is as clunky and old-fashioned as my grandmother's Chevy Impala. And efforts at radical change—such as the megachurch model—seem too transparent. It may look like fun, but the underlying messages of judgment and exclusion that so many Nones have rejected are still there, behind the cafeteria and stadium seating.

In addition, as such churches try to modernize and become "hip," many people are actually saying they prefer the traditional rituals and sacred space. In her book *Searching for Sunday: Loving, Leaving, and Finding the Church,* Rachel Held Evans, who left the evangelical faith of her upbringing for Episcopalianism, writes that Millennials like her are longing for the sacraments, not coffee bars attached to churches or light shows instead of sermons. But even beyond such rituals and traditions, it seems that many are longing for a religious figure who brings clarity and focus to what matters most.

A NEW KIND OF POPE

The most striking recent example of the way that religions must evolve or die can be found in the sense of hope many around the world see in Pope Francis. With his rise to the papacy, the enormously popular Jesuit from Argentina has shifted the dialogue from dogma and an enumeration of moral evils to service and humanity. Francis is known for his humility and his concerns for the poor, the environment, and religious freedom. He prefers to live in a simple guesthouse in the Vatican rather than the sumptuous papal apartments, and he rides in a Ford Focus. He welcomes interfaith dialogue and has said that even atheists can go to heaven. In July 2013, when asked about his position on homosexual priests, he replied, "If someone is gay and he searches for the Lord and has goodwill, who am I to judge?" This pope is changing with the times more rapidly than any previous pope. And he has touched a worldwide nerve.

When Pope Francis visited the United States in September 2015, the throngs lined up to see him could barely be contained. It seemed everyone—religious, nonreligious, Catholic, non-Catholic—could find something in Francis to relate to. His popularity reveals much about what many people are seeking in a religious leader today: authenticity and kindness, a goodness that goes something beyond religion itself.

On a clear day in April, shortly after Francis became pope, I took my seat in Gaston Hall at the center of the lush Georgetown campus in Washington, DC. The churchlike meeting hall was adorned with stained-glass windows and bright murals of biblical figures. I was joining the audience of three hundred for a daylong event sponsored by the Vatican and meant to bring religious and nonreligious people together in dialogue about the common good. How can people in a pluralistic society come to some agreement on how to address modern social ills? How do we bolster concern for others in an increasingly individualistic age?

The event was a roving spiritual talk show, drawing in cardinals, priests, rabbis, and even some atheists. The concept of the initiative goes back to King Herod's reconstruction of the Temple of Jerusalem in 20 BC. Though the temple had always been reserved for Jews, the king specified that he wanted a separate courtyard, called the

Courtyard of the Gentiles, where Jews and non-Jews could congregate and engage in respectful dialogue. The current program began under Pope Benedict and was broadened and invigorated under Pope Francis.

In Gaston Hall, Cardinal Gianfranco Ravasi, an animated figure in a long black cassock tied with a bright red sash, strode to the podium, smiling widely as he gestured toward the colorfully painted murals and windows. Ravisi spoke to us in Italian, while the priest beside him acted as interpreter, relaying his message on diversity and the common good: "Many coins are made at the same mint, but like coins we are all different," he said. He cited John Donne's famous "No man is an island" and urged us to see our similarities, not differences. "The common good includes values that are transcendental, infinite like the ocean, mysterious and secret," he said. "Those are core values for those who believe and those are core values for those who do not believe."

After this introduction, a group of panelists took their seats onstage. They included a priest, a scholar of Islam, a journalist, and a secular studies professor. Cokie Roberts, a popular NPR contributor, sat to the side of the panel and served as the moderator. She began by asking how we approach the common good in a pluralistic society. How do we resist the natural urge to favor our own tribe? One important shift by the Vatican is to take more seriously the nonbelievers who make up a growing minority here and abroad.

Phil Zuckerman, the panel's secular studies professor, wore white jeans and a casual short-sleeved button-down and had a bemused grin on his face. When asked where he saw evidence of the common good, he told a story of visiting a public elementary school science fair the night before in Rockville, Maryland, with the family of the friend he was staying with that night. The school gym was filled with kids and families from all faith traditions (and none at all), different ethnic groups, and a variety of languages. That scene, he said, was "the epitome of the founders' vision," a secular space in a public school funded by tax dollars, with no one religion privileged over any other. "Yay!" he said. "The First Amendment is alive and well."

What was more remarkable to him than that scene of the common good in action, though, was that he, an outspoken atheist, had been invited to be on the panel that morning. He saw this as a radical change showing how important atheists and other types of nonbelievers have become as a cultural force. "The secular population is growing," he said. "And people of faith are taking note."

Outside Gaston Hall later that morning, the conversation continued under white tents, in more intimate settings. From his seat on a small makeshift stage, Zuckerman told the smaller crowd that Christianity has great ideas, but that they don't come from heaven; they come from humanity. Many in the audience nodded. Later that day a selection of writers—Robert Pinsky, Alice McDermott, and Ayana Mathis among them—discussed how art, religion, and science are all after the same thing: a way to address the mystery of life and our wonder in the face of it. Robert Pinsky, former poet laureate of the United States, said, "I spent many years of my life in synagogue, and it is a great relief that I don't have to do it anymore. I'm one of those who find the courtyard more interesting than the synagogue." The religious on the panel and in the audience laughed.

The event demonstrated the ways in which some walls between different systems of belief may be coming down in the modern age. As knowledge and awareness of other cultures and beliefs spread, it becomes increasingly difficult to see your own way as the only right one. Religions have always evolved, and those that haven't have withered and died. Of course, some evolve more successfully than others. The balance between tradition and adaptation is tricky to achieve: One must hold to absolute moral truths created in a faraway place and time while also witnessing and responding to the practices and demands of contemporary life.

Time will tell whether Pope Francis can reconcile traditional Catholicism with the current culture, but many Catholics are hopeful. At the opening address of the extraordinary session of the Synod of Bishops in 2014, the first such papal event in thirty years, he exhorted the two hundred bishops from five continents in his audience to pay attention to "the beat of this age."

Anyone listening to the beat of this age can't help but hear the voices of the nonreligious rising to articulate their own stance. Religions must in turn try to evolve to draw people back into the pews. They may not always succeed, but the willingness to have the discussion across the aisle with those who don't share belief in their religion (or possibly in any God at all) feels new—and necessary.

The pope is popular, his inclusiveness refreshing—and while that is encouraging, it's clear that Catholicism still has its limits. For example, Francis maintains that the "door is closed" on women being ordained. For many, such a stance is a vestige of an ancient patriarchal culture that is long overdue for updating. People may admire Pope Francis as a person, but the religion he represents has a long way to go before people find their way back.

For the Catholic Church in parts of the United States, it may be too late. While Catholic membership is thriving in the South and the West, areas that boast large Latino populations, it is shrinking in parts of the Midwest and on the East Coast, where scores of parishes are merging, and churches are being turned into restaurants and condos. The lasting legacy of the sexual abuse scandal, not to mention outmoded beliefs on contraception and women's leadership roles in the church, has turned many Catholics away—and many of them, Pope Francis or no, won't find their way back.

What Francis's popularity shows, though, is how many people yearn for a church that leaves the dogma and judgment in the past. Perhaps the future of religion lies in something far less structured than traditional organized religion, in an experience of faith stripped instead to its essence. While some are trying to reinvent alternative or edgy religious practices to attract the modern believer, others are turning within, seeking what's essential.

SEEKING "THE MORE"

A friend suggested I call Pamela Shepherd, the senior minister of the United Church of Christ in Ashland, Oregon. Shepherd had left her own Protestant faith but later found her way back to religion through an unlikely route.

Shepherd said that she left the church when she "hit the age of reason," at thirteen. "I thought, 'This is nonsense, because this doesn't line up with the world I'm seeing and experiencing.' " She gradually wound her way back to religion in her mid-twenties by discovering a sense of the sacred through a Hindu guru, and by learning how to meditate from a downstairs neighbor who was Muslim. Sometimes after a long seated meditation, the neighbor would say, "You could be a very good Christian." Shepherd was surprised to realize that her friend knew more about her faith tradition than she did. Maybe she hadn't seen what faith had to offer her the first time around, she thought, so she decided to give Christianity another chance.

"The first time I had communion in church after years away, I was overwhelmed by the strongest sense of the presence of God in my life, and the sense that God had been present and with me through this whole journey," she told me. To her surprise, her interest in faith kept growing, and she ended up in the ministry.

Her church in Oregon is progressive, and many of the people who come through the doors have left other, stricter religions but sense they're missing something in their lives. "I see how many people have that same longing that I had," she said. "We long to be whole, and we long for the transformation of our lives from what's shallow to what's deep."

Shepherd said that religion offers a safe place to explore what's beyond rationality, what's beyond the material world, and "what's deeper than our little ticking brains." She said that her faith community offers people a means of transformation, a way to touch whatever it is they call God: "We all want the sense of 'the more,' which some call God. You just have to figure out what your way is, go on your way, and not stop."

Such a sentiment may sound like a kind of diffuse New Age seeking, and indeed "spiritual-but-not-religious" is a popular way for people to describe themselves when they've left traditional religion but not belief behind. But it's also what people across many lines are seeking as well, a greater authenticity, an experience that feels more direct and personal and less mediated by authorities and texts.

I asked Shepherd whether there was some way to get at that powerful experience of religion without all the architecture, both literal and figurative, that had been built up around it. She said that for her, the thing that sets religion apart lies in community and honest connection. "When you hear somebody really telling the truth, it's like an arrow to the soul. And you just go, 'Yeah, that's my truth, too.' That breaks down our Western sense that we're like individual little flesh pods that connect. You start to feel the oneness that belongs to us together." I thought of Glide, emergent churches, the pope's new openness, and the science fair in Rockville, Maryland. In all these instances, the shared theme was that of breaking down what separates us.

When I asked Shepherd what she thinks religion will look like in the future, she described a peeling back of all the labels we've put on things: "I remember somebody telling me they had been to Africa, and they were asking the people of a local tribe about their spirituality. The tribesman couldn't make sense of the word 'spirituality.' And so the visitor kept trying to explain what they meant by spirituality, and finally the man said, 'Oh, we call that life.' "

Shepherd said that if the traditional structures and language no longer serve us, religions should be open to evolving. "There are huge things about Christianity that are just dying and going away—in twenty-five years, they'll be gone," she said. At the same time, new aspects of religion are starting to be born: "Something new is happening now. And it's happening inside the churches, in the synagogues, in mosques, and outside them, and it's bubbling up because it belongs to humanity. So I don't think it's about patching together what used to work. I think it's about living into what's alive and letting what's dead fall away."

GOOD-BYE TO ALL THAT

CHAPTER 4

The Big Picture

Were one asked to characterize the life of religion in the
broadest and most general terms possible,
one might say that it consists of the belief that
there is an unseen order,
and that our supreme good lies in harmoniously
adjusting ourselves thereto.

—*William James, The Varieties of Religious Experience: A Study in Human Nature*

One day when my son was four, I was driving him home from a swimming lesson, along a winding road just off the highway, headed toward the sunset, with a big pot of macaroni and cheese in our near future. I kept checking the rearview mirror to make sure his sister, then just a baby, wasn't falling asleep. We were listening to music on the radio, when he suddenly turned from staring out the window and locked his eyes on mine in the mirror.

"Mama?" he asked.

"Yes?" I said.

"Are there going to be a lot of days?"

I paused, thinking I'd misheard him.

"What did you say?" I asked.

"Are there going to be a lot of days?

"A lot of days for what?"

"For us."

"For us to what?"

"For us to do a lot of things."

It was one of those moments when all the stuff of parenting—the driving, the cooking, the wrestling kids into and out of car seats—falls away and you face one of the big questions.

I looked back at him through the mirror and said, "There are going to be so many days that we won't know what to do with all of them."

I didn't know this, of course, but I wanted to give him a clear, strong answer to erase his worry. I kept driving as he looked out his window at the grassy hills and tall pines. He was reclining in his car seat, which resembled a small throne, with a relieved look on his face.

"And we'll go on forever and ever and ever and ever," he said.

KIDS ASK THE most profound, difficult, amusing, and sometimes annoying questions. They want to know why there are stars in the sky, why there are dogs, why we breathe, why people have to die. They ask the big questions about how the world was made, where we came from, and why we're here. Through the years, my own children have asked: Where do all the people come from? What's the meaning of life, anyway? Who named everything? Who were the parents of the first people?

It's not just kids who are asking these questions, of course. *Why are we here?* is the most fundamental human question. We ask it when we're alone reading a book or amid thousands of fans cheering at a football game. We ask it beneath starry skies and as we walk our kids to school and while seated on airplanes thirty thousand feet above the earth. We ask it when a woman gives birth, when someone we love dies, when an earthquake devastates a city or a terrorist bombs a building. We ask it when we stand on top of a mountain we've just climbed or sail a smooth stretch of sea. Even as science expands what we know about the physical world, the question of why we're here in the first place is the one question that remains unanswerable by pure observation, the one remaining mystery. For many people, religion has conveniently answered this big question that human beings have been asking for ages. This is one of the reasons religion has long been such a powerful cultural force.

Though many parts of the world are secularizing, 84 percent of the people around the globe still describe themselves as religious. Religion is powerful and pervasive because it provides so much that humans need, namely, identity, community, ritual, and a profound sense of meaning and purpose. Religion binds people in shared history, symbolism, and culture, and it is an important part of our inheritance. It instills a moral code in groups and sets norms and laws that organize and knit more tightly those within a community, who then benefit from the well-documented social and health benefits of a sense of belonging. And, at its heart, it helps us answer life's deepest questions about purpose and meaning. What happens to all of this when we let go of religion?

I often think of my grandmother closing her eyes and saying grace before each meal and how the practice forced her to express gratitude, savor hope, and acknowledge the pain of others. I think of my Catholic friends driving with their families to Mass every Sunday and how that gave them something unified and lasting to hold on to. I think of my own early religious experiences, scattered though they were, and of the comfort I once found in my belief, however fuzzy, in God. I gained meaning and community and identity from my Christianity. I sensed God's grace shining down upon me, chosen for his blessings. I and those around me were actively engaged with expressing thanks for that God-given grace—through prayer and song, ritual, and church attendance.

Now that I had released myself from those connections, I wanted to understand just what so many others and I were losing. It has been a testimony to the true power of religion that it has held on for so long and influenced so many. I wanted to know what we could learn about its unique contribution to human culture before it morphed, for my children and theirs, from distant memory to nothing at all.

WHO MADE US?

At the first, most basic level, religion satisfies our need to know our place in the universe. Religious belief in a deity (or deities), a divine, unfolding plan, and an eternal afterlife consoles us. According to scientists, the supernatural beliefs espoused by religion and taken on faith feed a biological hunger for hidden agents and a coalescing narrative that we all share. There's some science behind the notion that all of us, and children in particular, have an inherent interest in finding explanations for the mysterious. And traditionally, it's been religious beliefs that give us the answers we are wired to seek.

Deb Kelemen, a professor of psychology at Boston University, looks at how children develop what she calls teleological thinking—the belief that things happen for a reason, or that objects or behaviors exist for a purpose. I wanted to know why so many people, through history and across all cultures, developed such elaborate beliefs in God. So one day I walked over the Charles River bridge to Boston University to ask her. Her office lay at the end of a drab academic hallway, a nondescript space with a window, bookshelves, and a paper-covered desk. On that otherwise quiet afternoon, Kelemen was bursting with excitement about her research. Her work has shown that children differ from adults in that they have a "promiscuous teleological tendency," as she put it. This means they tend to think that both living and nonliving things exist to serve some purpose, perhaps because they believe they were created by some grand designer, like a God.

Kelemen was born in England and describes herself as an atheist. One day she and her son were playing outside when he noticed some flowers and asked her where they'd come from. She and her husband were raising their son to have a clear grasp of science, so she was intrigued to see that he was so attracted to finding a teleological answer to his questions. "He certainly hasn't been going to church or anything like that," she said. "And he gets these physical explanations from me and my husband for why things are as they are. So I was like, 'Oh, they come from the seeds. They get germinated when the rain falls.' And he said, 'But who made the seeds?' "

Kelemen understood that somehow design-based teleological thinking had taken hold of her son. Indeed, that's just what her research predicts would happen. "We ask kids, 'Why is this rock pointy?' " Kelemen explained. Her juvenile subjects are prompted to choose one of several multiple-choice answers. Possible responses include everything from "The rock is pointy because stuff has accumulated on top of it over the years," to "It's pointy so animals can scratch themselves on it when they have an itch." It turns out kids are much more likely than adults to choose the explanation that gives the rock purpose, apparently imbuing the inanimate object with agency or intention. In a kid's mind, it seems that everything is made—by someone, some god, or superior intelligence—for a purpose. To them, the world didn't just happen by accident.

Around the time kids turn ten, they usually show a decline in belief that there is a hidden purpose behind everything that happens. Kelemen said that by this time, kids are starting to learn a bit of science, which makes them focus more on finding answers through observation than teleological explanation. But that innate bias toward agency stays with them—and with adults, too—showing up when there's not enough time to work through a problem scientifically.

Even scientists, when asked to answer Kelemen's questions without much time for reflection, choose teleological reasons when they can't come up with another answer. In one study, scientists were asked to judge statements such as "Trees produce oxygen so that animals can breathe" or "The Earth has an ozone layer in order to protect it from UV light" under pressure to answer quickly. Another group of scientists made judgments of the same statements without any time restriction. The researchers found that scientists who were under pressure were much more likely to accept unscientific, purpose-based explanations than their colleagues who were given plenty of time to answer. Under stress, even the most rational human beings fell back on the human brain's natural bias to believe in hidden design or purpose.

WHO ARE WE?

It seems religious beliefs are rooted in the brain's desire for answers, but it's through the outward expression of those beliefs that religion has gained the most power. Religions, however they started, transmit culture through histories, stories, and practices. They feed people on levels beyond the inherent need to understand the mystery of the universe. It's through what people have done with their religious beliefs, how they have assembled and organized and reinforced their tribes, that religion has been able to wield the most power—for good and evil.

The religions in existence today are highly evolved mechanisms for binding people into tribes and reinforcing practices and beliefs through mythic narratives, elaborate rules and rituals, and established principles. If supernatural belief is rooted in the brain's need to understand creation, tribal religious practices are rooted in the group's need to come together for protection and survival.

Charles Darwin knew that even natural selection—often construed as survival of the fittest individual—favored cooperative groups. In 1871, in *The Descent of Man*, he wrote, "Sympathy . . . will have been increased through natural selection; for those communities which include the greatest number of the most sympathetic members, would flourish best, and rear the greatest number of offspring." Outward expressions of belief helped solidify the group's mechanisms for getting along together, strengthening them further.

WHY ARE WE HERE?

Beyond a sense of who made us and who we are, religions help us answer the big questions about the meaning and purpose of life. Religious conceptions of meaning come from the belief that we are part of God's plan. I wanted to understand how a sense of deep meaning and purpose changes when we detach from those conceptions. How do we as individuals and a society believe and behave differently when belief in God is no longer the only established route to meaning?

New England was going through a midspring gray spell when I met Sean Kelly in his office on the third floor of Emerson Hall at Harvard. Kelly was the chair of the Harvard Philosophy Department and coauthored a book on the secular quest for meaning called *All Things Shining: Reading the Western Classics to Find Meaning in the Secular Age*. I set up a meeting with him because I didn't understand how secular meaning could compete with God-given religious meaning—that sense that we are here on earth because God created us and that our lives are part of a divine, unfolding plan. I wanted him to explain how those of us who were leaving religion could address that loss.

When I met Kelly in his spacious office he was disarming and friendly, with a broad, boyish face topped with a thick flop of dark hair. His easy laugh echoed down the long hallway outside his door as he explained the history of the modern search for meaning.

To Kelly, one of the great contributions of monotheistic religion was a unifying sense of capital-*M* meaning. Believing that you are part of God's plan gives life a set meaning and purpose: Anything that happens to you or elsewhere in the world can be ascribed to God's will. Such a worldview can be comforting and even galvanizing; it removes the paralyzing existential angst of wondering why we're all here by providing a neat, premade answer.

During the Enlightenment of the eighteenth century, Kelly said, that unifying, God-centered view of the world began to give way to scientific understanding and the flourishing of humanistic philosophy. The Enlightenment impulse ultimately did away with the idea that there is one absolute truth, grounded in God. When monotheistic belief began to break down, the sense of a unifying order gave way. Without that order, Kelly explained, people start to see the universe as indifferent to their needs, and our traditional way of conceptualizing meaning changes radically. We lose the sacred beliefs and institutions we once circled around. Capital-*M* meaning splinters, and suddenly issues such as moral behavior become individual and fluid, not determined or governed by one all-knowing God and his rules.

That week, Kelly was teaching *The Brothers Karamazov* by the Russian novelist Fyodor Dostoyevsky. He described a scene at the beginning of the book when the father and brothers go to the monastery to see the elder Zosima. There, in that venerated space, the father calls himself a buffoon and begins to make fun of himself and everything around him. To Kelly, Zosima represents a profound cultural change in which people no longer take the sacred seriously. As one of the characters in the book says, "If God is dead, everything is permitted."

"I think Dostoyevsky sees this as a kind of turning point," Kelly said. "Already back in 1879, there is some sense in which the culture isn't taking seriously the spaces and the traditions and the things that it's always been obvious that you take seriously." He added: "A shared, monotheistic God that organizes everyone's life in a kind of unified and harmonious way doesn't really organize our lives anymore." And without one God to organize our lives, we see that there are myriad truths, that there are as many ways to believe—and things to believe in—as there are people to believe them.

Dostoyevsky, however, is hopeful that he can help people retrieve a sense of God. Even without the traditional belief in God, not everything really is permitted. Individuals are guided by their consciences and feel guilt and remorse when they do bad things. Recognizing this, according to Dostoyevsky, is the experiential core of religious belief, but we can do this even without God. People may feel their lives lack unity and harmony, but Dostoyevsky believes it's just that we need to look harder to find it. "And when we do, then that will redeem our understanding of God," said Kelly.

While Dostoyevsky and others tried to find a way to reanimate Christian monotheism, the overall trend since the Enlightenment has been away from it. In the secular age, we tend to think there is a plurality of good ways to live. This has some upsides. For example, we no longer have to dismiss or condemn people as less than human because they don't share our views of the sacred. We begin to see that there are other beliefs just as valid as ours that people can hold, and we can reject tribalism in favor of cosmopolitanism. We see a growing acceptance of those who choose not to call themselves religious and who choose not to believe in God.

The benefits of this are clear. "In the Middle Ages," Kelly said, "if you came upon someone who wasn't Christian, that was a reason to abominate them. To think automatically that they are so foreign, in the sense that they don't share your conception of what you can't laugh at, that they don't even count as human and you don't have to treat them as human. And religious wars result." We see such problems even today with fanatical religions.

But the loss of a unifying system to organize our lives isn't all positive. On the one hand, Kelly said, we have a greater respect for other people's traditions. On the other hand, it's less clear how to ground ourselves in common activity for the greater good if we no longer share a conception of what we hold sacred. "The sacred is whatever it is that you can't get the requisite distance from, at least in certain circumstances, and it's necessary to have something like that to ground meaningful choices in our lives," Kelly said. For religious groups, sacred ideals are like hard-and-fast rules—everyone agrees on them. In the modern age, we define the sacred in all sorts of ways. We may find it in time spent with family, in nature, or alone. We may find it through work, volunteering, or planting a community garden. Determining what we hold sacred helps us create meaning and connection in our individual lives, but it is hard without monotheism to unify around commonly held beliefs.

In fact, it can be paralyzing. After leaving Kelly's office that afternoon, I called another Harvard professor. Dan Gilbert, the famed happiness researcher and popular professor of psychology, had written an article on just the issue Kelly had brought up—what to do with all the choices we have in the modern world. We made an appointment, and I set out again to see what I could learn.

....

DANIEL GILBERT IS the best-selling author of *Stumbling on Happiness* and a world-renowned expert in what makes people happy. He also works in perhaps Harvard's most relaxing office, a large, dimly lit space on an upper floor of the building named for the philosopher William James. When I met him on an early summer afternoon, he was dressed in shorts and a T-shirt and was sitting still as a monk at his desk. Natural light from a wide window flowed over his neatly arranged book collection. He seemed to have honed his work procedure to just what he needed, and I wondered if his minimalism offered a hint at his approach to the glut of stimulation and choice in our times.

He told me that it's true that our very conception of happiness, satisfaction, and meaning has changed in our increasingly secular world: "For the first time in human history, large populations of human beings on our planet have everything they want, or at least everything they could reasonably want." And more and more people expect to find happiness here on earth, rather than in some afterlife. "There's no doubt that happiness was once thought of as something that doesn't happen in this life," he said. "It's what happens when you get everything you could possibly want, and that doesn't happen while we're here on earth. That's for the afterlife."

As more and more of us have direct access to what we want here on earth, he said, we lose the faith we once turned to for answers about meaning. "We lose faith in authorities. We lose faith in previous generations. We lose faith in the ability of others to simply tell us what must be so." Instead of turning to traditional prepackaged sources, we seek our own answers from an overwhelming set of choices, including those from a vast spiritual and commercial marketplace. A body of research has shown that if we are given choices without a good reason to choose one thing over the other, we'll just choose neither. "When you give people too many choices, they get paralyzed," he said. "They don't like it. They don't choose. They choose to do nothing whatsoever."

Choices, large and small, can overwhelm us. "The major decisions of life, until very recently, were all made for you the day you were born," Gilbert explained. "You're going to live here. When I die, you'll take the house, and you and your wife will move here, and you will do what your father did, and you will live in the town where your parents raised you, and your decision was 'Do I want sprinkles or not on my strawberry ice cream?' They were little decisions. Nobody had to say, 'Where do I want to live, whom do I want to marry, and what do I want to be?' Every one of us gets up and asks these questions. Until, what, a hundred and fifty years ago, nobody asked those questions."

It was true. And now one of those questions was: What do we do if we don't have religion anymore? How do we create a framework for how to live? Gilbert himself is an atheist who says he doesn't need religion to ground him; he derives meaning from work that he loves and colleagues who engage him. In many parts of the country and the world, however, religious belief continues to bring the most meaning to people's lives.

HUMANS ARE MEANING-MAKING machines, as Kelemen pointed out. We crave coherence and explanations over chaos and randomness. We like to tell ourselves stories about why things are the way they are and why forces that seem random are part of a larger plan.

When it comes to religion, research suggests that belief in God is a remarkably effective way to attain a sense of meaning in life. This is true even in poorer places, where life is defined largely by the struggle to survive. A study of 132 countries showed that people living in poorer, more religious countries report more meaning in their lives than those in rich countries. Using data from the Gallup World Poll, researchers looked at measures of self-reported feelings of meaning in life, along with religiosity, fertility rates, GDP, and suicide rates.

While richer nations tended to score higher on measures of *life satisfaction,* which reflect better objective living conditions, the poorer, more religious nations had higher rates of self-reported *meaning.* Countries like Sierra Leone, Togo, Laos, and Senegal, among the poorest in the world, were in the top 12 percent. Trying to determine why, researchers ran a variety of models, looking at the effects of such factors as education, fertility rates, and social support. The deciding factor was that the poorer countries were the most religious.

Other research shows a strong correlation between having a sense of purpose, which gives life meaning, and belief in God. Using data from the General Social Survey, which has been conducted annually in the United States for the past four decades, Stephen Cranney, a graduate student in sociology and demography at the University of Pennsylvania, examined the relationship between religiosity and a sense of purpose and found that the religious do have a deeper sense of purpose in their lives. Cranney then separated his subjects into four different degrees of belief: no belief at all, some belief coupled with doubt, belief in a higher power, and absolute belief in an entity called God. What he found was that definitive belief in God was like a jumper cable to meaning. This was not a gradually sloping graph; the effect was more like an on-off switch. Everyone from atheists to those who believed in an underlying energy or spirit *some* of the time fell at the low end of the life-purpose spectrum. But if a subject believed in God without any doubt, his or her sense of purpose spiked.

In *The Writing Life,* Annie Dillard writes, "How we spend our days is, of course, how we spend our lives." I think what my son was asking me that day in the car, without quite knowing it, was how we were going to make the most of the days—really, the life—that we had. Even as a young child, he sensed something special—about life, about time, about the love between parents and children—that he didn't want to waste.

How do we create a sense of meaning and purpose without religion? The key to meaning is the commitment to something of value. Only then will we know we are not squandering our time. Without religious belief, we have to redefine what is sacred and then commit ourselves to nurturing and maintaining it. In a secular age, we must seek to create our sources of meaning and sacredness elsewhere, lest we find ourselves unable to answer life's most fundamental questions.

CHAPTER 5

Moral Authority

Where there is no vision, the people perish.

—*Proverbs 29:18*

Years ago my mother was visiting from Arkansas, lounging on the couch in our living room as our two oldest kids pummeled each other across the room.

"You two need to practice the Golden Rule," my mother said in her soft southern drawl. They stopped fighting and looked at her quizzically.

My son asked, "What's that?"

She raised her eyebrows in my direction, and I felt a twinge of remorse. The Golden Rule—"Do unto others as you would have them do unto you" (in case, like my son, you don't already know it)—is a central tenet not just of the religion I was raised in but of every major religion in the world. It is the idea on which religious morality is based, and my kids had never heard of it. Not knowing the term didn't mean they were bad people, but the lack of such a basic moral vernacular symbolized a loss that went beyond just words.

Absolute rules, like the Golden Rule or the Ten Commandments, provide a strong framework for morality. Religion provides clear-cut reasons to be good and role models to follow on that path to goodness. Religious morality comes from a belief that you are compelled to be a good person because you were created in God's image and in order to please God (and get into heaven), you have to act according to certain laws. Congregations bind themselves around such rules into a moral community. Religions create ritualistic reminders of these rules as a way to solidify group identity around what is considered upright behavior. On the Sabbath, religious groups gather to worship gods who enjoin them to be good, one of many built-in reminders that meaningful life is about more than our own personal happiness. In fact, one of the reasons the monotheistic religions we know so well today developed the way they did had to do with creating common codes of behavior so that increasingly large groups of people could get along.

As far back as we can tell, small bands of people called on the gods to help it rain, preside over burial ceremonies, and protect them from their enemies. But these gods weren't concerned with behavior, sin, and redemption. The earliest religions were not concerned with morality at all. That's because those groups were small enough that individuals within them could monitor one another's behavior. People behaved themselves because they knew their reputations were at stake if they didn't. All that began to change when people started to gather in larger groups—around the time hunter-gatherer cultures were shifting to agriculture and larger, more permanent settlements. Because early humans were highly vulnerable to outside threats, they created tribes, religions, and other social constructs that bound individuals together into protective groups.

In her book *The Great Transformation: The Beginning of Our Religious Traditions*, Karen Armstrong examines how the three major faith traditions, and one philosophical one—Confucianism and Daoism in China, Hinduism and Buddhism in India, monotheism in Israel, and philosophical rationalism in Greece—all took shape around the same time, during what religious historians call the Axial Age, from about 900 to 200 BC. With large-scale agriculture emerging in the same period, the new, bigger societies needed to manage the increased size of groups, and these systems emerged as ways for individuals to manage complex relationships.

Such systems were necessary because good behavior results from a combination of innate empathetic urges and our concern for maintaining our own reputations and the reputation of our family. We treat others well in part because we hope they'll remember our upright behavior and do the same for us one day. But once the size of groups grew to the point where it became impossible to know and monitor everyone, the need arose for a common code of behavior. The bigger the group, the greater the opportunity for anonymity. And, as anyone who's read the anonymous comments section at the end of an online article knows, people turn vicious when nobody knows their identity. In each of the Abrahamic traditions—Christianity, Islam, and Judaism—a single, watchful God who monitors behavior and inflicts punishment on wrongdoers was created, and to resounding effect: These religions are among the most powerful and lasting that the world has ever known.

Religion, then, is less a set of beliefs than a set of practices through which people learn to create trusting bonds that extend beyond kin. Religion gives you a people beyond your family and a set of rules that govern everyone's behavior. Over millennia, tribes and groups created stories, practices, and moral laws to uphold the belief structure that increasingly bound them together. Mythic narratives also reinforced tribalism through the idea that the group was somehow chosen, by conveying the concept "We are the people who do this, as opposed to those people, who do that." Given such an elaborate, well-oiled machine honed over the ages, it's no wonder that religions are still strong and prevalent today.

IT'S NOT THAT religious belief makes people good, per se. We can read the headlines of any newspaper to see that plenty of religious people do bad things and plenty of nonreligious people do good things, and vice versa. But without these core beliefs, people have to come up with their own reasons and reinforcements for being good. Without the structure of religion to provide a code of conduct, complete with vivid parables and symbolic language as reminders, my own family's values seemed ungrounded, rooted in nothing more substantial than moment-to-moment feelings, subject to change with our moods. Were Michael and I raising children who were as practiced in and aware of strong moral values as kids raised within a religious fold? How could we be sure we were transmitting the same kinds of values to our children that had been transmitted to us?

"Religions exist primarily for people to achieve together what they cannot achieve alone," writes David Wilson in his book *Darwin's Cathedral: Evolution, Religion, and the Nature of Society*. So it's perhaps unsurprising that the religious are better at binding together to do good works. Belief in God is a remarkably galvanizing force for groups; perhaps this is why philosophical humanism has never reached the heights of the three great monotheisms in terms of group organization and dynamics. Research shows that churchgoers give more of their money, time, and energy to charity and volunteering than the nonreligious do. In fact, though religion's contribution to total charitable contributions in the United States has declined since the late 1980s, it still makes up 32 percent of all such contributions. And 33 percent of volunteer work is done through religious organizations.

The religious aren't just giving to religious causes and groups. They are more civically engaged and active as well, giving more generously and more often to secular causes and groups than the nonreligious. This makes intuitive sense, but research also bears it out. According to Eric Uslaner, a professor of government and politics at the University of Maryland, the structure of religion, with its rich history of charitable giving, makes it easier for people to train and be brought up as "givers." "Active membership in a church or synagogue lets people develop and practice skills (letter writing, organizing) that easily translate into civic engagement," he writes in a paper examining religious engagement in the United States and Canada.

The religious learn more than the nuts-and-bolts of putting together volunteer activities. Religion provides an added bonus that is hard to quantify: "Donors to charity and volunteers believe that there is a moral responsibility to help others, reject the notion that we should look out for ourselves first, and tie their beliefs to religious ideals," Uslaner writes. And research shows that the people who help others have a greater sense of meaning and purpose in their lives.

As we seek our own individual paths, we lose the tools and skills we need to foster greater civic connections. And the social capital that results from civic connections is missed most by the least fortunate among us. It's worth asking what secular people—and society—should be doing to mitigate the loss of communal giving that is the most obvious outward expression of morality. After all, it's one thing to believe you're living a good and ethical life and teaching your kids to be good people. But how do you put that into practice?

If we detach from religious rules and customs, what moral measurement sticks could we use instead? What motivates us to be better people? Religious community is about more than a feeling of belonging; it is also about the feeling of belonging to a group unified by moral purpose.

So, even though I no longer believed that God was watching me and keeping tabs on my behavior, I wanted, for me and for my family, a moral context in which to live. I didn't think we needed to recite the Golden Rule every morning. But I did think we needed reminders to think beyond our individual worries—to consider, more deeply and more often, the common good.

BORN GOOD, AND THEN WHAT?

The notion of original sin dominates certain strains of religion, but I've always believed that people are basically good—they just need structures in their lives to reinforce that goodness. It turns out that there is research that backs up this belief in original goodness. In her book *The Philosophical Baby: What Children's Minds Tell Us About Truth, Love, and the Meaning of Life,* Alison Gopnik, a professor of psychology at the University of California at Berkeley, challenges the idea that humans are wild, selfish beasts who have to be trained through vehicles such as religion to act kindly toward others. Instead, it's more likely that we're wired for compassion. In her research, she observed that babies as young as eighteen months old exhibit empathetic and altruistic behavior. "The new research shows that children have some of the foundations of morality from the time they're very young, even from the time they're born," she writes. "They identify with other people and recognize that their own feelings are shared by others. In fact, they literally take on the feelings of others."

I've seen this in my own children. When our older daughter was a year and a half, she would toddle over to her older brother when he was having a meltdown and offer him one of her stuffed animals. She was barely two feet tall, but she was already displaying an understanding of another person's discomfort and taking steps to try to alleviate it. Even as a baby, she seemed to possess the urge to help others, alleviate suffering, and do good.

Gopnik writes that it's possible that babies can't see any difference between the pain others are feeling and their own. In fact, part of the growth process in infants includes a transition from thinking that they and their mother or primary caretaker are one and the same to seeing that they are separate entities. It seems we are born with this profound feeling of connection, and our development rests on our growing apart, though never completely away. We retain those initial empathetic instincts, but they are only part of what makes us moral. Gopnik writes that these instincts aren't lodged in our brains like a capacity for grammar. Though we are born with fundamental moral ideas, our moral compass develops over time.

In other words, even if we are born with the capacity for empathy, there are tools for broadening and strengthening it, and religion has historically been the biggest, most authoritative tool of all—a large-scale organizing force that holds as its premise the sanctity of human life, the primary building block of civilization as we know it. Religion can be used for terrible outcomes, but at its best religion gives people a story that binds them to one another, and from that story a command to take action. Religion also provides built-in mechanisms for dictating morality when human desire for it fails. Without a religious identity grounded in practices and codes, we have to develop that sense of giving and connectedness on our own. Unfortunately, we live in a culture that doesn't always make that easy.

By the time children grow up to be teenagers, it seems, the innate goodness scientists have pinpointed starts to fade without strong social support, such as religion. Social scientists who study teenagers have noted a frightening sea change in adolescent values in recent decades. While at some level we know kids' obsessions with selfies and documenting their every move on social media smacks of simple teenage self-absorption, researchers say the problem is serious—and will likely have serious consequences. The evidence is everywhere:

- A recent study of fourteen thousand university students between 1979 and 2009 found that students have become dramatically *less* empathic over the years, particularly since 2000—in fact, they are 40 percent lower in empathy than their counterparts of twenty or thirty years ago.
- A 2006 survey showed that 81 percent of eighteen- to twenty-five-year-olds think getting rich is an important goal, and 64 percent think it's the most important goal, while a mere 30 percent believe that helping others in need is important.
- A study published in 2015 found that children develop narcissistic tendencies when parents overvalue them, and that this trend is increasing as hyperparenting, with the primary goal being the establishment of self-esteem, rages on.
- Two-thirds of children today think it's more important to pursue their own personal happiness than to be good people, a complete reversal from a college freshman survey in 1970.

As I read those dire statistics, I had to wonder if my fellow nonreligious parents and I were part of the problem. I went to visit Richard Weissbourd, a lecturer at the Harvard Graduate School of Education, because he's a tough critic of modern-day parenting styles as a contributing factor to our societal drop in moral values. In his book *The Parents We Mean to Be: How Well-Intentioned Adults Undermine Children's Moral and Emotional Development*, he presents research he did in five US high schools showing that the teenagers there prized achievement and personal happiness over being kind to others. I met Weissbourd in his office in the main building at the Harvard Graduate School of Education, where he chairs the Making Caring

Common Project, a program that works with parents, schools, and communities to combat bullying and encourage healthy, caring relationships in and out of schools. Weissbourd is an affable guy, tall with a thick head of ginger-colored hair. But he didn't mince words when he placed much of the blame for the change in adolescent values squarely on our indulgent parenting culture, which he said is more winner-take-all than do-unto-others.

In his research he has found that 80 percent of kids say their parents care more about achievement than kindness. When he interviewed parents, they said, "No, we really care about kindness." But that's not the message parents are sending—or that the kids are getting. Weissbourd said our intense focus on our children's happiness and achievement makes them hyperaware of their own feelings and desires—to the detriment of caring about other people's feelings. The irony is that, over time, such focus on the self ends up making them less happy. "We've elevated happiness and achievement as our primary goals, and we've demoted morality as our primary goal in child raising," he said, adding, "I think that morality should be the prime goal."

Weissbourd believes that if we want our children to flourish, we should encourage them to have fulfilling relationships with others. Rather than encouraging accomplishment and self-fulfillment, parents should spend more time helping kids learn how to tune in to other people, accommodate those around them, and be more generous. The result? "They're going to have better relationships their whole lives," he said, "and that's the strongest source of happiness there is."

I thought of all the times I've said that all I care about for my children is that they grow up happy, but how they become happy is what Weissbourd is turning on its head. Many parents seem to be *over*-compensating for whatever lack we sensed in our own childhoods, and this helicoptering makes kids think they are the center of the universe. Between the 1990s and early 2000s, college-educated mothers came to spend an average of nine hours more per week with their kids than their mothers had spent with them; fathers spent an average of five more hours. Even after they graduate from high school, we micromanage their lives to the point that colleges now stage official parental farewell ceremonies at the beginning of the school year to help moms and dads say good-bye. We show up alongside our adult children for their job interviews and help them negotiate their benefits and salaries. But our over-involvement and drive to inculcate positive self-esteem are precisely what may keep our children from deepening their relationships with others and developing their moral selves. Weissbourd said parents should be talking to their kids less about their happiness and more about whether they are committed classmates and team members.

Overparenting isn't the only driving force behind the narcissism epidemic documented by researchers. We're also not creating contexts where our children's moral development is encouraged. That doesn't have to be a religion. Often schools work on character development. Weissbourd's Making Caring Common Project provides discussion tools to help schools encourage empathy and respect among students and to create safe and caring communities.

With people leaving religion for their own spiritual pursuits and disengaging from civic institutions, Weissbourd warns, the traditional contexts for moral development are evaporating. As a result, we need new moral orientations to fill that void.

"I'm not a big fan of heaven and hell as moral orientation," Weissbourd told me later, "but it *is* a moral orientation. It's not 'Who has the most toys or things or money or the most achievements?' " Losing ties that once grounded our values means we must create them anew. And that work starts with the stories we tell ourselves about who we are as a people.

....

FAITH TRADITIONS AS "STORIES OF US"

Religions accomplish much of what they do—binding people together in groups and providing a moral framework—through shared story. Beyond creation myths that help people understand how they got here, religious narratives help people make sense of who they are by tying them into larger, ancient stories of challenges overcome, God-given miracles, and helping the less fortunate. Sacred stories unite followers with others—past, present, and future—in common purpose. They give individuals a "story of us."

Morality begins with a statement of values; story reaffirms those values and helps make them manifest. To grow up Jewish or Catholic or Baptist can give a person a sense of how she is expected to behave and what values she is expected to hold—because that's what her people have done through time. A Quaker, Jesuit, or Buddhist can tap a rich tradition of teachings and history around issues such as peace and war, service and compassion, or just getting through the small struggles of each day. Religions give people not just an individual set of rules to abide by, that moral framework with absolute laws, but the powerful group identity that comes from being part of a long history, passed down through generations via story.

Marshall Ganz, a senior lecturer at Harvard's Kennedy School of Government, believes in the power of religious stories to define a moral vision and to inspire action around that vision. He thinks the question of how to find those coalescing forces for moral vision in ways that may transcend particular religious practice is critically important. In fact, his popular course "Public Narrative: Self, Us, Now" is focused on this very question. Students in the course learn to craft their own "public narratives." Ganz instructs them first to articulate their most deeply held values, then to communicate those values in a way that will engage a range of listeners, and finally to use that connection created through story to encourage moral action.

Ganz was introduced to the power of narrative as a child raised in a Jewish household in the 1940s and '50s. He met Holocaust survivors when his father, a rabbi and US Army chaplain, was stationed in Germany to counsel displaced people after World War II. He believes his sense of social justice grew out of hearing these survivors' stories and remained a primary part of his own story of self, which is the story that explains why each of us does the things we do, our starting point.

As a Jewish child, he was also intrigued by the story of Passover, which tells of the emancipation of the Israelites from slavery. The story provided him with an understanding of how social change works: One cannot rely on outside sources to gain freedom; real change has to come from within. And that change begins with a galvanizing narrative that gives the group its identity, a common past, and a moral vision. This is the story of us, the story that binds groups together through common values and history. In Ganz's case, that identity led to his leaving college early to join the civil rights movement in Mississippi in 1964. He became an organizer for the United Farm Workers of America and went on to train organizers in a variety of campaigns, including Barack Obama's campaign in the 2008 presidential race, in how to engage others through the use of public narrative.

I called Ganz to ask what happens when we detach from religious story. We look to religious stories for our moral sources and to locate ourselves within community. When we lose aspects of story, we begin to detach from the overarching narratives that give shape to individual and communal lives. Those of us who have left religion may rue our forgetfulness as we start to lose the stories that once tied us to a religious group—and stand slack-jawed in the face of the evidence that our children will never know them in any meaningful way at all.

Ganz said that even if you have left religion, those stories are important as a part of your cultural and moral heritage. "My father was a rabbi, and after bar mitzvah, I wanted nothing to do with it for thirty years," he told me. "But you know, at the same time, it shaped my sensibilities in very profound ways. It enabled me to understand the role of faith in movements I became involved in, the civil rights movement, the farm worker movement, in which faith was absolutely central to what was going on."

How do we form a story of us if we are averse to joining not just religious institutions but all institutions? What are the particular challenges the Nones will face when it comes to forming bonds based on common moral values?

"The question of religion is less about 'What is God?' than it is about 'Who are we in relation to each other?'" Ganz said. He argued that one of the values of religious practice is learning to manage our relationships with others as well as our own hearts, and this focus on relationships with one another makes religion an inherently ethical project. But, he said, we can find other ways to replace religious stories—for example, within the context of what he calls a public narrative.

At Harvard, he teaches his students that public narrative is a framework for turning our core values into action, for taking our story and doing something with it. He teaches students to construct their public narrative in three parts: a story of self, a story of us, and a story of now. The story of self communicates personal values and experiences and is created by exploring one's past and determining the most personally resonant moments. Ganz's students are encouraged to craft this story in preparation for public work in which they'll be called to account for who they are and why they do what they do, as well as their aspirations.

Once that first story is established, we must connect it to a wider group. This is the story of us, in which we join a larger story that bears out our values and validates our experiences. This story enables us to work toward a purpose larger than our own immediate circumstances. Only in binding with others into a larger narrative, Ganz argues, can we make our highest values manifest in the world. For Ganz, this "us" was Judaism, the civil rights movement, and the United Farm Workers of America. In all of these communities, Ganz's own values were merged into a larger structure, which allowed him to express his personal values and to draw strength from the size and richness of the groups. The story of us, however, is not categorical, in that it is based on certain traits, but experiential, in that it is based on shared values or experience.

When bound into a story of us with those with whom we share values, we meet the story of now, which is the nexus of a present challenge, choice, and hope. This is where it all comes together—the intersection of an "us" with the surrounding circumstances, e.g., the interaction of the civil rights movement with the social and political climate in the United States at the time. Religious traditions are exquisite examples of stories of us that, used in the right way, can motivate people to social action. That's because religious traditions tell powerful stories of us. They bind people into groups with a shared identity, values, and history, which in turn teaches people how to face life's challenges—how to confront their story of now.

According to Ganz, however, we can't access that story of now without some foundation from the past, some collective identity around which we circle and from which we draw strength. In the text of one of his speeches, he quotes Proverbs 29:18: "Where there is no vision, the people perish." If we can't articulate our moral sources, and our set of beliefs and values, we more easily lose our way. And once we articulate those sources and values, we have to act on them. Religion has long done that; the challenge for the nonreligious is to develop the same ability to come together for moral action. "Unless we make commitments to each other," Ganz said, "we don't have anything."

CHAPTER 6

Religious Literacy

Stories save us from the smaller versions of ourselves.

—Julia Alvarez, from her Muse and the Marketplace keynote speech, 6 May 2012

Three winters ago our younger daughter, then two and a half years old, and I were visiting the garden store to pick out a Christmas wreath for our front door. As I was browsing the selection, she wandered off and found a statue of an angel kneeling amid some ivy with her hands clasped in prayer. "Look, Mama!" she yelled across the outdoor lot. "That girl is doing yoga!"

I walked over to her and bent down to whisper, "Sweetie, that girl is an angel."

"Oh!" she said brightly. "What's that?"

I laughed, but I was also shocked. How could she not know such an essential symbol of the Christian faith? She wasn't missing just the stories of the biblical angels but all that these figures symbolize. When I was a child, my grandmother would brush her hand across books of religious paintings and say, "Look at those beautiful angels." I marveled at the smooth, cherubic skin, the silken curls arranged to look like small, soft crowns, the eyes wide and the lips thick and red as strawberries. Nestled alongside my grandmother in her bed as she read to me, I thought of those angels as a promise of safety and care, babes in heaven looking out for me. Long after giving up religion, I still feel a flood of recognition upon seeing any religious painting, sculpture, or architecture. The vocabulary of religion—verbal, visual, musical—surrounds all of us, including the nonbelievers, and enriches the scenery even for those who don't see God in a soaring steeple or a stained-glass window.

But we are losing that vocabulary—and the stories it represents—as we exchange Sunday school for youth soccer games and trips to Target. It's not as if my children might forget a few lines of the Lord's Prayer or get hung up on one of the four Gospels. They will have no sense—felt or remembered—that these spiritual reference points were ever there. They have no religious knowledge to forget. As the philosopher Charles Taylor writes in *A Secular Age*, "Massive unlearning is taking place."

Religion has created the world's most lasting narratives, stories that have helped people make sense of birth, death, and everything in between, and that have guided and consoled people in the same fundamental way for thousands of years. The holy texts assign meaning and purpose to the human condition, provide a set of moral codes, and tell us how to live. They do this through metaphor and imagery, characters and conflict, rhythm and poetry. But the real power of religious stories stems from the depth of the questions they raise and the topics they cover, matters of the human heart. Spiritual cultures come together around these powerful tales and hand them down to younger generations as a way of explaining life. Religions established themselves in the imagination through story.

"Story—sacred and profane—is perhaps *the* main cohering force in human life," writes Jonathan Gottschall in *The Storytelling Animal: How Stories Make Us Human*. "Flip through the holy books of the three great monotheisms—Judaism, Christianity, and Islam—and you will be flipping through anthologies of stories. . . . Religion is the ultimate expression of story's dominion over our minds."

Those stories are part of the religious literacy that enriches our understanding of art and culture. Even though religious stories and codes were born in a time before science and modern thought, we live amid the remains of their enchantment. Religious iconography speaks directly for the ideas and values that drove the creation of the Western world. But when I led my older daughter's first-grade school group through the Museum of Fine Arts in Boston, only one girl in our group of six recognized the figure of Jesus in a collection of paintings depicting his crucifixion and resurrection. The others called him "the naked guy."

Flannery O'Connor. Johann Sebastian Bach. Michelangelo. Could such masters of their crafts have accomplished what they did without faith in God? Would Michelangelo have had the galvanizing energy and devotion to paint the ceiling of the Sistine Chapel as he did if he hadn't been motivated by desire to please God?

Religious stories and images are losing their hold on contemporary America as they compete to capture the attention of a more diverse, competitive, and distractible population. Some feel excluded by these ancient stories, others attacked by their moral implications. Religious myths are easy prey for a rational mind looking to pick apart discrepancies and identify historical impossibilities. Even if we embrace a metaphorical reading of these texts, they still are often lost on us, so we seek other narrative sources of meaning. We look for authentic and timeless stories in modern books, movies, and song instead.

What are we, individually and as a culture, religious and nonreligious alike, unlearning, and at what cost? What is lost—and gained—when we leave behind the inherited stories and rely only on our own? As more and more Americans grow up without a working knowledge of religion, not to mention a grasp of what religion means to the people who practice it, how do we develop a nomenclature for spiritual metaphor and a bridge to those who do believe?

RELIGIOUS ILLITERACY, BY THE NUMBERS

In 2010, the Pew Foundation conducted a poll of Americans, asking twenty questions such as: What is the Islamic holy book? Who was Martin Luther? What religion does the Dalai Lama practice? More than 50 percent of respondents correctly answered only eleven of them. Everyone else fared worse. In his book *Religious Literacy: What Every American Needs to Know—and Doesn't,* Stephen Prothero, a professor of religion at Boston University who co-led the study, defines religious literacy as "the ability to understand and use the religious terms, symbols, images, beliefs, practices, scriptures, heroes, themes and stories that are employed in American public life." He argues that large numbers of Americans, notoriously vocal in their religious views, have no idea what they're talking about.

Prothero's interest in religious illiteracy began after he started working at Boston University, having moved from Atlanta, and noticed that his students couldn't grasp basic religious references in his lectures. "When I would say things like 'In Matthew, blah, blah, blah,' the students would get that look like they sort of knew what I was talking about, but they really didn't." He realized that he would have to fill in the knowledge for them, piece by piece. "I would have to say, 'Matthew, which is one of the four Gospels, which are books in the New Testament, which is a scripture in Christianity, which is one of the world's religions.' "

As Prothero's experience shows, increasingly secular generations are losing a working knowledge of religion. Because of this, Prothero's students share no common texts. They can't discuss much of the literature of the Western world in a deep way because they don't have knowledge of basic tenets and texts of the religions of their own ancestors, not to mention those of others. They're also missing the stories that have been passed down through the ages.

Religious illiteracy cuts us off from our history, from an understanding of the spiritual impulses that once structured the societies of our ancestors, and from a working knowledge of how Western art and literature came to be. It's impossible to understand Western culture without religious literacy—not just the past but the conflicts making the news today. If you don't understand religion, you don't understand a lot of what's going on in the world. We lose greater awareness of how we fit into a larger cultural framework and inheritance that connects us through myths and symbols.

Religions transmit more than values to children. So much of our shared culture and understanding of world events is rooted in religious knowledge. If our kids aren't being raised with an understanding of religion, will they still be able to understand the essential history that religion imparts, not to mention the dynamics on the world stage?

SOMETHING BIGGER THAN YOURSELF

When my older daughter was seven, I added an illustrated children's Bible to the stack of books I read to her every night before bed. I had high hopes of weaving an essential text in with those about historic American Girl doll characters, fairies, and dogs.

She loves animals, so I chose the story of Noah's Ark, figuring she'd be taken in by all those goats and giraffes and elephants lined up safely two by two in the hull of the boat. But I'd neglected to consider how Noah and those animals got there in the first place. I read the opening lines: "So God said to Noah, 'I am going to put an end to all people, for the earth is filled with violence because of them. I am surely going to destroy both them and the earth.' "

My daughter stiffened. I quickly turned the page, skimming over the phrase "every living thing wiped out" and the picture of the tumultuous waves surrounding the boat. After two pages, she put her hand over the book. "I don't want to read this anymore," she said, her voice trembling. "God's too mean."

The idea of a wrathful God was utterly alien to our children, and I realized I'd forgotten it myself—the humbling presence of this omnipotent being with the power to obliterate or redeem us. This is a greater loss than simple religious literacy. This kind of God stands in for a structure that lets people know they are part of a unifying whole, a power that holds and nourishes them, and also threatens them if they do wrong. For thousands of years, religion has bound people together largely by reminding them that such a God was watching. Somehow this story still felt important to me. Not that God would come down and flood the earth, but that we should be mindful of forces larger than ourselves, and learn that we are accountable to them in our actions.

That night, nestled on the couch with my daughter in relative safety, I realized I couldn't explain to her the theology behind God saving some and destroying others. I closed the children's Bible and placed it on the bookshelf, where my own Bible had lived throughout my childhood. I asked her what she wanted to read instead. She chose our collection of Greek myths—the more palatable stories of gods, goddesses, and fantastical man-animal hybrids that were almost human in comparison to the God of the Bible. We spent the next hour amid gods and goddesses who did beastly things to one another, tricked and punished and betrayed each other, but never with the same terrifying authority or finality.

Her choice seemed a desire to remain close to the ground, alongside stories of mystical beasts of nature and gods who were like characters in a play rather than those of a people under the severe hand of a single, ultimate God. But this desire suggested to me the loss of an inner architecture, a sense of awe and fear before the vastness of God, the uncertainty of our lives, the unknowability of the world. Would my daughter's spiritual terrain and moral core develop only through what she could see in front of her?

On one level, religious literacy is about knowing the stories themselves, all those cultural references our children will come across throughout their lives in literature and art and music, but on another level it's about the messages captured in those stories, born from another time and way of thinking about the world. Shouldn't our children have a sense of how religious people then and now have conceived of the world, and answered life's big questions?

THE ROLE OF SCHOOLS

As essential as religious literacy is to our understanding of our past and our present, it doesn't have to be learned in houses of worship. One finding from the Pew survey of religious knowledge is that the more education a person has, the higher he or she will score on the religious literacy quiz. Thus, the highly unlikely combination of Mormons, Jews, and atheists, all groups characterized by high levels of education, scored in the top ranks on the survey.

I tested my own religious literacy on the Pew website and was shocked to have answered fourteen of the fifteen questions correctly, putting me ahead of 98 percent of the population. I don't think of myself as religiously literate, but as I answered questions covering a range of religious history, literature, and practice, I was borne back to different places and times in my life. Like most Nones, I had a hefty dose of religion growing up, spread out though it was. I recalled learning about the Catholic belief of transubstantiation back in my all-girls Catholic high school, where I couldn't take communion during Mass (because in the Protestant religion, the bread and wine are symbols, not the real thing). I'd learned during an early American history course in college that Jonathan Edwards participated in the Great Awakening. My father is a scholar whose specialty is Martin Luther, so I knew who started the Protestant Reformation. And I had to credit my regular yoga practice for my knowing that Vishnu and Shiva are Hindu dieties.

Requiring religion as a cultural study in American schools is the most obvious way to create a space in children's minds for the role that religion has played and continues to play around the world. That's because our schools are where our democratic vision of plurality most clearly plays itself out in children's lives, and where they come up against ideas other than their own. If religious literacy is to be fostered in the public square, we must start with schools.

But schools shy away from this. Many public school teachers are afraid to broach the topic of religion for fear of violating the separation of church and state mandated by the Constitution. They don't realize there's a big difference between teaching and preaching religion, or they fear they'll cross that line inadvertently. Many Americans conflate the ban on school prayer, which was handed down by the Supreme Court in two decisions in the 1960s, with a ban on any discussion of religion at all, even in the form of a comparative studies course. Pew found that only 36 percent of respondents knew the difference between the two.

In fact, the two Supreme Court rulings state clearly what can—and should—be taught in school with regards to religion. A closer look at the pivotal decisions on school prayer shows that the justices encouraged teachers to instruct their students on what religion is. In *Engel v. Vitale* (1962), Justice Hugo Black wrote, "The history of man is inseparable from the history of religion." And in *Abington School District v. Schempp* (1963), Justice Tom Clark wrote, "One's education is not complete without a study of comparative religion."

While schools shouldn't proselytize, they can teach religion as a cultural study. Schools can make space to talk to students about the role of religion without promoting any particular ideology. It's important for kids to learn about other religions in the world to understand our history, present conflicts, and diverse points of view. Shielding kids from the study of religion only closes them off from exploring how and what others believe. You can preserve the church-state divide and still teach the role of religion as an ongoing factor in the lives of many.

One proponent of mandating religion as a cultural study in schools is Daniel Dennett, a professor of philosophy at Tufts and an outspoken atheist. Dennett argues that all religions should be taught as part of cultural literacy, and that, in fact, parents have a responsibility to teach their children about religion even if they aren't religious themselves: "Religions are an important natural phenomenon. We should study them with the same intensity that we study all other natural phenomenon, like global warming," he said in a TED Talk. Dennett, though adamantly opposed to religious influence in society and government, knows it's a part of the social fabric that we misunderstand at our own peril.

"Today's religions are brilliantly designed," he said. "They are immensely powerful social institutions, and many of their features can be traced back to earlier features that we can really make sense of by reverse engineering." Parents, as stewards, have a responsibility to teach their kids about religion. "You have a responsibility to the world, to the state, to them, to take care of them right," he told his audience. "You have a responsibility to let them be informed about all the other creeds in the world, too."

Many private schools teach religion as a cultural study, but few public ones do. A few courageous public schools are trying to teach religion as a history course. In Modesto, California, ninth-graders have to take a nine-week survey course in world religions to graduate. Studies of the program have shown that students come out of the course with greater respect for a diversity of religions, as well as for First Amendment rights.

Religious literacy is strengthened when we have relationships with people who come from different religious backgrounds (including none at all). It happens through discussion and sharing and respectful debate. It happens when we are not afraid of people whose faith is different from ours, and we can allow ourselves to hear what religion means to them.

"Interfaith dialogue" is a buzzword on college campuses these days. Groups of college students come together to combat common misperceptions of different faith traditions and explain what their faith or atheism means to them. Programs like the Interfaith Youth Core attempt to tear down walls we put up when we're ignorant about religion and choose not to learn more. Perhaps it's easier, for students and instructors alike, to navigate the potential conflicts of such discussions in college than in K–12 settings. But by the time kids get to college, it may be too late.

ON A VISIT to New York City, several friends and I took a trip up to Washington Heights to visit the Cloisters, a museum established to exhibit medieval art and architecture. It was a crystal-clear fall day, with a hint of summer humidity still hanging in the air. My friends and I walked up the well-worn stone steps to reach the twelfth-century Spanish chapel where forty black speakers were set up on tall, skinny stands in a circular formation, part of an unusual musical installation created by Janet Cardiff called *The Forty Part Motet*. The first contemporary art ever presented at the Cloisters, it was based on a motet by the Tudor-era composer Thomas Tallis and sounded as it did in the Middle Ages, with each speaker playing one part from the forty-part song.

About thirty people had gathered. One woman held a very small baby; another sat in lotus pose, hands resting in her lap, eyes closed. A few older couples stood stooped and still. The music rose and fell around us, the trills of a Christian choir that resonated so deeply in me it was as if I'd heard those sounds all my life. The music was sacred and captured something unnamable yet overpowering. I felt connected to that music because the sounds had been so threaded through my life. The same was true of the religious art and architecture there. The museum was not just a pretty place to me. It was imbued with a feeling I understood on a deeper level, a feeling that the mere recitation of religious facts could not convey. I wondered if my children could ever feel what I felt there, if there was anything that would give them such a sense of solace and connection.

After the music ended, I felt renewed, the way I sometimes used to feel after church. As my friends and I walked around the grounds and through the exhibits of the museum, I was stunned by how much beauty had been created in the name of religion. I tried to capture some of it in photos on my phone, but later that night, when I viewed the photos, I realized that the true power of the place—like much of religious culture—had to be sensed firsthand to be understood. You had to walk through it to feel it. I realized religious literacy was not simply something you know but also something you feel.

My friends were moved as well, and I had to wonder if, when my own children were adults and looking for a nice way to spend a Sunday morning, it would occur to them to come to a place like this. I decided to work harder to expose them to religious art, iconography, and music so they might come to appreciate the rich heritage that belongs to all of us.

CHAPTER 7

A Sense of Belonging

To think about home and the departure from home, about not going home and no longer feeling able to go home, is to be filled with a remarkable sense of "afterwardness": it is too late to do anything about it now, and too late to know what should have been done. And that may be all right.

—*James Wood, The Nearest Thing to Life*

One afternoon seven years ago, I was in my son's bedroom, putting his clothes in his dresser drawers as he played with Legos on the rug. He was six years old then, and it was the quiet time before dinner when there's nothing much to do. As I tucked his dinosaur pajamas into his top drawer, I heard him say, almost to himself, "I feel homesick."

I inched the drawer closed.

"Can you describe the feeling?" I asked.

"It just feels . . . empty," he said.

I sat down beside him and leaned against the side of his bunk bed, brushing some scattered Legos into a loose pile. I tried to act nonchalant, as if the word "homesick" weren't coursing through my head like a snake. "Homesick" was exactly the word I used to describe the emptiest moments in my life. Not a literal homesickness. The feeling had nothing to do with being, or not being, home. It was something larger—an ache beneath the surface that emerged at random. It would strike at the dinner table on trips home from college, in the middle of nights out with friends, or on long Sunday afternoons when worries about Monday morning loomed.

Now my son was feeling it, too. A child's tantrum I could handle. Boredom, anger, sadness—like any other parent of two small children, I dealt with their emotional ups and downs every day. But "homesick" felt like a different register, the kind of spiritual gap that a parent could not easily remedy.

"Is there anything I can do to help make the feeling go away?" I asked.

He stared at the floor, and tears formed behind his small wire-rimmed glasses.

"I miss our cousins and Grandma and Grandpa and uncles and aunts and, just, well, just everyone," he blurted, looking down at the floor. "I just want us all together in one place," he said.

I plucked a Lego Storm Trooper, no bigger than my pinkie, from the pile and straightened its legs. My children had been born into a loving family; we visited grandparents, aunts, uncles, and close friends. He had his younger sister (and another one would soon be on the way), friends at school, and kindhearted babysitters. But both Michael's family and mine were broken up and flung apart. Michael's parents, each an only child, had died before I met him. One of my brothers had also died, when I was in college. Nearly all of our extended family lived out of state, so we saw them only on holidays. And on my side of the family, divorce runs so rampant that even the thought of getting everyone together in one room would send the adults into a panic.

That tribal force of family togetherness didn't come easily to our fractured clan. As he and I sat there alone on that quiet afternoon, I wished, not for the first time, that we had a people. And I worried that he was wishing it, too.

I looked around at the toys and books that Michael and I had bought to enrich his young life. We checked out parenting guides from the library, ate dinner together as a family, and read to the kids every night before bed. But we both also wondered if we had failed to give our children something bigger than our love. They were growing up without *communitas,* the term the anthropologist Victor Turner uses to describe a richer form of community than what we find through friendship, work, and school. Communitas is a group bound by the shared quest for values, purpose, and meaning.

Did we lack the coalescing force that such a group could give us, an identity rooted in such strong yet invisible bonds that our children would not feel alone even when they were? What I heard my son wanting, and what I wanted as well, was the sense that we were part of some larger, lasting whole. I had witnessed all my life how religion gives people that feeling. But we were not religious, and I suspected we weren't going to change. What I wanted to know was if, for families like mine, religious belonging could be replaced.

THE IDEA OF belonging is rooted in the word "religion" itself. It comes from the Latin *religare,* meaning "to bind," and religion's ability to bind people to one another in common belief and purpose has made it, for good or ill, the most powerful cultural force the world has known. Like a ligament (from the same Latin root), religion holds the individual parts of the whole together so it can function.

Throughout history, religion has been the greatest provider of a sense of belonging outside of the family itself.

Belonging matters in ways that go beyond the evolutionary urge for group survival. Humans have a fundamental need to feel we are accepted members of a group, which starts at birth. Religious parents welcome their children into the fold soon after they're born. Long before children even know what religion is, they are christened, circumcised, or otherwise marked as members of their religious tribes. In Judaism, parents hold a baby-naming ceremony or bris. Christian ministers use water as a symbol of washing away sin. In Islam, a prayer called *Adhan*—"God is great, there is no God but Allah"—is whispered into the newborn's ear, and the same prayer is whispered again at the end of a person's life. Through these rituals, religious families and their congregations pass along not just specific beliefs and practices but also a powerful sense of belonging.

The human need for interpersonal attachments continues throughout our lives, as a basic human motivation. Many of the emotional problems people suffer, including anxiety, depression, grief, loneliness, and relationship problems, stem from a lack of belonging.

A new field, social neuroscience, is proving that belonging is key to our physical health, not just our mental well-being. Research shows how humans evolved biological mechanisms to ensure our safety within a flock. John Cacioppo, the director of the Center for Cognitive and Social Neuroscience at the University of Chicago, discovered that our body chemistry changes depending on our interactions with others, or lack of them. Outside the safety of trusted friends and family, our bodies go into alert mode, exhibiting a series of negative changes: Our arteries tighten, raising our blood pressure; our levels of cortisol and epinephrine, hormonal signals of stress, go up; and inflammation diminishes our immune function. Loneliness and isolation make people sick. When we interact with others, immunity levels, hormones, and blood pressure respond positively.

Our bodies possess a biological system of punishment and reward to ensure that we socialize. It's not an exaggeration to say that the difference between a life of isolation and one of community can be the difference between life and death.

Such effects aren't so much about the quantity of connections we have as they are about the quality. Our experience of connection to others is subjective. Despite the actual number of social or family connections we have, to reap the positive biological benefits of interacting with others, we need to feel these others are people we can truly count on. In other words, we are nourished and healed by being close to "our people." Our bodies reward us for finding and connecting to a tribe.

To reap all the physical benefits of belonging, you have to go beyond the feeling of belonging to a group and act on it—in fellowship with others. "Congregating physically may actually play a role in an association found between religious observance and decreased morbidity and mortality," writes Cacioppo. Citing a study by Lynda H. Powell, Leila Shahabi, and Carl E. Thoresen, Cacioppo explains that only in coming together in community do people experience the benefit of belonging. The authors found no connection between spirituality and health. Instead, it was the act of attending religious services that reduced mortality. Those who attended religious services in community with others lived longer. The same wasn't true of just any group. "Weekly attendance at the Rotary Club may also be good for you," Cacioppo writes, "but the findings by Powell and her colleagues indicate that there may be something unique about regular attendance at *religious* gatherings."

What does participation in a religious community in particular add to our well-being? Cacioppo surmises that church attendance often has bonuses, such as reinforcing family connections and presenting people with an array of trustworthy friends. And the altruistic focus at the heart of much religious charity work "fosters feelings of self-worth and control while reducing feelings of depression."

The community connections people find through religion also increase what sociologists call our social capital, a measure of both economic and social value derived from networks based on reciprocity and trust. Our social capital comes into play when friends put the word out when you're looking for a new job, a PTA member asks other committee members for gardening tools for a neighborhood planting project, or a church announces that a family has lost a loved one and could use some help. These connections make our lives easier and make us healthier as well. But as more and more of us leave institutions like religion, they are diminishing. The loss of such connections doesn't just decrease our sense of happiness and belonging. The loss is bad for our health, and it affects us on a cellular level.

WHEN WE FEEL we belong to a group, we experience greater meaning in our lives than when we are isolated. True "belonging" is more than just hanging out with friends, though. A study led by Roy Baumeister, a professor of psychology at Florida State University who specializes in the study of belongingness, demonstrated that the more friends a person has, the greater his feeling of happiness. What Baumeister wanted to know was what kind of relationships promoted the greatest sense of *meaning*—and why. In particular, he investigated which characteristics of one's relationships created the greatest sense of meaning: a sense of belonging, feelings of social support, or high social value, which is essentially the self-esteem that comes from having a lot of friends.

Baumeister and a team of social psychologists divided 105 participants into three groups. The members of the first group were asked to close their eyes and think of two people or groups to whom or to which they felt they truly belonged. After the subjects had a few moments to contemplate their feelings of belonging, researchers asked them how much meaning they felt in their life. Then researchers asked the second group to reflect on the help or social support they had received from others, followed by the question about how much meaning they sensed in their lives. Finally, they asked the third group to think about the compliments they had received from others—in other words, the social value they accrued from their friends—and again followed up by asking them how much meaning they felt. Of all the groups, those who were asked to consider their sense of belonging reported the highest rates of perceived meaning in their lives.

The study showed that a sense of belonging is not the same as simply having an active social life and a lot of Facebook friends. True belonging does more for us. Baumeister says that when we feel it, we gain a sense of continuity, even permanence, the very things that religion is so good at bestowing. Once people have that sense of belonging, the benefits to their social lives and health accrue—especially if the group to which they belong is a religious one.

Just what is a true sense of belonging? How strong and enduring do groups have to be to give us the positive physical, emotional, and social effects of belonging to a community? It turns out that it's important that the group be lasting—that you have faith that it will continue and will be there when you need support. Historically, groups with that degree of longevity have tended to be religious ones. Richard Sosis, an anthropologist at the University of Connecticut, compared two hundred American utopian groups, some religious, some not, from the nineteenth and early twentieth centuries, to see which ones had the most staying power. He found that the secular groups did not have the same staying power as religious groups. In fact, nine out of ten of the secular groups he studied were gone within twenty years. The religious groups, on the other hand, lasted an average of twenty-five years, with nine out of ten breaking up within eighty years.

Religion strengthens communal bonds through rituals. People mark their lives from baptism to First Communion or bar or bat mitzvah to marriage and death in religious institutions. Participation creates an ongoing sense of security and belonging. Synchronous group rituals like singing, chanting, and prayer have also been shown to bind people more fully. In fact, a study of a religious firewalking ritual in Spain revealed that the heart rates of practitioners and audience members began to operate in sync during the ritual, rising and falling in tandem.

One essential factor in religious groups' longevity and stickiness is trust, which is also cultivated through the use of ritual. The practice of any religion requires commitment, and the higher the cost of that commitment—unconventional dress, significant time allocation, or painful ritual—the greater the trust it establishes among members. Those who don't demonstrate commitment are let go; you can't belong if you don't fall in line. This cutting out of the "free riders," as social scientists call those who seek to reap the benefits of group membership without doing any of the work, makes religious groups stronger.

Sosis found that the religious communities that enforced the strictest rules lasted the longest. But that wasn't true of secular communities, which disbanded despite costly rituals and behaviors. He concluded that true binding required an additional reinforcement: The rules had to be sanctified by God, made holy in the name of some force larger than the group members themselves. Sanctification allowed the group to experience collective transcendence, a sense of operating on another plane of existence, out beyond the typical concerns of the day. Once religious groups come together around whatever it is they call sacred, self-interest diminishes and the group experiences an elevated sense of collective purpose.

IT WAS ONE thing to study the academic perspective on what religion gives us in terms of belonging, and what we risk losing when we leave religion, but I wanted to step out of academia and into the religious world to understand what's lost on a more emotional level. A friend who is a member of St. Bartholomew's Episcopal Church in Manhattan suggested I talk with the popular rector there at the time, Buddy Stallings.

On one of his rare days off, I visited Stallings in his well-appointed apartment with a picture window overlooking the East River. He wore glasses, had thinning gray hair, and played the avuncular guide as he reclined on a tan couch in his art-filled living room, his shoes off and his pale blue golf shirt open at the collar. In the comforting southern drawl of his Mississippi roots, he explained what the church had given him—and how it sometimes loses its way.

Stallings told me he understood why people like me would leave religion. He knows that the church has failed at times to make itself relevant to many. In fact, Stallings understands acutely the ways in which Christianity doesn't always follow its own instructions to love others. As an openly gay minister, he is at the hot spot of right- and left-wing church debate. In addition to the troubling issue of politics infecting religion, Stallings said that ancient religious texts can be challenging to apply in the modern day—impossible if we take them literally. He sees why people who have only a cursory understanding of the Bible reject it. To him, the Bible requires so much annotation and interpretation that it should come with a warning label that says, "Don't read this by yourself."

Yet, despite the many ways religion can be mishandled and misunderstood, Stallings still thinks it can and should hold a crucial place in our lives. He grew wistful when he told me that his son, who lives in Mississippi with his wife and three children, stopped going to church because it no longer mattered to them. His son said he just didn't see the point of getting the kids dressed up and off to Sunday school each week.

"That makes me just want to lie down and weep," Stallings said, shaking his head. He feels the church contributes so much to the lives of those who belong to it. "I want to be giving my life to something that makes a difference in people's lives," he said.

Stallings knows firsthand that the investment people make in a religious community often sustains them through the struggles we all inevitably face. At funerals he doesn't tell the grieving that he knows why things happen as they do; rather, his faith calls on him to be there with them in their pain and to remind them that God is with them, too.

An extreme example of confronting deep pain was the Sandy Hook murders, when a twenty-year-old shot down twenty children and six staff members in an elementary school in Newtown, Connecticut, one of the deadliest mass shootings in a school in our history. "Every funeral for the children eventually took place in a community of faith," he pointed out. He wasn't saying that religion could explain why such a terrible thing had happened, but that it can be a comfort, especially in times of extreme grief, to connect to the mourning rituals and spiritual guidance of a faith tradition.

"I've been a pastor long enough to know that when people's lives have blown up, we should be there in an honest way that doesn't say, 'Here are the answers,' but instead says, 'What I believe is that God is with us, that God is utterly powerless in any human understanding of power, but the presence of God, not just literally present, but in other people, is what will eventually sustain us to get through whatever comes.' "

During difficult times, Stallings reminds his congregation of the literal stone foundation of their church. He uses the stones of St. Bart's, which were set in place a century ago, as a metaphor for the lasting nature of religious tradition and the strength it has to bear individuals through suffering. He sees those stones as the tangible reminders that religion offers a container for even seemingly unbearable grief.

"I talk sometimes in funeral homilies about how the stones of St. Bart's are filled with emotions—penetrated with the hopes, dreams, fears, and anguish of so many generations before us. I tell them that that matters," he said. "And I believe it does."

To Stallings, the church is an institution that can be supremely helpful in people's lives. As we leave it, we should consider where we can find similar sources of strength, especially in the face of great challenges.

WHEN WORSE COMES to worst, where do we who are without religion turn? Without a spiritual tribe tied to ancient texts and rituals to call our own, we join temporal communities—sports clubs and hobby groups and work communities. If these communities had doors, they would not be the big, solid ones of Stallings's church. They'd be the beaded kind that were so popular in the 1970s—alluring, but a lot less substantial. A weekly yoga class may teach us to be patient and calm, but it doesn't bind us to other people in a lasting way. A Little League baseball team provides an education in patience, struggle, and teamwork, but at the end of each season the players and their families disperse. If my son were sick, would people from his basketball team show up to sit with him while he recovered? When he tells me he's homesick, how do I help him transcend the walls of his Lego-strewn room to connect to something larger? Were something truly devastating to happen, where would we turn? So often I find myself longing for a foundation as large and lasting as the stones of St. Bart's.

It's clear how important a sense of belonging is to people who are religious, and how it supports them in their lives. For my grandmother, it meant that everyone showed up at her house late in the night when her husband died. In congregations across the world, people come together to help members who have had setbacks, financing their education, rebuilding their homes, supplying meals, and offering prayers. The religious feed and clothe others in their faith in faraway countries, people they've never even met. They give more of their time and money not just to their own religious groups but to their wider civic communities. Belonging to a faith community confers enormous social, emotional, and even biological benefits.

Without religion, it's difficult for many people to find communities that give them the same sense of belonging and meaning in their lives as their faith group once did. In some religions, the worst punishment is shunning, forcing members out of the fold. Many people are choosing to do that themselves, when they no longer have faith, but they, too, suffer the consequences of no longer belonging.

BY THE TIME I'd lost religion, I was surrounded by others like myself. My sense of belonging, to some degree, came from not being part of a religious group. I wanted to know what it would be like to turn your back on your religion if you lived in a very strong religious community, where the consequences were more overt—and devastating. One answer came from Neil Carter, who lost everything when he left his religion. I met him at the American Atheists National Convention, where hundreds of atheists, freethinkers, and skeptics come to share in a weekend of speeches, workshops, and camaraderie all centered on their nonbelief. That year, it was held in Memphis, Tennessee.

Neil is the father of four girls and lives in Jackson, Mississippi. He was raised in the Southern Baptist tradition and continued in it until he realized he didn't believe in God or the teachings of the Bible anymore. A plainspoken forty-something with sandy hair and an easy drawl, he was one of the three panelists on a panel called "Southern Atheist Living." He told the thirty or so people assembled in the small ballroom that after leaving his religion, he didn't have anybody. His religion had been his whole life, and he was suddenly alone. He lost his wife and his community, and he left his job as a teacher at a conservative school to work elsewhere after a student discovered he was an atheist. When asked what it was like to be an atheist in Jackson, he did not mince words: "Mississippi is the most religious state," he said. "It's social suicide to come out as a nonbeliever."

Leaving religion was such a seismic change in his life that he compares it to the moment in the movie *Toy Story* when Buzz Lightyear realizes he is not an elite intergalactic space ranger but a simple child's toy. Like Lightyear, Neil fell to earth, losing the sense that he was part of a divinely inspired cosmic drama. But the loss of his community was even worse. Though he felt relieved that he no longer had to do mental gymnastics to reconcile the biblical teachings of his faith with contrary evidence from science and reason, he paid a huge price with his friends, family, and community.

Like many nonbelievers who live in highly religious areas, he turned to the Web to find a like-minded community. "The religious go to church," he said, "and atheists to the Internet." He started a blog about his experience, *Godless in Dixie,* which has become so popular he was featured on *CBS Sunday Morning.* He has drawn in readers who tell him his story has helped them. But the Internet didn't hold all the answers even for this popular blogger. He told the crowd that it's hard to create online relationships. For one thing, it can be a challenge to find other atheists through social media without everyone else finding out, too. Many in the audience also shared stories of wanting to keep their nonbelief secret. Despite rising acceptance of atheists on the two coasts, and an increase in the numbers of Nones in every area of the country, including the South, being an atheist in certain regions is much more challenging than in others. In some places, it's not just a liability but also a danger.

So while the Internet allowed Neil to communicate with like-minded others, it didn't solve the problem of having lost that sense of belonging. What Neil said he missed most about religion had nothing to do with belief. It was the connection to a community. "The problem with social media is your friends can't cook you dinner if they're six states away," he told the audience. Though he has begun to make a new life for himself with a new job, partner, and friends he's met mostly online, when it comes to community, he added, "it's just not the same."

MARCI OLSEN ALSO knows the pain of leaving a faith that is so centered around community. She left the Church of Jesus Christ of Latter-day Saints as a teenager and spent a decade trying to find a community, and even a name for herself, that would help her recover the richness of her life as a Mormon. I met Marci in Santa Fe, New Mexico, in the home of the local head of the atheists Meetup group, over coffee and quiche one Sunday morning.

Marci told me that after leaving her home and her faith, she attended community college in Cheyenne, Wyoming, then moved to Missoula, Montana, where she tried for five years to find her people. But Missoula was more a college town than a place for postgraduate twenty-somethings, and she found nothing compared to the community she'd had through her Mormon identity. When she was growing up, nearly every day included some activity arranged by or at the church. Now, there was no driving force or central meeting place organizing a group of like-minded people.

"I was lost as far as community goes," she said. So, after college, she packed her life into her pickup truck and spent a year living in it, eventually finding her way to Santa Fe after a series of bad relationships. Shortly after landing there, she started scouring the Meetup website for a group of people to go hiking with. She found an event listing from a community of atheists but was skeptical. She took atheists to be angry and militant, the typical stereotype. But a friend encouraged her to go, and she soon realized her preconceptions couldn't have been more off base. Several of the people she met that day have become her closest friends. They gather every other Sunday for brunch in someone's home. After eating, they break out instruments and play music. Marci sings like she used to do in church. These are her people now. "The community we've created is the closest I've had in my adult life," she said.

Even so, Marci still doesn't quite know what to call herself. Her identity growing up was so tightly tied to Mormonism that it's hard for her to articulate who she and her people are. She wrestled for a long time with the right word to capture her identity and finally gave up.

"I think we'd be better off if we decided it didn't matter what we called ourselves," she told me. "We are never really one thing anyway. We are an aggregate of things." For now she has settled on a label that reflects that. She calls herself an "agnostic with atheistic and Buddhist tendencies." It is the kind of identity more and more people are searching for—a word, phrase, or sentence that captures the complexity of a human life.

While some people resist a label, finding one can be important. The term "None" itself is problematic, defined via the absence of religion for many who don't even think about religion at all and therefore don't feel any absence. With so many leaving religion, reinterpreting religion, or determining their own understanding of who or what "God" is, "None" is no longer adequate.

Even the term "nonreligious" is a misnomer: It suggests that the absence of religion is a defining element of a person's life even if it's not, reflecting religion's longtime dominance. We don't yet have terms to reflect the variety of secular communal life or to signify nonreligious experiences of transcendence and grace. Finding adequate language and labels is a first step in finding a clear voice, and also in beginning to draw others together in community.

WHO AM I?

For millennia, religion has given people a sense of identity through the powerful vehicle of belonging. When you have a people, you have a name that suggests certain beliefs and practices. When you leave your people, you lose all that. Along with gender, family, and nationality, religion has been a defining characteristic of individuals throughout history. For millions of people, religion is and has been a safe harbor in a new world, a membership card to a trusted tribe, a vertical stake connecting temporal experience here on earth to both a rich history and eternal life.

Back when most people belonged to an established religion, we *inherited* our identities, and along with them our sense of meaning, our commitment to others, our ways of celebrating and dying. Because religion has dominated the cultural landscape for so long, our connection to the past is likely a connection to religion. Our sense of identity, passed down through families over generations, has typically been rooted in the religious past.

But that's less and less true today. We are now less tied to tradition, and to the past. The word "secular" comes from the Latin *saeculum*, meaning this age, this century, this generation. The definition connotes present time, the here and now, not eternal or religious time. We think in terms of our immediate concerns, of how to flourish here on earth, not in some believed-in afterlife. To think about time this way changes everything—and it means we can more easily lose a sense of our histories, communities, and identities.

In a society where we can come and go from religion, move from one to another, or abandon the practice altogether, our identities are more fluid. Those who quit religious institutions may still define themselves by what they left behind. We tell people, "I was raised Christian," but then add that we no longer practice. We call ourselves "lapsed" or "lazy" or "fallen." Unless a person is firmly atheist, many religiously unaffiliated adults will cling to a slim trace of their first religious identity, even if it's defined in the negative—"ex-Catholic" or "former Muslim," for example. Many of us live in that kind of liminal zone, where identity hinges on the loss of something we once had.

This loss of a sense of belonging and identity crosses many religions. In general, the stronger and more fundamentalist the faith, as Richard Sosis discovered, the more it creates an all-encompassing sense of identity. For some people, leaving a religion isn't just a matter of going to a different church than your parents or sister; it means leaving your people entirely. For many Muslims, for instance, the sense of loss of community and identity can be profound.

Mohamed Abdelziz remembers the moment he left Islam. He was kneeling before his prayer rug, facing Mecca from his apartment in Michigan, preparing to pray. He had recently been wrestling with his faith. As a college student taking classes in philosophy, science, and religion, he had been soaking up all the knowledge about the world that he could in the hope of validating his faith. But as much as he wanted to continue to believe in God, the evidence from his studies kept pushing him in the opposite direction. He realized he couldn't adapt his faith to the new ideas on evolutionary biology and philosophy that he was learning in school. He was losing his grip on God, and religion no longer made sense to him.

According to the strictest interpretation of Islamic tradition, Muslims can miss a prayer session if necessary but can't actively choose not to pray. That is considered disobeying God. For Mohamed, who was praying five times a day and trying to follow all the rules, not praying meant violating his relationship with God in an unforgivable way. And so, as he knelt before his mat that day, he knew that if he decided not to pray, it would mean he was deciding to leave Islam. "I thought to myself, 'If I reject this now, this is a big deal.' "

He chose not to pray. When he stood up and walked away from the prayer rug that lay beside his bed, he knew he had left his faith, a heritage that extended back to Egypt, where he was raised, and through his ancestral line as far as anyone in his family could remember. "For a long time I walked around like, 'Okay, I guess I'm an atheist,' " he said. "After a while, I was like, 'What does that even mean? What do I do now?' "

I met Mohamed at a meeting of the Ex-Muslims of North America, a group with fifteen chapters that was set up as a safe community group for open discussion about the rejection of Islam. On the evening we met, the group was gathered in the basement room of an Italian restaurant in downtown Chicago. As drinks flowed and heaping plates of pasta and grilled fish were served, Mohamed and others shared their experiences of leaving religion, particularly the feelings of isolation that followed. Several members of the group came in secret, saying that their families might harm them if they learned of their participation.

A twenty-one-year-old college student in Kalamazoo, Michigan, Mohamed is at once boyishly energetic and thoughtful beyond his years. He has long waves of thick black hair, cut to his chin, and wears large glasses. He told me that he has always been the type of person who asked big questions about life's meaning and purpose. Though he was raised Muslim, his parents weren't outwardly religious. His mother didn't wear a headscarf, and his father didn't pray five times a day. Faith for his parents was vitally important, but they were not conservative. Religion was more a matter of the heart.

As a teenager, Mohamed began practicing his faith more rigorously. He decided that if he was going to be a Muslim, he was going to go all in. The more he learned, the more he saw that to be a Muslim meant he would have to practice certain rituals, such as praying toward Mecca five times a day, which he did. Then he entered college and started taking classes in philosophy, science, and history, which came up against his faith and eventually won out.

Soon after he walked away from his prayer mat that day, he entered a period of despair, which he was still feeling when we met. "It was really disastrous," he said. "It was a feeling of being all alone." He said that a lot of people he knew sugarcoated their atheism, but for him, the process had been anything but easy. "It's better to know that my views are more aligned with the way the world is and what the truth of the world is," he said. "But it's a painful process."

That process was made more painful by knowing he was cutting the spiritual branch off his family tree. "Islam was the foundation for everything," he said, "especially for the people in my community and my culture." And it was threaded through every moment of his day. Rigid Islamic faith of the sort he was practicing dictates small prayers during even the most practical matters of everyday life—eating, brushing your teeth, and showering. To leave the faith meant removing the practices that gave inherent meaning to everything he did. The character of each moment of his life changed.

Leaving faith also shattered the bigger picture of life's meaning. "Islam says that you go to heaven and everything that you ever wanted will come true," Mohamed said. He loved the idea of a father figure watching over and protecting him, punishing those who wronged him and keeping track of all that he had ever done. "Nothing other than religion can give you that," he said.

Mohamed is trying to come up with a new framework for his life, but he isn't sure how to do it. He's the first in his family line to step outside his faith, and he wonders what he'll teach the children he hopes to have one day.

"When you move that brick, the whole building crumbles, and then it's just really hectic to know how to build the building back again, to build meaning and purpose in life, to build a whole system or way of living," he said.

Creating that new life is especially challenging because Islam is imprinted on him in his very name. One of the questions he asks himself is "What does it mean that I'm Mohamed, but not a Muslim?"

Without religion, and without the community religion provides, many people experience a kind of existential crisis, wondering who they are after they disaffiliate. When people lose faith in God, they lose a key framework for coherence, a narrative in which all our actions are watched over by a benevolent God who cares for us and may even intervene on our behalf. This helps us believe that our lives have meaning and, importantly, that our lives will never end. Perhaps the greatest innovation of monotheistic religions was to give people this consolation. Without it, some move on easily; others struggle in anguish.

But losing one's whole world—the religious narrative and all it gives people—shouldn't have to render people hopeless. People like Neil and Marci and Mohammed were already finding new avenues for meaning and belonging for themselves. And talking with them made me wonder how many Americans were finding such a sense of identity and belonging without religion—and where.

THE PATH FORWARD

CHAPTER 8

Morality Without a Map

It is a fine thing to establish one's own religion in one's heart, not to be dependent on tradition and second hand ideals. Life will seem to you, later, not a lesser, but a greater thing.

—*D.H. Lawrence,* THE LETTERS OF D.H. LAWRENCE

Religion has been creating and cultivating elaborate frameworks for belonging, meaning, and morality for millennia. But when it comes to morality, there are other sources we can easily look to, such as philosophical humanism, reason, common sense, and reflection. Still, most Americans continue to believe that the nonreligious are less moral than the religious. A 2014 Pew study found that the least trusted group in the United States is atheists. Add to that a 2006 research study showing that Americans rate atheists as the group least likely to care about their country and as the ones people are least likely to want their kids to marry (not to mention select as president).

There is a long-standing belief that religion leads to morality. Without religion, the theory goes, flawed humans born of original sin are tempted to commit immoral acts. God's grace alone saves us from ourselves. Even if you don't believe the supernatural aspect of this rendering, the practice of religion itself has as its bedrock the kind treatment of others, at least in principle if not always in practice.

Religions do provide a moral orientation. They create important reminders for people to think beyond their own individual interests. And religions often espouse absolute laws that leave no wiggle room, no guessing about what's right and what's wrong. But none of this means you need God to be good. In fact, despite what most people in the United States think, religion is not necessary for moral development.

A RESEARCH TEAM at the University of Chicago recently ran an experiment to see if there was any difference in measures of altruism between religious and nonreligious kids. The study, led by Jean Decety, looked at 1,170 families from a variety of countries and religious and nonreligious backgrounds. Researchers focused on one child between the ages of five and twelve from each family. Each child was allowed to choose stickers from a selection—but told that the researchers wouldn't have enough time to give stickers to everyone in their school. The researchers then gave each child an opportunity to share some of his or her stickers. Altruism was measured by how many stickers the child gave up—if any. It turned out that the nonreligious kids were 23–28 percent more likely to share their stickers than the religious kids. In addition, the more religious a family was, regardless of which religion, the less generous the child was.

Studies like these open a new and interesting vein of research into what actually makes us moral. If religion is not the main influencer, then what is? New research is showing that parents have a profound influence on the moral development of their kids. An earlier study by Decety and Jason Cowell showed that an infant's morality was shaped by his or her parents' sensitivity to others and sense of justice. Studying children between one and two years of age, the researchers found that all exhibited distinct brain activity and eye movement when watching videos of characters acting either pro-socially or antisocially. Then the children were offered toys depicting the characters whose behavior they had just seen. The babies of parents who measured higher in empathy, justice, and fairness were more likely to make a negative judgment about the antisocial character by not choosing that toy. The researchers concluded that the response those children had was a result of more complex reasoning.

We are learning that we don't need God to be good. Parental influence matters, however, perhaps more than ever. People who study adolescents say there is much to be worried about—narcissism, depression, and a loss of concern for others, among other things. When it comes to creating a strong moral framework for younger generations, there may be no better time than now to seek alternatives to religious moral teachings through ingenuity, reflection, and a more authentic expression of values. And there's perhaps no better place to begin than in our first community—our homes and our families. It is there that our values take root.

HELPING CHILDREN HELP OUT

Focusing on others doesn't have to be packaged in a religious saying like the Golden Rule. Simple compassion can be and is modeled everyday by thoughtful parents, religious or not. In fact, though the motivation for moral behavior may differ between the God-fearing and secular, I suspect we all live by some version of treating others well. The trick is modeling it in such a way that the kids take notice. At church, you can force them to sit through a sermon. That's harder to do in your own home, but it doesn't mean we shouldn't try.

Articulating our sources of morality means teaching our children the story of who we are as a family, our family's connection to the past, and respect for the histories of our relatives who came before us. Parents have to own their values if they want their kids to grasp them. In our family, that means stressing kindness, empathy, and honesty. And we have to model these values every day to fight the cultural tide of narcissism. My younger daughter's preschool has a "mood meter" posted in the room, so kids can monitor how they're feeling throughout the afternoon. But, mindful of Rick Weissbourd's thinking about how we raise kids to have meaningful relationships, each day I try to ask her—and her siblings—how the other kids they interacted with were feeling instead. But is it enough? And how do I know?

One Sunday our older daughter found a magazine cover that perplexed her. She asked me what the Voting Rights Act was and why the magazine article said it was being thwarted. I gave her my down-and-dirty explanation, and she seemed satisfied, but after dinner I heard her asking Michael about it, and he went into even greater detail about racism and civil rights and our country's history of inequality. Listening to them, I thought of Michael's Jewish upbringing, his parents' liberal Judaism, and his own cultural identity as a member of a group that cares deeply about justice and civil rights.

Later, when I was tucking her into bed, she asked, "What can we do about people not being able to vote? How can we change that?"

I told her we could support the groups waging the battle in the courts. She could set up one of her unusually lucrative lemonade stands and, instead of giving the money to the Ronald McDonald House or the nearby animal shelter as we'd done in the past, she could learn more about this particular cause and the best way to support it. I told her that when she was older she might want to find work that would build on her seemingly innate desire to help others.

As I turned off her light and left the room, it occurred to me that our family hadn't stepped foot in a church or synagogue that day. No one had said a word about God, read the Bible or Torah, or prayed. Yet somehow our values of fairness, equality, and, yes, the Golden Rule, had come to the surface on their own. *How can I help other people?* our daughter had wanted to know. She was developing her moral compass from what she gleaned as she watched and learned in her home, school, and wider community. Our job was to keep those kinds of questions and concerns coming, and find a way to channel them so they wouldn't fall away unrealized.

Creating those frameworks for ourselves is not easy. And yet the newness of the challenge brings opportunities for ingenuity, reflection, and authentic expression of values. In small-town Minnesota, one spiritual-but-not-religious mother I met creates a DIY religious and moral framework deliberately for her family—around the kitchen table.

KITCHEN TABLE SUNDAY SCHOOL

Sarah Aadland was raised in a predominantly Lutheran town with a population of three hundred and fifty in North Dakota, but she left religion in college because she couldn't square her understanding of the world with a belief in God. After she and her high school sweetheart were married, they moved to Minneapolis and started a family. Longing for a values-based community in which they could raise their kids, they joined a Unitarian Universalist church, which gave them a like-minded community that didn't require belief in God. Ten years later, they decided to move an hour north to a small rural town called Taylors Falls to escape city life and start a hobby farm, growing plants and vegetables for fun. The area was far more conservative, and once there, the Aadlands struggled to find the same kind of diverse, progressive community experience that they had found in the Unitarian Universalist church.

After the Haitian earthquake, Sarah's older daughter, then four, heard the news on the radio and started crying. She asked her mother how they could help. They made a donation, but it seemed intangible. So Sarah started piecing together a more conscious practice of instilling values in her growing family. She decided to re-create what she'd loved most about the Unitarian experience through her own homeschool version of Sunday school. And she has been blogging about her experience ever since on the website of a nonprofit organization called Doing Good Together, which provides parents and schools with information about upcoming volunteer activities in their area. Her blog, called Big-Hearted Families, provides parents with resources and ideas for building empathy in kids.

Sarah practices what she preaches with her three young children. The family has a donation jar that they put extra money into throughout the week; from time to time they decide which charity to give it to. They talk about and practice values that matter to them. Sarah says her kids' teachers tell her they are peacemakers in the classroom. And every Sunday, Sarah, her husband, Joe, and their three children set aside two hours to take a collective breath and discuss what matters most to them. On a sunny morning in March, I joined them.

After blueberry muffins and orange juice, Sarah's family gathered around the wooden table in the light-filled room just off the kitchen, and she rang a chime to signal the start of their family version of Sunday school. They began by reflecting on the joys and sorrows of the week. Each child scooped up a handful of dried black beans and, when it was his or her turn, placed one on a plate bearing a happy face or a sad face. With each plunk of a bean, the children took turns sharing what events of the week had made them either happy or sad. Everyone was sad that Monkey, the cat, had contracted Lyme disease, but school projects and the start of spring made the happy pile. Already, they were talking about things that mattered most to them.

Then Sarah popped a children's meditation CD into the CD player. She lay on the floor with her son, Max, the youngest of her three kids, and we all closed our eyes and stayed at the table for the guided meditation through the Spaghetti Test, where you make your body as loose and relaxed as cooked spaghetti. When we opened our eyes, the couple's older daughter said, "That really worked!" And it had—everyone, including Max, seemed calmer and more centered. Joe read a book called *Two Old Potatoes and Me,* a secular parable about new growth from old, unpleasant experiences, which was the setup for the garden planting we then went out in the backyard to do.

On the back deck, surrounded by the bucolic landscape, we pressed seeds into small plantable pots that the kids ferried over to the fenced garden to plant. Sarah said her daughter had been told on the bus on the way to school one day that she was going to hell because she didn't believe in God. To Sarah, it was crucial to develop the values to counter that kind of bigotry. To her, religion wasn't necessarily the source of moral behavior. "I'm trying to teach them acceptance, tolerance, thoughtfulness, and critical thinking," she said, stating the values she holds most dear—her own moral framework.

For this family on their small farm so far from the city, who had left first the Lutheran faith, then the Unitarian one, the weekly ritual was how they filled the gap left after religion. As I drove the dirt road away from the Aadlands' home, I thought that some of the good that comes from religion—rituals that ground and connect us, the practice of compassion, the honoring of stillness—could be created in other ways. Anyone could develop and reinforce values within her own family through deliberate practice. The most important thing wasn't whether you were religious or not. It was what you modeled within your family, the way you embodied your own values and transmitted them through your actions.

KICKING AWAY THE LADDER

The truth is that belief in a supernatural god or gods works exceedingly well when it comes to cultivating morals within a group. We act better when we feel we are being watched, as by a God. Want your kid to behave? Hang a poster of two eyes on the wall in his bedroom, and research shows he'll hew more toward the straight and narrow.

But societies begin to let go of religion as a way to structure and reinforce good behavior when they no longer need it. So says Ara Norenzayan, a professor of psychology at the University of British Columbia in Vancouver and author *of Big Gods: How Religion Transformed Cooperation and Conflict.* Once the elements of society that religion was critical in creating—social norms, moral codes, and communal protection of individual members—have been replaced by trusted secular institutions, adherence to religion starts to give way. Institutions like governments, police forces, and courts work together as a secular safety net, a civic alternative to the guidance and controls religion originally provided.

"Now we have an interesting social transition in some places," Norenzayan told an online interviewer. "This isn't happening everywhere, but in many parts of the West, we have strong secular institutions that seem to take away the function of religion." Over the past hundred years, as people have begun to trust these secular institutions, levels of cooperation have gone up and religiosity has declined. Norenzayan points to countries in Scandinavia, among the most peaceful and well-functioning in the world. Places like Norway and Finland took what they needed from religion, he says, and "kicked away the ladder."

As we wrestle with the big questions in new ways, it doesn't take belief in God to make us good. But attachment to some moral framework, such as philosophy, reason, or individual family values, can go a long way toward helping us feel less alone as we deepen that innate sense of morality to meet the complexities of the real world. I thought of one of the ladders Sarah Aadland had kicked away, though not by choice. When she and her family left the Minneapolis area, they also left the Unitarian Universalist church. Much of the home Sunday school program she'd created was modeled on that church's own practice. What was it about UU that so easily transmitted to the secular realm?

A STRUCTURE TO GROW UP IN

A friend was raising her two sons in a Unitarian Universalist church in Arlington, Massachusetts, and suggested I visit their teen group that met on Sunday nights. I wanted to see how the Unitarians build moral community in a creed-free religion that welcomes believers and nonbelievers alike.

Secular people who don't subscribe to stringent religion but desire an organized spiritual community often find their way to liberal Protestant congregations such as the Unitarian Universalists. Perhaps the oldest Protestant "church" open to atheists, Unitarian Universalism is eclectic, offering people of all faith backgrounds—and none at all—just the right balance. Instead of guidance from a sacred text or creed, Unitarian Universalists center their faith around seven principles, or moral tenets, including the worth and dignity of every person and the free and responsible search for truth and meaning.

One winter night, I drove to the First Parish Unitarian Universalist Church in Arlington to meet thirteen teenage youth-group leaders in a basement lined with old couches and strewn with empty pizza boxes. The teen leaders come every Sunday to plan community service work and other functions. Once a month, they meet for evening "worship," during which they delve more deeply into problems they are having and show their support for one another. The night I visited, they shared with me what they most prized about their membership at the church: The bonds made there were deeper than at school, the place was a true community, and it gave them the sense that they were not alone.

When I asked what they thought my young children would miss out on if we never joined any religious group, they told me that they couldn't imagine their lives without their church—and, in particular, this group. A blond-ponytailed girl in a blue sweatshirt said, "This church creates a structure for us to grow up in. There's no book to follow. It's about a general love for each other and wanting to be part of something larger than yourself." She said that they are called there to act in love.

That calling, which came from being a part of the community there, galvanized them toward action that was greater than what they might accomplish alone. Each year, for example, the youth group went on a service learning trip, building houses in Appalachia or helping repair parts of New Orleans. But perhaps they gained the most from the lessons of care and generosity they gathered in that room, among their peers. One boy said the camaraderie he found at church was something altogether different than what he found at home, at school, or on his sports teams. He felt accepted at church in a way he didn't anywhere else.

A FEW DAYS later I met with Marcie Griffiths, the adviser to the youth program, who was raised in a Unitarian church herself. She described the parish as a community of care and said they put their values into action through service learning, whether it's volunteering at homeless shelters, building houses for people in need, or helping with a blood drive through the American Red Cross.

"I think you could piece a lot of it together on your own," she told me. "I think you could take the good things from it if you didn't want the religion." But the community aspect is what she sees as the true benefit. "Especially once they are teens, having this kind of supportive place that's not school, not work, and not home—I don't know if they can get that elsewhere."

She told me more about the monthly teen meeting of "worship." Worship takes many forms, but it is usually a breakout workshop session in which the members explore things like fears and struggles. At the end they light candles and share something positive from their lives for which they are grateful—events like college acceptance or a parent recovering from surgery. Griffiths said that at one of the recent candle rituals, a boy came out as gay for the first time. She said that normally the group snaps their fingers to show support, which is "less disruptive in the sacred atmosphere," but this time everyone erupted in loud applause and hoots and hollers.

"It's things like that that make me feel nothing else matters," Griffiths said. "You've learned that you can be who you are, and that's the most powerful thing that I can hope to create out of this program."

Leaving the Unitarian church that day, I thought maybe this job of raising good kids—not to mention trying to be a good person myself—was too much to take on alone. I knew Michael would never join a Unitarian church because it was too steeped in the Protestant religion. Though plenty of Jews attend UU churches, along with expats from many other traditional faiths, it wasn't the right fit for us. As much as I admired the sense of mutual care and respect I'd observed in the teen group, as well as the group's engagement with community service activities, the truth was that Michael and I would probably never join a religious group, no matter how open-minded. And yet it was the dynamic of the group—belonging to it, caring for it, allowing it to hold you accountable—that shaped and guided moral behavior beyond innate goodness and individual reason. The kids in that room were called to act in love by their faith. What was it that called my kids to act in love—beyond their own small voices?

CHAPTER 9

Do-It-Yourself Religion

The way things are, are not the only possible way they can be. Stories are the first way we figured that out.

—*William Alexander, from his National Book Award acceptance speech, 2012*

Years ago, when Michael and I were living in Northern California with our two young kids, we decided to host an impromptu Passover dinner, or Seder, with friends—most of whom, like me, hadn't been raised in the Jewish faith. Now that I think about it, I had no idea what faith any of my friends had been raised in, because we never talked about religion. Instead, we talked about our kids, work, books, movies, or music. We shared stories from our past, most of which featured the many ways our parents had neglected us throughout our childhoods, and yet how such neglect had turned out to be a good thing. We talked about everything, it seemed, except religion.

But Michael and a close friend of his from high school, also raised Jewish and no longer practicing, were feeling nostalgic and wanted to hold a Seder. We prepared for the meal in our own busy, secular way—ordering the food from a nearby deli and downloading the Passover manuals from the Internet. We concocted a shortened version of the ceremony by crossing out the long, boring parts, threw some pasta into the unleavened mix to make the kids happy, and zoomed through the ceremonial meal with the speed and efficiency of a brainstorming session at work. We ended the night as we ended all nights together, sitting around telling stories and drinking wine while our children fought with plastic light sabers and watched reruns on the Cartoon Network.

As we settled into our overstuffed faux-leather couches, hand-me-downs from one of Michael's fellow graduate students, someone brought up religion. Fresh off the secular, store-bought Seder, we asked one another: Did we need it? Did it matter? Were we missing something? That's when Michael, who has a maddening-yet-lovable habit of trying to provoke people with outlandish questions, said he had a proposition. We all looked up from our wineglasses in anticipation.

"Why not start our own religion?" he said. "Just us. We'll meet every Sunday for dinner." He went on: No theology or dogma or strict rules. We wouldn't even need the excuse of a holiday like Passover to gather. Instead, we'd be just a group of friends who enjoyed sharing in one another's lives in a more regular, formalized way.

Everyone smiled and nodded and agreed the idea sounded good in theory. We were close friends who'd known one another's children since birth—we were practically family. But the conversation quickly reverted back to seemingly more pressing matters. *Who's going to be the Democratic nominee in the next election? Who's the best rock band of all time?* Without saying why, we all knew that religion was different from a group of friends getting together once a week. As lovely as the vision sounded, such a group could never be anything close to the equivalent of joining a church, synagogue, or other religious institution. Friendships, even deep ones, couldn't provide what organized religion had been offering people for so long.

For one thing, I was pretty sure we wouldn't keep it up. There would be new jobs and relocations (in fact, we moved to the East Coast the following year), conflicts and excursions. One of our friends was an avid surfer. Would he show up even on days when the waves were just right? Another friend pursued romantic relationships as if it were his full-time job. Would our regular Sunday dinners be tantalizing enough to woo him from an intriguing match on an online dating site? Our children would have soccer games and birthday parties, fevers and stomach bugs. Life, quite simply, would get in the way—and, unlike the religious, we wouldn't have a solid foundation that stayed put when individual commitment wavered. No God would command us to come.

As our friends left that night, we hugged at the door and spoke enthusiastically of our next get-together: likely another impromptu gathering thrown together that day or the night before in a flurry of phone calls and mad dashes to the grocery store for food to grill and wine to drink. We'd pick a venue—a house, the beach—and gather at no specifically set time. I loved our friends, but I knew as we said our good-byes that we couldn't make a religion out of a dinner party, or a religious community out of a small group of friends, beloved though they were.

But I also wondered if Michael's proposition represented some hole we were trying, consciously and unconsciously, to fill. How many of the religiously unaffiliated sought a community more structured than a collection of friends but less restrictive than a religious tribe? Was it possible to have all the good of religion—without the parts we didn't like?

As I traveled the country, I began to find a surprising number of people looking for that sweet spot of secular identity and community that went beyond just friends. In all corners of the country, groups are trying to create replacement communities for what religion once gave them. Some are just starting out. Others have hundreds of members. What they show is that secularism is surging, and people now have enormous freedom to seek their own forms of meaning and create their own types of communities. But what are the risks of trying to cobble together one's own secular "religion"?

SHEILAISM TODAY

In the 1960s, when the number of people leaving religions began to spike, the influential sociologist Robert Bellah described how the counterculture was breaking down many of the communal values shared in religious groups in favor of a do-your-own-thing ethos. In their 1985 book *Habits of the Heart,* Bellah and his coauthors describe interviewing a nurse named Sheila Larson, who said she called her faith "Sheilaism." Sheilaism was a mix of ideas with no connection to texts, values, or community beyond herself. "My own little voice," she called it. To Bellah and his colleagues, Sheilaism suggested the breakdown of that unifying power of religion to give us something we all agree on and revere—and "the possibility of over 220 million American religions, one for each of us."

Since the publication of *Habits of the Heart,* the move away from institutions that bind individuals together is even more widespread.

Today, anyone can be his own guru, get a mail-order certificate to officiate at her friend's wedding, or create individualized rituals. In fact, it's common. We are far freer to piece together our own private religions, to find sacredness wherever we like—or not at all—and a kind of Sheilaism is now practiced by more and more Americans. A 2009 study by Pew showed that Americans increasingly mix and match elements of diverse religious beliefs and practices, even from conflicting faiths, to create their own DIY religion. We curate our experience in ways that meet our highly individual needs, retreating from the commons to protect and nurture our own. In essence, we're all Sheilas now. But a custom-made spiritual practice does not solve the desire for belonging. In fact, it isolates us. What's missing is a sense of community—which is one of the most important features of religion when it comes to making people's lives more positive.

Until recently, no one could say exactly why religious Americans tend to be happier, healthier, more charitable, and more socially connected than their nonreligious peers. Was it something about religion itself that conferred these benefits? Though there were copious studies that correlate positive effects with religion, no clear cause-and-effect relationship had been established. Which comes first: religion or health and happiness? Maybe healthy, happy people are better able to get themselves to church on Sunday, which explains the happiness boost. Or maybe a belief in God makes us want to exercise to demonstrate our gratitude for life, which accounts for the apparent health benefit.

For a long time, no one knew the answer to this chicken-and-egg question about religion and its benefits. Then, in 2010, Chaeyoon Lim, a sociologist at the University of Wisconsin–Madison, along with Robert Putnam, published the results of an experiment in which they asked regular church attendees about their beliefs, religious activities, and social networks. They found that the boost in life satisfaction the religious have long been known to receive didn't result from prayer, beliefs, or the feeling of God's presence. Instead, the level of happiness that religiously affiliated people felt was directly proportional to the number of friends they had in church.

In fact, for every two to four friends a person had through his or her religious congregation, the resulting measure of life satisfaction increased by nearly a percentage point. Lim and Putnam found that people with ten or more friends in their congregations were almost twice as likely to say they are "extremely satisfied" than those who have no friends through their congregations. Those who attended services but sat alone didn't experience any boost in life satisfaction from going to church. What it comes down to, ultimately, is community. We are geared to be social, and when we join with others, our bodies reward us for it. This dovetails with John Cacioppo's research on how community affects us on the cellular level, as well as Baumeister's demonstration of how greater meaning comes through connecting with others. On so many levels, we humans really are social animals.

But what if we don't want to go to church? What if we don't believe in God or don't like the pope's politics or find ourselves yawning during stale rituals? Can secular people come together in a way that mimics what religion gives people? If it's really about the community, couldn't the nonreligious have some of that on their own, without the sacred texts and dogma?

Across the country, all kinds of groups are creating secular community in an attempt to fill the void left after religion. Groups such as Alcoholics Anonymous, adult recreational sports leagues, and Weight Watchers have been binding people in common purpose for some time. But now new, values-based groups are seeking to provide something more than what book clubs and yoga classes have to offer. Newly emerging secular groups, and revitalizing older ones, are developing into full-fledged alternatives to religion. But they face the challenge of trying to unite people who don't necessarily want to be united. So I set out to see just what made do-it-yourself, nonreligious communities work—or not.

SUNDAY ASSEMBLY

Sanderson Jones and Pippa Evans, two British comedians, were driving through the English countryside one afternoon in 2012 when Jones said he wished he could go to a church without the religion. Evans thought this was a wonderful idea, and the concept for their godless Sunday services, dubbed the Sunday Assembly, was born. They found an unused church and rented it, posted details of the upcoming event on Facebook and Twitter, and sketched out a program of singing, stories, and cake. The motto they created for their group was "Live Better, Help Often, Give More."

Within a week, news of the Sunday Assembly had spread around the world. Jones and Evans scrambled to create a website and launched a Kickstarter campaign to start Sunday Assemblies in other countries. Two years after its inception, there are 68 affiliate Sunday Assemblies around the world.

Though it's called an "atheist church," most Sunday Assemblers don't call themselves atheists. They'd rather say what they do believe in, not what they don't believe in. In fact, when a group in New York City tried to open a Sunday Assembly chapter and called itself an "atheist church," the founders balked and said they couldn't use the Sunday Assembly name. They also veer from the term "secular humanism," because, as Jones once said, the label bears a whiff of intellectualism that turns people off. Whatever it chooses to call itself, Sunday Assembly is meant to give people who have left religion a soft place to land.

On a Sunday in March, I walked the bridge across the Charles River to find out what Sunday Assembly was all about. In the basement of the arts building on the Boston University campus, a group of smiling thirty-somethings welcomed me. They were standing beside a table covered in cakes and cookies for the reception after the secular services. I took my seat with about thirty other people, and our emcee, a balding, fortyish guy named Bob in a collarless purple button-down shirt and black suit, welcomed us. "The big thing here is about celebrating life," Bob told us. He explained that he grew up religious and loved the communal aspect of his faith, but he didn't like the tribalism.

"What if we could have the good stuff but with a radical acceptance?" he asked. "No matter who you are, what you believe, or where you're from, we welcome you." He summed up the Sunday Assembly philosophy by saying that life can be hard but connecting to others in a community like this one can help. To get things started, he asked us to turn to our neighbor and participate in an icebreaking game. We were going to thumb-wrestle with our partners, he said as laughter broke out. He explained the goal of the game: to get as many points as possible. He told us to start, and I found myself locked in thumb combat with a young woman with a slight frame and surprisingly strong thumb. After several minutes of boisterous play, Bob told us to stop. He asked who had the most points and found one pair in the group who had gotten to three hundred points. "How did you do that?" Bob asked. The man said that he and his partner had purposely let each other win instead of competing. "Yes!" Bob exclaimed. He told us that the pair had unlocked the secret to the game—to work together, not against one another—and that their strategy was a metaphor for creating community.

Next up was a scruffy band called Pet Jail, which led us in a loud sing-along to "Love That Dirty Water" and "Joy to the World." A local poet approached the podium and read one of his poems, and a young speaker from Rhode Island told us about her experience demanding that her school take down a publicly displayed prayer. During a segment of the program called "This Much I Know," a Sunday Assembly board member came to the podium to tell us about how her marriage fell apart and she realized she loved another woman. For years she and her mother battled over this, until her sister brought them together. When her mother invited her and her girlfriend to her home, she felt she finally belonged.

At the end, Bob tried to knit together the various parts of the service into some unified meaning. "Whatever your comfort zone is, step out of it to make things better. Whoever you are, whatever you believe, you're welcome." He asked us to take a moment of silence to reflect. Then, taking a page from a Quaker meeting, he asked audience members to stand and spontaneously share their thoughts. One woman said, "I may not need to be here today, but someone else may need me to be here." One said, "I have a problem with angry atheists." Another: "I was nervous to tell my boss, who's religious, about Sunday Assembly. But she got it. She said community is the thing she loves most about church."

After the service, the organizers passed around a plastic collection cup, which we filled with fives and singles. A woman announced that all those who wanted to form a Schmoup (small group dedicated to something—karaoke, guitar jam, craft beer) should write the name of their proposed Schmoup on a helium balloon in the back of the room and stand with that balloon until others joined them. Afterward, we ate cake and drank juice in the tradition of churches everywhere, united in a dizzy kind of postfellowship bliss.

As novel as the experience was—at least for me, who spent most Sunday mornings reading the newspaper—I left feeling vaguely unsatisfied. I knew that many Sunday Assembly affiliates were sprouting up in cities across the United States and that some of them drew large, steady crowds, offered childcare during services, and sponsored regular volunteering activities. The one that I attended, however, seemed unsure of itself. It hadn't held the reverent power of a church service—not even close. It seemed that what was missing was any semblance of the sacred. Everything on offer there—the music, the games, the discussion—could have been had somewhere else. I wasn't sure it was compelling enough to propel me to come back for more.

But, as I was leaving, I saw two young men walking just ahead of me down the long basement hallway. They'd been standing a few rows ahead of me during the service, singing, dancing, and embracing. Now they were quiet, their arms wrapped around each other as they walked down the hall. I thought that even if this particular Sunday Assembly wasn't for me, for those seeking a welcoming community that doesn't discriminate, it could be essential.

PARENTING BEYOND RELIGION

San Diego is home to a major military base and, though teeming with Nones, has a thriving Catholic community. Certain parts of the city are religiously conservative, so atheists, agnostics, skeptics, and other nonbelievers have created secular havens where they can go to be themselves without fear of judgment. One of these groups, Parenting Beyond Religion, began as a local atheist parenting collective and has grown to more than a hundred members of all types of freethinkers living in the San Diego metropolitan area.

That March I flew to San Diego to find out what the community gives its members. Two hours before the group was to hold its first secular Nowruz celebration, I met group leaders James and Anjali Murphy. They'd come to the park early to secure some picnic tables and set up for the party, their nine-year-old daughter, Chandra, in tow. Planes from the nearby airport flew constantly overhead, leaving criss-crossed white ribbons; below their paths, brightly colored kites floated on the wind. And every hour, the bells of a distant church rang. Nowruz is the Zoroastrian spring festival, a Persian ritual that predates all Abrahamic religions and welcomes the spring equinox with food and fire dancing. One of the organizers of the group is of Persian descent, and she proposed the ritual for the group less as a religious idea than a cultural one. Because the group doesn't have its own space, they'd planned to meet in a public park that day.

Sitting at one of the tables as we waited for the others to arrive, the couple explained how they had come to the group. Anjali told me she was raised in California by her mom, a Buddhist, and her father, who was Hindu. Her maternal grandfather became a Buddhist monk, and her paternal grandfather was an ascetic who gave all his money to his ashram and lost touch with his family. Because of this, her parents rejected religion when they had their own children, choosing to raise Anjali and her sister without religion. But as an adult, her sister joined a Christian cult in New York, where she stayed for twenty years before the family finally had her kidnapped and deprogrammed. That was why Anjali had become so active in the Parenting Beyond Religion group: She longed for a values-based community to fill that void, not just for her and her husband but for their daughter as well. She also wanted to join a group that would encourage critical thinking skills as applied to religion, along with religious literacy, so that her daughter would never fall prey to religious indoctrination. James came from an Irish-Portuguese background—each with strong Catholic traditions known for their focus on community service. He said that the group gave him the opportunity to volunteer with others in serving the community, which can be hard for untethered nonjoiners.

Soon about thirty parents and their kids began to arrive with folding tables, chairs, and trays of Persian foods—baba ganoush, dolmas, pita bread, and salad with fresh mint and tomatoes. The parents I met told me that this group was the one place where they didn't have to pretend to be something they weren't. One mother, the wife of a navy doctor, told me that she would never tell her military wives group that she's a member of Parenting Beyond Religion for fear of being shunned. Another mother said she doesn't mention the name of the group at her children's school; she and her husband just say they're part of a "parenting group." Several of the parents said that when word got out that they belonged to a group with "Beyond Religion" in the name, their children were told they were going to hell because they don't believe in God.

Most of the parents said they'd been raised with religion and left. They described conflicts with their own parents over this decision and said they either don't talk to their parents about it much or just shrug their shoulders when the arguments start. One mother said she was headed out of town for two weeks and her mother, an evangelical Baptist who lives in Florida, was flying in to watch the kids. She was worried about what her mother would tell them. Another said her aunt sent her a religious book of children's prayers, which is now her two-year-old daughter's favorite book. One said her parents keep trying to take her kids to church. Nearly all of them were the first in their families to leave religion, and one of the main things they liked about the group was getting to know so many others who were walking the same difficult path.

In addition to get-togethers like this one, organized volunteer activities, and moms' and dads' nights out, the group hosts a regular fellowship meeting, modeled on Sunday church services. At the fellowship meeting, the group gathers to discuss issues that concern them—everything from navigating the fraught world of social media for their kids to how to talk to children about death. These fellowship meetings were Kimberly Hansen's idea. Kimberly is a no-nonsense mother of two who works for an advertising firm. As her young son clung to her thighs (clad in solar-system leggings), she told me she was raised Methodist in small-town Pennsylvania and had left religion but wanted her children to have a values-based community group to counter the idea that nonreligious people were somehow bad. When she joined Parenting Beyond Religion, she asked the organizer if she could start a Sunday fellowship meeting to foster regular get-togethers with a core group of parents.

Despite the stigma some of the members feared from their association with the group, it was thriving. Some members were creating a website to provide resources for other parents, with the hope of drawing in even more people. Anjali pulled a printout of a new logo for Parenting Beyond Religion from her bag: three black figures with their arms raised in joy. I thought of how hard it is to build a lasting community from scratch. Religious groups enjoy millennia of built-up resources, rituals, and teachings for children, not to mention soaring cathedrals and historic temples in which to gather. Would this group that Anjali and James and their friends were starting be around for their children to enjoy as grown-ups?

The three tables set aside for the secular parenting group in the expansive park were but a tiny segment of the nonreligious pie in this country. But to the adults gathered around them, that space was a vital source of connection and meaning, not to mention a safe and accepting place for their children.

Parenting Beyond Religion is not exactly a replacement for religion, but it provides its members with much of what they long for in their postreligious lives: fellowship, support, and an outward expression of shared values. That outward expression was what made it different from most of the other groups of friends and families gathering in that park that day, the ones who were there for volleyball and cookouts. From across town, the ringing church bell reminded us that many were gathering in religious houses of worship. Parenting Beyond Religion was something in between.

As the party wound down, the parents folded blankets and packed up food, dutifully separating trash from recyclables. Two women discussed the next event—a camping trip with all the families—and asked if I could come and bring my kids. I told them I wished I could, but I lived across the country. I'd have to find my people back there. After I left the group, I strolled past other families out in the park that day. Parents were packing up their coolers; children were taking final rides down silver slides, their bursts of boisterous laughter like bells. The kites had been pulled back from the sky by then, and the sun appeared to be hovering just a few hundred yards in the distance over an ominous gray-black Pacific. A man walked past me pulling two small girls crouched back-to-back on the wide plane of a pink scooter, all laughing. I thought: If we strip away the layers of religion, most of what we all value most—family, friends, laughter, food—is the same.

THE CHURCH OF STORY

Farther up the West Coast, I visited Ashland, Oregon, a city of twenty thousand set along the Siskiyou Mountains, to observe how another group is trying to create community through the sharing of stories. The group is called the Hearth, and the intent of its founder, Mark Yaconelli, is to increase a communal sense of compassion and inspire the same sort of charitable action as any religious organization—without the set dogma or tired rituals.

Southern Oregon provides one of the best visions of how secular community develops when organized religion isn't a large part of the social fabric. Institutional religion holds such weak ties in the Pacific Northwest that sociologists have dubbed the region the "None Zone." Most people in the liberal tourist town of Ashland fall under the "spiritual but not religious" label. While they don't join religious institutions per se, many believe in a God-like force they might call energy. I was told there are three healers for every one person living in Ashland, and the smattering of shop and home windows bearing signs offering such services as aura readings, Reiki sessions, and healing crystals seemed to prove the point. The first bumper sticker I saw when I drove into town was a quote from the Dalai Lama: "Kindness is my religion."

But I hadn't come to explore the New Age in particular. I was interested in how the four hundred people who regularly attend the Hearth were tapping into something religion has always understood: the power of story to connect us.

LIKE PARENTING BEYOND RELIGION, the Hearth has no physical meeting space of its own, so the event was held in Temple Emek Shalom, an airy, clean-lined synagogue set on a rural highway on the edge of town. But neither Judaism nor any other religion was mentioned that night. In fact, the rabbi's lectern had been pushed to the back wall, replaced by a teenager's drum set. The rabbi himself, a young newcomer to town with long hair and a charismatic smile, was seated in the audience with his wife.

Mark Yaconelli approached the microphone at the front of the sanctuary. Dressed casually in jeans and a black button-down shirt, he commanded the room with an intense, brown-eyed gaze, saying, "What makes us human is our capacity to love. Love is the center of the spectrum of all of the emotions. And, as e. e. cummings said, 'Unless you love someone, nothing else matters.' So tonight we're going to explore our capacity for love." We would do that, he explained, by listening to six storytellers, each of whom would come up on stage to tell a true story of a time when he or she learned an important lesson about love.

One by one the first three storytellers took the stage—regaling the crowd with sad and funny tales of love gone wrong, love nearly missed, and love found in a surprising place. The tellers were by turn nervous and serene, joking and serious. The audience responded with rapt attention, a reverence for the courage it took to make oneself so vulnerable onstage before friends and strangers.

After the first set of stories, we broke for intermission, and I met a woman named Maddy DiRienzo, a blue-eyed, blond-haired mother of two. She told me that after years of searching for a sacred secular experience, the Hearth had become like her religion. Though she admires people who possess blind faith in God, she had come to realize that it didn't work for her, saying, "we all have to create a story that makes sense for us." Having abandoned the strict Catholicism in which she was raised, believing it was too judgmental, she and her husband had dabbled in New Age spirituality and read all the popular books about atheism that appeared shortly after 9/11, before finding this community. She and her husband attend every Hearth event and bring their two sons.

"There's a feeling I get at the Hearth that I never got at church," she said. She thinks the feeling comes from the personal nature of the stories and the audience's openness about them, which she called an "energetic exchange" that moves her. Of all the religious alternatives she'd tried since leaving Catholicism, the Hearth gave her the greatest sense of meaning and connection. This was precisely Mark Yaconelli's goal.

When I met him later over a glass of wine in town, I asked Yaconelli why he started the Hearth. "We don't know our neighbors anymore," he replied. "We don't know who to call if we're in trouble and we need someone to watch the kids or help take the spouse to the hospital. We don't have that kind of connection with people anymore." He said he sees spiritual poverty all around him. "We are living on this very narrow band of a pragmatic functional hyperactivity, like we're caught under a spell," he said, pointing to our winner-take-all culture of busyness and distraction. Even his teenage sons were experiencing an existential crisis: "My sons were complaining last night, 'I have to get good grades in high school so I can get good grades in college so I can get a good job so I can get a good retirement so when I'm sixty-five I can live,' " he said, shaking his head.

Trained as a Christian minister, Yaconelli worked for years with troubled youth, teaching them exercises in self-compassion, such as meditation and deep listening. He longed to use the community-building and healing skills he learned in seminary in a new way. When he heard about the Moth, a nonprofit organization that sponsors storytelling events around the country and produces the weekly *Moth Radio Hour* for NPR, he saw an opportunity for his own city of Ashland. Within weeks, he rented out a bar, tapped potential storytellers, printed flyers, and created a website. He wasn't trying to make money, so he decided that the five-dollar ticket price would go to a local food bank. Eighty people showed up at the pub, which had a posted maximum capacity of fifty. The attendees packed onto windowsills or stood in the doorway, and the owner left abruptly for the night, afraid he'd be fined for exceeding capacity. Six people told their stories. At the end of the night, the pastor from Yaconelli's church approached him and said, "I think this is your ministry. Your church is the church of story."

From there the Hearth grew quickly. Yaconelli and his board members expanded the program, creating big quarterly events and smaller storytelling workshops, as well as programs for teens and families. Yaconelli thinks the Hearth can address suffering by helping people find deeper meaning and connection in their lives. He has modeled the storytelling ritual on religious structures, in particular Protestant testimony, in which the congregation comes together and bears witness to the stories of others. And he said it's working.

"People who have been coming for a while say, 'I'm less irritable with folks at the grocery line or in traffic because I realize after hearing all these stories that everyone has a story and might be struggling with something,'" he said. The moment of transaction between teller and listener, he believes, increases participants' capacity for compassion, which they then take with them, and which appears in their interactions with others. In this way, this type of storytelling is less about binding people together into "a people" or tribe in the religious sense, and more about peeling away layers to reveal our similarities so we feel heard and understood. Beneath the artifice of our constructed identities, the stories told at the Hearth remind us how much we have in common. Though religious himself, Yaconelli believes people don't need to practice religion *in toto* to get the good out of it. "I'm just taking all the best stuff that religion has to offer as it goes into decline, and I'm giving that out to the next generation to do whatever they want to do with it," he said.

The Hearth has become enormously popular in Ashland. Joshua Boettiger, the rabbi at Temple Emek Shalom, told me that when he first started donating his synagogue space, the number of people who showed up for the Hearth rivaled the crowds he drew on the high holidays—Rosh Hashanah (the Jewish New Year) and Yom Kippur (the Day of Atonement). Now the Hearth crowds consistently surpass even those numbers. Attendees crowd onto the back of the stage and line the walls.

"I'm not used to seeing this many people in the synagogue, ever," Boetigger said when I reached him later by phone. He thinks the Hearth taps into the human longing for direct experience, as opposed to experience that is mediated by religious leaders and traditional rituals. "We're finding ourselves in the story," he said—which we don't always do with religious storytelling. "I think that's what we in the religious world have to get better at doing."

Back at the Hearth, for the final story of the night, a man wearing a long-sleeved gray cotton shirt, wire-rimmed glasses, and jeans walked up to the mic. He told the story of his exuberant son, who loved to surf and play ball and practice on his bass guitar but who developed cancer in his twenties and passed away before he could finish college. After the father finished his story, he picked up his son's worn bass and joined two other musicians, a violinist and guitarist, onstage to perform a cover of the Dixie Chicks song "Godspeed (Sweet Dreams)," an alternative pop lullaby about a parent's love for his child. Listening to the song, I felt as if I'd known the boy and his father personally. Beside me, a woman wiped her eyes.

"Through all our suffering and loss, there is love," Yaconelli said from the stage after the musicians had finished their song. He wrapped up the evening by reminding the audience of key parts of the stories we'd heard and tying them together in a universal message of hope, in the way that the message of all religions is ultimately a message of hope.

After we'd filed out and the organizers were stacking up the chairs, I stood just outside the entry of the synagogue, talking with a few of the people I had met. A fog had settled like thick steam over the hills that surround Ashland. It was starting to rain, but several of us lingered, replaying the highlights of the evening as small beads of water spread into dark blots on our jackets.

I recalled Buddy Stallings, the minister from New York City, telling me that he consoles his congregation by reminding them of the lasting nature of the stones of St. Bart's, a metaphor for how religion has always been there to contain our suffering. A hearth, too, is a metaphor, and often made of stone. For the people there that night, it was fast becoming a strong and sure container for their deepest emotions. The only question was whether it would endure. Would the

Hearth continue long enough that Maddy DiRienzo's children and those of everyone else in that room could one day call it their own?

GIFT CIRCLE AT THE ETHICAL CULTURE SOCIETY

Though they're newly proliferating, secular communities like the Sunday Assembly, Parenting Beyond Religion, and the Hearth are not without historic precedent. Values-based community groups have vied for the hearts and minds of the nonreligious for centuries. Unitarians, describing themselves as "heretics," from a Greek root meaning "choice," began their church in the sixteenth century in Transylvania and have been welcoming atheists and agnostics into the pews ever since. Humanistic Judaism, started in 1963 by Rabbi Sherwin Wine, offers congregants a celebration of Jewish culture without the need for God. And Ethical Societies have provided an alternative to religion since 1876, when Felix Adler, a son of a rabbi and training to be one himself, gave a sermon omitting God at his father's synagogue. When he didn't find a warm reception, he started his own group in New York City. The premise of Ethical Culture philosophy is that people create meaningful lives by striving to live more ethically and treat others with inherent worth and dignity. The group prides itself on "deed before creed," and Adler's "supreme ethical rule" to "act so as to elicit the best in others and thereby in yourself." Though still relatively small in number at twenty-one nationwide, Ethical Culture groups were pioneers in the values-based secular organizations we see proliferating today.

One evening in spring, I ascended the creaky wooden stairs of the Brooklyn Society for Ethical Culture in Brooklyn, New York. The group has been meeting since 1947 in a neo-Jacobean-style brownstone mansion. I was there to attend a monthly practice called a Gift Circle. The Gift Circle is a ritual popularized by Charles Eisenstein, whose book *Sacred Economics: Money, Gift, and Society in the Age of Transition* proposes an economy based on trust and sharing. Eisenstein believes money issued as debt creates scarcity and promotes suffering. If we shed our current construction of debt-based currency, he believes, the gifts we offer one another would proliferate, and there would be far less suffering in the world. The idea of sacred economics may be utopian, but the Gift Circle ritual calls on participants to demonstrate empathy, compassion, and selflessness.

On the second floor of the Ethical Culture Society, nearly twenty people took their places in a circle of mismatched chairs. The room was messy in a homey way, a library with books haphazardly arranged on shelves, worn furniture tucked into corners, and paintings slightly askew. Twenty-somethings, baby boomers, and a few elderly folks filed in, some placing refreshments on a small table at the center of the circle: plump strawberries, dark chocolate truffles, and shiny tins of nuts.

The moderator, Helen Zuman, was a young woman wearing corduroys and a T-shirt. She welcomed everyone and explained what the Gift Circle was and how we'd do it: We would go around the room one by one, and each person would name one or two things he or she needed. After each of us had expressed our need, we would go around the circle a second time, naming things we could offer someone else. And with that instruction, we began.

Some requests were personal: computer software, a cat-food bowl, help decluttering. Others were for a wider community: help digging a community garden, legal advice for starting a communal living space. Some revealed difficult situations—an older man who was looking to make ends meet said he needed piecework. As we listened to each other, the quiet in the room deepened.

If the first go-round in the circle brought out the vulnerability of human need, the second demonstrated old-fashioned generosity. One woman offered a healing massage, another lessons in container gardening, others a place to sleep, or paid work helping with a website. The digging for the garden materialized, as did the piecework. Each offering was a testament to the human ability to solve our own problems. All we had to do was sit still long enough to listen to one another, then consider how we might be of service. With every statement of need, I asked myself: How can I help this person?

Because I didn't live in New York, I couldn't offer the woman seeking furniture the futon we no longer needed back home. As a traveler, I had no material goods to give then and there, so I offered to listen to people's stories about leaving religion and finding their way to Ethical Culture.

After the circle wrapped up and we'd chatted over the snacks people had brought, I descended the stairs and left the building. Walking out into the dark night toward the subway station, I realized that the secular ritual had softened something in me. I'd long been aware of how much I have and how fortunate I am, but I had no structure through which to engage in direct conversation with strangers about their basic needs. Though I wanted to help others, I often did so in a random, scattershot way. The Gift Circle worked because it created a sense of connectedness among the people in the room, many of whom didn't even know one another. When we begin to tap into that connectedness, we sense the potential to participate in some bigger purpose that both humbles and elevates us. We don't need religion to find that feeling, but we do need a context in which to channel our empathetic urges.

After that night, I e-mailed Helen Zuman to ask if she would share with me her story of how she started holding Gift Circles in Brooklyn. She said that she had long since left religion but missed the communal aspects of it. She sometimes finds herself singing as she walks alone around her neighborhood. The words of the hymns she learned growing up in the Catholic Church come to her unbidden, and the songs take her back to what she loved about religion. "It was a swelling of joy in our voices together," she said. "I loved singing with people in church." She described the sensation as agape, an intense feeling of love for the world and everyone in it.

Despite how much she loved that feeling, she didn't stay in her faith. The priest's homilies never spoke to her. She recalled her first-grade teacher telling her that God decided who went to heaven or hell and was keeping a list of all the good and bad things people did, and for her, that knowledge grew over the years into guilt. Like many other people I had met, she said her religion teachers didn't like it when she asked too many questions.

When she turned twelve and was preparing for confirmation, the priest told her and her peers that this was the ceremony where the Holy Spirit appears. With excitement, she prepared herself for the overwhelming power of the Holy Spirit coming to her. But during the ceremony, nothing like that happened. Everything felt the same. After that, she continued to attend church with her parents and sisters and went on to a Catholic high school, but her faith was already gone.

Helen couldn't find a place for herself in the Catholic Church, but her urge for connection and belonging remained. The first time she spoke with the director at the Ethical Culture Society about hosting a monthly Gift Circle, she felt welcomed and was impressed that all the leaders were women, something she'd never seen in church. She said that during the Gift Circle rituals she had glimmers of that same "oceanic feeling" she'd felt while singing at church, a feeling of deep connection to others. It was those moments when she realized that she didn't need religion to tap into that feeling. "It's there and accessible," she said. "It's part of life."

HELEN WAS DESCRIBING the kind of collective ritualistic experience many people crave. But, detached from the powerful institutions of religion, it can be hard to come by. I recalled that when I interviewed Robert Putnam at Darwin's café in Cambridge, I'd asked him if secular people like me could form communities that would ever rival religious ones.

"Can there be a church of the Nones?" Putnam had asked with an intense gaze as he considered the question. I leaned closer, pen poised. I thought maybe he was going to give me the clear-cut answer I was looking for.

Instead, he shrugged and said, "We won't know for another three hundred years."

CHAPTER 10

Almost Church

I recommend that everybody here join all sorts of organizations, no matter how ridiculous, simply to get more people in his or her life.

—*Kurt Vonnegut,* PALM SUNDAY: AN AUTOBIOGRAPHICAL COLLAGE

I was daunted by the problem of secular community that Putnam raised, an issue I'd gotten glimpses of in the groups I'd already seen struggling to put down their own roots in a world in which religion is still powerful and pervasive. It would take time (at least three centuries, according to Putnam) and effort for such groups to build themselves up, and it would take introspection for individuals to find their way there. I realized that in order to answer my children's questions—and my own—about who we were and where we belonged, I would have to dig deeper. I would have to figure out what I myself believed.

A friend had told me about a website called Beliefnet, which caters to a pan-spiritual crowd and has a quiz to help you figure out your spiritual identity. The quiz, called the Belief-O-Matic, consists of a series of questions—such as "What is the nature and number of the deity(ies)?" and "What happens to humans after death?"—meant to determine which religion most aligns with your beliefs. That such a quiz even exists speaks to the fluidity and variety of spirituality today. On the site, I found a smorgasbord of faiths. There were so many choices that scrolling through them all was like standing in the grocery aisle trying to pick out a cereal. I could immediately do away with Falun Gong and Zoroastrianism—couldn't I?—but I still didn't know where I would best fit. Was I "Earth-based"? I love nature, but is that really a religion? How about Buddhism, since I take yoga classes and have a meditation app on my phone? Was I still Presbyterian after all this time? Did my Calvinist work ethic make me a Christian? Was I a little Jewish through osmosis because I was married to Michael? I had no idea where I fit, so I took the quiz.

After I answered the questions—it took about five minutes—and hit ENTER, an e-mail popped into my in-box. I was almost afraid to open it. What would it say about me: "Heathen Yogini"? "Wiccan-Wannabe"? "Just Plain Lost"? I summoned my courage, clicked on the message header, and read the e-mail: Secular Humanist, 100 percent. A pureblood? I felt a strange rush. Having been raised in such a tangle of Christian strains, I'd never felt like a pure part of any specific group before. I'd always wanted a clear-cut identity, and here I was something through and through.

But what, exactly?

According to the e-mail description, a secular humanist is an atheist or agnostic who prizes rational thinking and considers the scientific method "the most respected means for revealing the mysteries of the origins of the universe and life." Secular humanists likely have no "concept of afterlife or spiritual liberation or salvation." What matters most is what they do on earth: "Realizing one's personal potential and working for the betterment of humanity through ethical consciousness and social works are considered paramount, but from a naturalistic rather than supernatural standpoint." In my religious past, I'd believed that if you accepted Christ as your Lord and loved others as he loved you, you would gain entrance to heaven after you died. It was a highly motivating setup—and terrifying when you did something wrong and believed you were going to hell. Secular humanism offered a different rationale for being a good person. Instead of holding out a big stick, it said that being kind to others and alleviating pain when it was in your power to do so was in and of itself the whole point. There was no prize for that—you did it because it was the right thing to do as a sentient being sharing the planet with other sentient beings.

The words made perfect sense, but I couldn't quite imagine what the secular humanist label meant in practice, much less what kind of church (or gathering) I was supposed to attend, which holidays I should celebrate, where I'd find my people, or how I was going to eventually be cremated or buried. What songs would I sing over the holidays? Would we hunt for Easter eggs, eat bitter herbs, take communion, or pray to the goddesses of the four directions? Secular humanism sounded good in theory, but what did it really mean?

I called Phil Zuckerman, the secular studies professor from Pitzer College in Claremont, California, who'd spoken so enthusiastically about atheism at the Courtyard of the Gentiles event at Georgetown University. I told him about the night at the window watching the Greek Orthodox procession with my son and how, when my son had asked me what we were, I couldn't answer him. I said I was disappointed in myself. Just because Michael and I had left religion shouldn't mean that we'd fallen into a black hole of nothingness. But how could we describe ourselves without the old labels?

"You're human," Zuckerman practically shouted into the phone. "You're not nothing."

I told him that I'd taken the Belief-O-Matic quiz on a bit of a lark but that the answer it had come up with seemed serious: secular humanist. Was being a secular humanist the same as having no religion at all? I suspected that's what my grandmother would have thought. The label sounded fine for me, but what would being a secular humanist mean for my kids, and for us as a family?

Zuckerman told me that nonreligious parents face a unique conundrum. They are so wary of forcing beliefs on their children the way religion was forced on them that they are often reluctant even to describe their worldview. He urged me to banish fear and plunge in, embracing my identity as a secular humanist—if, in fact, that's what I was.

"You need to tell your kids that you're a secular humanist and tell them what that means," he said. "You need to say, 'We believe in making the world a better place, we believe in evidence over faith, we believe in reason as a way to address problems, we believe in helping others because that makes the world better for everybody. This is what we believe.'" He was growing passionate as he spoke, like a preacher building to the end of a fiery sermon.

I nodded along as I listened to him list the foundational beliefs of secular humanism. They sounded true to who I was. I did believe in science and rationality, and that human beings have a duty to others, particularly those less fortunate. I believed in education, in preserving the outdoors, and that our most important concern should be the world before us, not some imagined afterlife. Hearing my own worldview recited back to me so clearly was a revelation: Of course I had beliefs. I had ethics and values. I knew myself to be a good and moral person. But without a label and the structure of a community, I had no validation for my way of living and seeing the world. Listening to Zuckerman, I saw that it didn't have to be that way. Just because I wasn't religious didn't mean I was nothing.

For me, connecting my identity to some philosophy was a first step to untangling where I fit now that I'd left religion. Secular humanism wasn't the only answer. I could see from Beliefnet that there were many other secular identities my family and I could just as easily embrace: Ethical Culture, Humanistic Judaism, and religious naturalism, to name a few. What these philosophies offer are systems defined not simply by the absence of religion but by the *presence* of something in its place. Secular humanism is a philosophy without a God, but it has a moral center. Now that I was armed with an example of how the loss of religion could be about being something rather than nothing, the next question was obvious: If I was a secular humanist, did that mean I had a people?

WE'RE NOT ALONE

As a logical next step, I went to visit Greg Epstein, the humanist chaplain at Harvard University. Dressed in blue jeans and black Converse high-tops, Epstein ushered me into a conference room in the basement of Memorial Church, which sits in the center of Harvard Yard. As an organist rehearsed for Sunday services above us, I told him about some of my fears around losing my religion. I worried that if my husband died, as my grandmother's had, there would be no one waiting at our house after the long drive home. There would be no tradition to tap for comfort, no spiritual leader or set of rituals to guide us.

"You're absolutely not alone," Epstein said intently, his clean-shaven head gleaming beneath the overhead fluorescent light. "There are millions of people in your position, whether they've all realized it or not. And we feel we are just beginning the process of meeting those people's needs."

Where were those people? I'd never met any of them. Epstein told me that there was a growing movement of secular humanist groups in the country who were trying to provide community for those who leave religion. For his part, Epstein led a weekly meeting of the Humanist Community at Harvard in addition to a Wednesday night meditation group, a book club, and a burgeoning secular Sunday school. From his point of view, a group of secular humanists could provide much of what religion has to offer people. In his book *Good Without God: What a Billion Nonreligious People Do Believe,* he points out that all the good parts of religion people enjoy—things like belonging, ritual, meaning, and community service—can be had through a values-based group like his, without the need to believe in God or practice religion.

"A lot of times you have pretty nonreligious people who sort of hold their nose and get involved in religion because they want community so much that they're willing to look the other way about the parts they don't believe in," Epstein said. Secular humanists, on the other hand, are trying to create a community where people's nonbelief is not just respected, it's embraced.

Epstein's aspirations are modeled on the humanist movement in Norway, where he said 72 percent of the country is secular, and the official humanist association comprises almost 2 percent of the country's population, a greater percentage than anywhere else in the world. The Norwegian association, he said, has been effective at creating rituals for major life events and replicating the close community ties that religious institutions have traditionally built and nurtured. The challenge, he said, is getting people who no longer buy the religious doctrine to abandon their faith community for something more authentic to what they do believe. As though to prove his point, he suggested I come to a meeting.

A few weeks later, I took my seat in a folding chair in a cramped room at the top of a small, oddly shaped building on a street not far from the heart of Harvard Square. About fifteen people wandered in, wrote their names on stick-on name tags, and took their seats in a circle. Epstein stood at the front of the room and led us in a discussion of what it means to be good without God. The meeting was equal parts youth group and grad school. As Epstein stood at the whiteboard and wrote down our comments and suggestions, the discussion veered from intellectual diatribes against the idea of God to heartfelt expressions of gratitude about the humanist group even existing. I was relieved not to have to bow my head and pray, but seated in that small room I had to wonder whether this enterprise was really going to catch on and compete with Christianity.

Maybe not, but such organized secular groups are sprouting up. Between 2005 and 2015, the American Humanist Association saw the number of its chapters rise from 59 to 180, in forty-six states and the District of Columbia. Where secular humanist groups of the previous century could be characterized as composed of graying members hashing out the implausibility of God's existence, today's groups attract Millennials, college students, and parents of young children through a wider array of activities, including opportunities for community service, secular rituals, meditation groups, and coming-of-age programs for teenagers.

Participation in secular humanist groups among students is skyrocketing, with 244 college groups and 19 high school affiliates now registered with the national Secular Student Alliance, up from 80 such groups in 2007. And thanks to the Internet, secular community groups like these are more visible, better organized, and easier to access and join than ever before. These groups are often passionate advocates for issues like the separation of church and state, the importance of reason, and a desire to clear atheism of the negative perceptions that hound it. But they are also trying to do something more. They are trying to help millions of Americans who've left their faith find a new home—a values-based community that has all the trappings of religion but none of the dogma or belief in the supernatural.

A few weeks after the meeting, I took my kids to one of the group's volunteer activities, a park cleanup day. I was glad to have a place where my children could do some volunteer service. It's important to me that they learn to get involved in their community and give back to it, and without church this can be hard to orchestrate alone.

We put on blue plastic gloves and each took a trash bag. The kids were too cool to act very enthusiastic, but I could tell they were taking the task seriously by the quiet that came over them as they worked—plucking miniature liquor bottles from the park's shrubbery and gathering candy wrappers and strewn newspapers and stuffing them into the bags.

In one corner of the playground, picking at some broken glass lodged in the dirt, I met the group leader, Mark DeSanto, who was there with two of his kids. He told me he'd been a part of the community for about a year and attended as many of the family-friendly events on weekends as he could. We agreed that offerings like the park cleanup were great opportunities to lure our kids away from screens and sports activities so they could think beyond their own needs and do a little work out in the world.

When we were done, we placed our filled trash bags in one towering monument to be picked up later by truck, collected the rakes, and stripped off our gloves. It was a sunny day, and as I walked home with the kids, they asked when we could do another cleanup. The event, which lasted a little over an hour, gave a deeper sense of structure and purpose to our day. I could tell they liked that, and so did I.

Before leaving, I'd asked Mark if he'd have coffee with me sometime to tell me more about how he found the Harvard Humanists and what the group means to him. A few weeks later, we met at a Starbucks near his office. Mark, a thirty-five-year-old biologist at a Boston university, told me he was raised as "a quasi-fundamentalist" member of the Church of the Nazarene in a small town in Vermont. His large family, like his church, was very conservative. His parents didn't believe in evolution, abortion, or equal rights for gays and lesbians. But for a boy growing up, it was the church's control over his own personal behavior that was the real problem.

"I grew up hearing things like 'Is that really what Jesus would want you to do, Mark?' or 'If Jesus was here watching you, would you go to the school dance?' It was that kind of powerful manipulation," he said. "Dancing, movies, rock music—anything that was related to secularism—was frowned upon. I still did those things, but I had to really push and manipulate just to be a normal kid. I grew up fearing hell, and feeling very guilty."

In college Mark started to learn how to develop theories based on the scientific method. He soon started to apply his new way of thinking to his fundamentalist religious beliefs, reading Bible stories for their instructional value rather than as literal history. "Satan became decentralized as a character in the narrative, and it became more about us being the authors of sin and evil," he said. He considered ideas he hadn't before: Noah's flood might be a symbolic cultural narrative, not a true story. Even as his doubts began to slowly take root during college, Mark married a conservative religious woman he'd met at an evangelical summer camp as a kid. When they ran across each other again during college, he thought it was God's will that they be together.

"It felt right," he said, "so why not follow through and really just commit to that faith of believing that we were meant for each other?" Still, he couldn't stem his growing doubts. By the time his first child, a son, was born, his climb out of his faith was escalating.

"We had him baptized, and I put together this big musical celebration," he said. "But there were times when I would hold him and look at him and think about my theology." In particular, he thought about the Christian concept of original sin—that we are all born into sin because of Adam and Eve's rebellion in the Garden of Eden and that only God's grace can save us. "I was trying to think about how my baby was broken," he said, shaking his head. "But there was nothing broken. There's no way that you could convince me that my baby carried the burden of original sin."

His doubts grew until one Easter many years later, when he couldn't bring himself to take communion because of the disgust he felt at the symbolic eating of the flesh and blood of Jesus's body. He didn't understand why a loving God would require a human sacrifice for us to be saved. He realized he no longer believed in God. But he knew he needed community. When he went searching online for atheist communities, the Harvard Humanists website popped up.

"I laughed to myself," he said, describing the first time he scrolled through the website. "Growing up in the church, 'secular' and 'humanist' were naughty words." He wasn't all that interested at first. But then he clicked on the section of the website labeled "What is humanism?"

"I read that," he laughed, "and I was like, 'I'll be damned. I'm a humanist.' It just cracked me up to no end."

His wife and friends didn't find it so funny. When Mark outed himself as an atheist to their church community, he lost both his marriage and most of his friends. Greg Epstein provided one-on-one counseling sessions and sometimes helped him deal with crises over the phone. Soon Mark, a newly single dad, brought his children to their first Harvard Humanists event, a beach cleanup. Just months before, he'd been convinced that he'd never find a community like the church he had belonged to for so long. But as he watched his children play Frisbee with the other members of the group, he started to feel better.

He attended regular humanist meetings and volunteered in the family programs, leading science experiments with kids on Darwin Day and making sure there were enough rakes to clean the parks. Driving home after one such event, when he asked his eight-year-old daughter why she thought people believe in God, she told him she thought people probably believed in God because miracles happen and people want to know how to explain them. That response made Mark smile. When I asked him why, he said, "Because it's harmless, and she's eight. But, also, she didn't say, 'Because if we don't, then we go to hell.' It gave me hope."

Mark was still struggling through a difficult divorce and custody agreement. ("My wife is leaving me for her invisible friend," he said, meaning God.) "I was a mess," he said of losing his faith. Yet, despite what he went through, he wouldn't call leaving religion a loss. "Some would call it a downward slope," he said. "But it was an upward climb for me."

SECULAR EASTER

As comfortable as I felt with the secular humanist philosophy, I wasn't sure that humanist meetings could replace some of the magic I associated with religion growing up. One of my favorite holidays was Easter. When I was a child, my father and stepmother took me to Macy's weeks before Easter to find me a dress and a bonnet tied with a silk ribbon. I wore patent leather shoes and white tights. There was a pageantry about the day. The floral arrangements on each side of the altar were taller and more brilliant, the pews more crowded; the music soared higher. The ritual spoke to that swelling of hope and relief that comes with a break in the winter, with new light, with spring. Easter to me felt in sync with the natural movement of the seasons, and so with my own mood. It didn't matter that I didn't believe that Jesus literally rose from the dead, that I still couldn't hear God talking back to me or imagine his existence. The day was about communal celebration, and the experience of it was transforming.

I recalled one Easter, a few years before, when I'd risen early, placed the Easter baskets in my kids' rooms, and gone to a yoga class as usual. On the way home after class, I was standing in sweaty clothes, a yoga mat slung over my shoulder, scrolling my phone, when the doors of the church across the street burst open and organ music flooded out. I looked up, stunned by the scene. Parishioners dressed in their Easter finery stepped out, celebrating spring and, for them, the Resurrection. The sight took my breath away. I'd been fine with my morning yoga ritual until I remembered that sense of renewal that always came to me at church on Easter Sunday. Could I find that sense of wonder among secular humanists?

That year, I decided to go to a secular Easter celebration to find out. On Easter morning, I went through the usual basket ritual, then left my family at home, with the kids and Michael scheduled to join a neighbor's egg hunt. Afterward, our son would head to baseball practice, our older daughter to a friend's house for brunch, and our youngest would nap. We would all be flung in different directions that day, a metaphor perhaps for how we'd lost religion in the first place. But I promised Michael and the kids that I'd be back as soon as I could.

I then made my way to the new Harvard Humanists headquarters, itself a testament to the growth of secular humanist groups in the United States. Since my first meeting two years before, the Humanists had moved out of the shabby walk-up with the secondhand furniture into the new Humanist Hub, closer to the center of Harvard Square and housed in a streamlined, contemporary office space above a Bikram yoga studio and a Lush soap and bath salts emporium. I emerged from the elevator into a large meeting room, with smaller offices set along a corridor, including two rooms for kids' classes decorated with whiteboards and colorful rugs. In the main room, four middle-aged musicians with rough beards and faded T-shirts were playing "Home" by Phillip Phillips, an ode to finding one's place in the world. The first stanza, which the lead singer crooned as I walked in, seemed apt:

> *Hold on to me as we go*
> *As we roll down this unfamiliar road*
> *And although this wave is stringing us along*
> *Just know you're not alone*
> *'Cause I'm going to make this place your home.*

Above the musicians hung the words CONNECT ACT EVOLVE in large wooden block letters. About fifty people were seated in folding chairs set up in wide, arcing rows. I took my seat toward the back.

Mary Johnson, who served as a nun with Mother Teresa's Missionaries of Charity for twenty years before leaving the convent and eventually losing her faith, led the event. Johnson went on to write a memoir called *An Unquenchable Thirst* about her experience breaking up with "Mother." She wrote that she had come to believe not in the God of the Bible but in a God that is simply "the best parts of you."

Exuding joy in her teal tunic, her reddish hair styled in a curly bob, Johnson stepped to the podium on the small stage. "I don't believe in religion anymore," she said, "but I have the Holy Week blues. I miss all the stuff I used to do."

As a group, the humanists are not typically nostalgic for religion, but I saw some people nodding their heads in agreement. She told us she had moved on: "I don't want to do *that*," she said, referring to the Catholic Easter rituals she performed for many years as a nun. The crowd laughed, already in her palm.

She explained that, after unraveling herself from her strong ties to faith, she decided that it was senseless to ignore religion. She hoped that today she could help those of us in the room reflect on what comes up at this time of year, and not judge ourselves for feeling longing or confusion. Instead of drumming up more ideas and thoughts, as the highly analytical humanists are wont to do, she asked us to take this springtime ritual—she never used the word "Easter"—as an opportunity to reflect on what we already knew and had inside us. The prime vehicle of our reflection would come through poetry. "Religion has its scriptures," she said, commanding the room, "and humanists have their poets."

We spent the next thirty minutes listening as community members read the words of poets who celebrate a secular understanding of the world. Mary Oliver, Robert Pinsky, and Esther Cohen were our prophets. At one point I was invited to stand at the podium and read a poem called "Lilies" by Kate Gale. I stepped to the stage and steadied my breath. In my experience with religion, I had never been called upon to participate in shared authority. It was empowering, a strange shift from my role as a quiet, seated parishioner in the congregations of my youth. The poem was about praying even after leaving religion, and it reflected that half-in, half-out feeling of the newly unaffiliated. After I read it, I stepped down from the stage as another woman approached to read Mary Oliver's "Mindful," a poem imploring listeners to notice everything in nature with heightened attentiveness, a spiritual practice without God or dogma.

After the readings, Johnson asked us each to stand and take a tulip from the table at the front of the room. The twenty-something man next to me groaned and said under his breath, "I guess we have to." I suppressed my own cynicism and tried to remain open to the ritual. A young woman stood at the end of each row in turn and gestured to us to begin walking to the front of the room. One by one, each of us stepped forward to take a tulip, in a quiet procession that reminded me of Holy Communion. Once we were all seated, with tulips in hand, Johnson asked us to feel the stem and leaves, then the petals. She asked us to smell the tulip, and fifty heads bent forward to inhale. She asked us to study the stamens and pistil and said we might notice that our tulip isn't perfect. I traced the cracked petals and the torn, arching stem, glossy as sealskin, and a star-shaped blister of brown and yellow around the stamens.

She ended the program by telling us about a poem written by Nick Flynn, a writer from Boston most famous for his depiction of a homeless shelter in the memoir *Another Bullshit Night in Suck City.* After the Boston Marathon bombings the year prior, when two brothers planted homemade bombs on the sidewalk where fans were cheering on runners crossing the finish line, Flynn wrote a poem about the event called "Marathon." Johnson read it, lingering on one of the final lines: "everyone we've ever known // runs without thinking // not away but *into* the cloud . . ."

The cloud is the smoke that rose when the two bombs detonated. Beneath that cloud was a grotesque and terrifying scene. And yet the story of how Boston ran toward the destruction, of how the city grew strong in that moment of terror, will forever be an example of people coming together to battle the worst of humanity. Johnson urged us to live our lives running into the cloud. Humanist philosophy puts human agency, not God's will, at the center of understanding how the world works. In this view, no supernatural power will swoop in and make everything right. We have to do it ourselves.

Johnson closed the ceremony by telling us that her only requirement was that we no longer had our tulip when we went to sleep that night. We could pass it on to anyone or anything we chose. I said my good-byes to the few people I knew and walked out into Harvard Square, where I found my favorite statue, a whimsical little creature that looks a bit like a hedgehog sitting on a tiny pedestal. The statue was erected in memory of a popular street performer who died young, and I'd always liked it for the contrast it made to the imposing statues of Revolutionary War heroes erected around

Boston. Here was a statue for the rest of us, the people going about their business, doing their jobs, caring for their kids, making their little bit of beauty in the world. I placed my tulip in the creature's unassuming little arms in the hope that the patch of brilliant color would bring a smile to someone's face. I boarded the subway back to our neighborhood.

I found my older daughter at our neighbor's house having Easter brunch among a group of our neighbor's college-age relatives. Talk revolved around summer internships, cafeteria food, and choosing majors. Though the family hosting the event was Catholic, no one at lunch talked about Easter, and none of the college students I met had attended services that morning. After dessert—an Easter cake and miniature cream puffs—I left my daughter with the neighbors, who would walk her back later. I walked home to find Michael playing basketball with our son behind our house while our younger daughter decorated the back steps with colorful sidewalk chalk.

I felt the rush I always get when I see my family before they see me, as if I'm holding a precious photograph. They are my solar system, my closest and most lasting tribe. But that day I'd moved beyond my small orbit. I'd given myself over to a new ritual, led by a wise stranger I admired. I'd observed moments of silence and reflection in a community of like-minded people, then returned to my neighborhood, more aware than before of its own bonds and protections. The day was infused with a feeling of gratitude and care. It felt like something in me was changing. But what?

My grandmother believed that God looked down on her and blessed each moment, freely, from the infinite well of his great love. She didn't ask for grace—that wasn't how it worked in her construction—but it was hers all the same. And it infused her life with meaning.

I had felt a bit of what I thought of as grace—an abundance of gratitude for something freely given—that day gazing at my tulip and, later, at my family from across the street. But it wasn't related to God. It was a wholly secular experience. What was it I was feeling? Could I train myself to recognize and prepare for such moments of secular grace—not to just wait for them to wash over me, but to create them myself?

For my grandmother, receiving and being thankful for God's grace was part of her many rituals, whether at regular Sunday services or with her own kitchen-table blessing before each meal. So I decided to investigate rituals. What were mine and how might they bring me closer to this feeling of grace?

CHAPTER 11

Ritual Without Religion

To experience grace is one thing; to integrate it
into your life is quite another.

—*Christian Wiman, My Bright Abyss: Meditation of a Modern Believer*

Each year, for weeks after putting up our Christmas tree, I rise before anyone else, go downstairs, and plug in the tree's lights. I stand in the living room, savoring the glow in the quiet moments before the morning rush to work and school. I remember my childhood experience of Christmas, the sweet sound of the all-boy choir in church, the soft crush of my velvet holiday skirt, and the nativity scene on the town green, with a wooden baby in a manger that I adored. All that remains of the enchanted religious rituals of my childhood now is the tree itself, a semireligious symbol erected by me, my Jewish husband, and our secular kids. As far removed as it is from any direct religious symbolism, the tree fills the psychic space of our living room during the holidays the way ritual fills the open, neutral spaces between us. My breath deepens as I take in those white lights twinkling in the dark. It's an experience I can only define as sacred.

I couldn't help but wonder if my children would experience these feelings of sacredness around the holidays if they grew up without religious rituals. Those of us who have left religion seldom completely detach from the religious roots of our rituals. We can't just wipe them from our memories. Though for some such memories may be painful, for many they add depth and a feeling of nostalgia. That tree means something because of all the trees that have come before it and all the religious experiences that have surrounded each one. Will something be lost when all my children know of Christmas is a tree and the gifts beneath? When Passover is the rare Jewish holiday we celebrate in a mad dash to Whole Foods to pick up the haroset and matzoh rather than an integral part of a yearlong religious practice? How will we pass along the wonder of ritual to our children without a constant, meaningful practice of the ideas and values that we're ritualizing? I was seeking nonreligious ways to convey the same sense of religious grace and connection.

Some research suggests that secular rituals are powerful indeed, helping us express and contain our emotions during life's most difficult passages. Professors at Harvard Business School used three examples to study the effectiveness of rituals in overcoming grief and disappointment. The researchers asked participants to perform a ritual after experiencing a loss ranging from significant (a loved one) to mundane (the lottery). One participant explained her ritual after her mother died: She would play "Miss You like Crazy" by Natalie Cole and allow herself to cry. Another participant explained that after a breakup he took all the photos of him and his girlfriend, tore them up, and burned them in the park where the couple had shared their first kiss. Despite the range of situations and rituals, the effect was the same: Those performing such rituals experienced a greater feeling of control over their lives, regardless of whether they believed in the power of the ritual.

Ritual is how we mark time and make meaning. Rituals celebrate the milestones of our lives: birth and birthdays, coming of age, marriage, promotion, retirement, and death. Collective rituals provide vessels for human emotions, public spaces for the formalized expression of values, practices for working through difficult passages and transitions. Rituals force us to forget ourselves and give ourselves over to practices meant to knit people together into a common identity. They are how we make the invisible visible even more directly than with words. Rituals are symbols, shortcuts to the human mind and heart. When Christians give up chocolate for Lent, they are practicing sacrifice and self-control. When Muslims fast for Ramadan, they are demonstrating the belief that they are part of something larger than themselves.

Certainly, there are plenty of secular rituals, from high school graduations to quinceañera parties when Latina girls reach fifteen to bachelor parties and housewarmings. But can secular rituals be as meaningful and lasting as religious ones? Outside the framework of religion, secular people are left to cannibalize the rituals they were raised with, or create new ones from scratch. Or they can walk away from ritual, disavowing it as old-fashioned and out of touch.

But many secular people still seek meaningful rituals in their lives. They want practices that don't feel stale or oppressive and yet somehow maintain the heft of tradition behind them. Often what gives traditional rituals their gravitas is the very thing that secular people don't like about religion: associations with ancient norms that also contain prejudices, repression, and constraint. As with other aspects of secular life in America as it takes shape in a new age, pioneers have emerged to navigate between the abandoned past and the uncertain future. They are creating new and powerful ways to meet a human yearning for ritual.

CULTIVATING AN "AS-IF" WORLD

Before I set out to look at whether secular rituals could be as powerful in our lives as religious ones, I wanted to understand the primary purpose of ritual. I went to visit Michael Puett, a professor of Chinese history at Harvard and coauthor of *Ritual and Its Consequences: An Essay on the Limits of Sincerity*. Puett has spent his career examining the philosophy of Confucius and his contemporaries. He believes that ritual is fundamental to how we see and shape our behavior and our relationships with others, with or without religion. The path to a meaningful life, Puett says, starts with ritual. If we abandon religious ritual, so be it, but we abandon all ritual at the peril of devolving into meaninglessness.

On a dark fall evening, my feet swished through the fallen leaves along my own small path as I walked to Andover Hall at the Harvard Divinity School, a hulking stone monolith that seemed out of place tucked away on a leafy, residential street. Puett was the keynote speaker for a group of divinity school students from around the world who had come to attend an annual colloquium. Tall and gangly, with a Cheshire cat grin and a thick pair of glasses, he spoke at high energy, as if each thought were a new discovery for him.

He told the thirty people in the audience that in the traditional Chinese world he studies, rituals were performed in a separate space, an arena set aside to enact the understanding of how life *should* be. This, he said, is the true benefit of formal ritual. Everyone who inhabits the ritual space behaves as if he or she is in a completely harmonious relationship with everyone else there. Such harmony doesn't exist outside the ritual space, and so we perform the rituals to realign ourselves, to be trained in how to act in the real world. Then, when we walk away from the ritual space, we do so with an understanding of the reaches of our best selves and our most harmonious society.

In effect, we become actors moving through a set piece, and the actions in the ritual space allow us to bring order to what is otherwise the chaos of being alive. Back outside, we reenter the wild flow of life, safe in the knowledge that the "as-if" world exists in the sacred space and that when necessary, we can return to it. Ritual gives us something solid and unchanging to hold on to.

Rituals and ritual spaces can also act as pockets of order and safety in the world. Some of the most powerful of these are not religious at all. Puett gave the example of the practice of elaborate "changing of the guard" ceremonies in ancient China, when power was passed to a monarch after the death of his father. These were dangerous junctures, when rivalries, hostility, and sadness hung heavy in the air. But the ritual space acted like a protective bubble, keeping the threats and jealousies from crashing in. When he talked about this function of ritual, I couldn't help but think of 9/11, when, after the Twin Towers were struck, our leaders—Democrats and Republicans—gathered for a memorial service at the National Cathedral. Regardless of politics and the fights that would ensue, here was a space in which, at least on the face of it, they were united, however briefly.

Puett explained that the prime goal of ritual is to cultivate harmonious relationships with others. If you want to find meaning, if you want to connect with others, if you want to create a sense of sacredness and grace, you have to start with ritual.

....

SECULAR SOLSTICE

People all over the country are trying to create new rituals where blank spaces have opened up. Times of high religious participation—Christmas and Easter, for example—can be lonely ones for those who don't practice faith. Individual family celebrations provide a treasured pause from work and school responsibility, but without the traditional structures, it takes discipline and planning to establish new rituals. Sometimes we need a visionary leader who can rally the group.

It was snowing when I ducked into a concert hall on the Upper West Side of Manhattan and handed my ticket to an usher, who placed a plastic, battery-operated tea candle in my palm. In the main auditorium I joined about 150 people, each also holding a small plastic candle, and took a seat. I had come to attend a secular solstice event called Brighter than Today, to learn how atheists and others were coming together to create their own rituals. Several microphone stands and a drum set sat on the spare wood stage. Glowing crystal salt lamps lined the front rim. The audience buzzed excitedly. It was December 14, near the time of the winter solstice, and I had come to participate in a secular ritual run by a crowd of twenty-something computer geeks and skeptics.

Raymond Arnold had organized the event, and he came to the stage in a suit coat a tad too large for his slim frame. He told the crowd that the winter solstice is the longest night of the year and pointed to the creators of Stonehenge as early geniuses set on measuring the passage of time. He blended into his homily the quasi-religious elements he believes our hyperrationalist world needs more of.

For one, he led the group in the Serenity Prayer practiced by members of Alcoholics Anonymous. Tentative at first, the audience gradually joined him: "I seek the serenity to accept the things I cannot change, the courage to change the things I can, and the wisdom to know the difference." He asked the audience to reflect on what we would like the courage to change in our lives.

As the evening proceeded, we listened to music, learned scientific explanations for natural phenomena, and sang along with everything from "The Times They Are a-Changin'" to the humanist anthem "Home" to a somewhat surprising ode to Jesus, "Do You Hear What I Hear?"

Before we sang "Do You Hear What I Hear?" Arnold deadpanned, "Some of you might be, like, I came to a secular solstice, what up?" Everyone laughed, but quieted as he explained that while the song may be about Jesus being born, it is at its heart about the birth of an idea.

"The idea starts small and touches the people, and the idea reaches the king and changes the world," he said. The song doesn't mention Jesus explicitly. It says that there's a child in the cold who needs us. Raymond asked the audience to sing the song with that spirit in mind, not the song's religious connotations. It's the idea at the root of the song, he said, not the religious specifics, that is universal. We don't have to toss out everything about religion just because we no longer practice religion. On a deep level, we still understand and relate to the inherent ideas.

I had met Arnold online, via a friend from the Harvard Humanists. He said he was "agnostic-atheist-humanist" brought up by a family of Catholics and atheists. His motivation to provide a secular alternative to Christmas was born of love and nostalgia. Ever since he was a child, Raymond's grandmother had hosted Christmas sing-alongs for extended family and friends at her house. Though Raymond is an atheist, he treasured those holiday experiences and couldn't find anything else like them in the atheist community in New York. So he created his own Christmas sing-alongs for the nonreligious. When I met him, he had launched a Kickstarter campaign to raise money for the event.

"My family has a Christmas Eve celebration each year, which is very nice," he told me. "We get together, we sing Christmas carols for hours, and we have a nice family meal." He said he always valued the warmth and beauty of this ritual and assumed everyone, no matter their faith or lack of it, held such celebrations. But a friend who joined him one year said he didn't do anything nearly as meaningful. "He and his family just wake up late on Christmas morning and give each other presents, and call it a day." His friend's family lacked the rituals Raymond's family had practiced, and to Raymond this was a lost opportunity.

The more he talked to others in his rationalistic, thirty-something technology world, the more he realized how rare his big family celebration was. So three years ago, he put together a ceremony in a friend's apartment. Scores of people showed up, and each year since more have come. In 2013, he decided it was time to expand. "I wanted a holiday that made us feel connected, and feel connected to the world," he explained. So he started the Kickstarter campaign and raised $8,300 to bring fellow nonbelievers together for a night of readings and Christmas carols in Manhattan.

"I don't believe in the literal message of the more serious Christmas carols," Arnold told me when I'd talked to him on the phone before the event. "But whoever wrote them clearly wrote them from a position of caring deeply about the story they were telling." He said he could sense the feeling of transcendence that people who'd written the Christmas music had felt, even if he didn't believe we could transcend this world. He was more interested in it as a feeling: "What I looked to do with the first solstice party was capture that sense of transcendence." He thought humanists should try harder to connect to rituals that moved people. Speaking of those who'd written the carols he'd selected for the program, he said, "I can feel a reverence there, even though I don't believe in those ideas."

....

THE LIFE AND TIMES OF THE MODERN RITUAL

Where we go to feel that reverence is another question secular seekers must find better answers for. The religious have cathedrals, mosques, synagogues—spaces wholly devoted to worship and collective transcendence. Look at the architecture of a cathedral: the soaring dome reaching up to the heavens, the cross front and center, the rows and rows of pews that collect and order the group. Within religious space, everything has meaning. Ritualistic objects and practices convey values on sight. If you pay attention in a religious space, you will quickly come to learn what the group worshipping there values.

Where do secular people go to celebrate and transmit their values? Where is the nonreligious ritual space? Burning Man, the annual gathering of artists, techies, and temporary free spirits on the huge playa in the Nevada desert, is essentially a place where people can come together and create art and ritual. On Saturday, the night is lit up, ritualistically, by a burning man effigy. It's an enormous expenditure of time and energy for everyone involved, and it seems to express a hunger for such a ritualistic secular space.

One challenge of the secular age is finding a more permanent space that allows for the reverence so many people long for. Sometimes this means reimagining the spaces we already have. For Raymond Arnold, the primary function of his Kickstarter campaign was to raise funds for the rental of the auditorium. The Hearth in Ashland, Oregon, shares space with the local synagogue. The Harvard Humanists were able to expand their quarters due to generous benefactors. Parenting Beyond Religion sets up tables in a park, and Sarah Aadland converts her dining table. None of these places were passed down or inherited.

Jim Lasko is a rugged-looking Chicagoan who has made a profession of creating new approaches to ritualistic space through his experiential theater group, Redmoon. When I met him at the Redmoon offices—in an enormous warehouse in an industrial area of Chicago—a heavy metal band was making a video upstairs, students in an after-school welding class were learning how to meld metal, and office workers were preparing the summer camp curriculum. Lasko and I ducked into his office upstairs, and I listened as he explained what Redmoon is all about.

"Our mission, which I love," Lasko told me, "is 'engineering new ways of being together.'" The statement reflected Redmoon's strategy of reclaiming public space for collective ritual experience. Lasko wants to wrench public space from strictly commercial interests and give it back to the community in a way that makes people see it anew. Using puppetry, fantastical props, and storytelling, Redmoon has been going into parks or central squares across Chicago for decades and performing pop-up theater that encourages neighborhood residents to reimagine their parks and spaces. One year Redmoon rolled an enormous speaker into Washington Park, on the South Side of Chicago. They set up a stage and open mic as curious onlookers gathered. Soon the park was filled with people talking, dancing, and enjoying the public square. But it was when the people truly took ownership that Lasko knew his group had succeeded. Two teenage boys asked if they could sing into that mic onstage. Redmoon organizers welcomed them up. The young men, who'd just come from the nearby church, sang a gospel song that held the whole crowd rapt.

Lasko believes the opportunities of a thriving public space are now being diminished by our private connections. We are all in our technological pods, glued to our iPhones and iPads. We're in our own worlds instead of interacting. At the same time, the places where we once gathered as groups are being privatized. Sports and entertainment are all run by big business, and childhood is overscheduled and oversupervised, drained of the spontaneity that once defined it. "It used to be that all those spaces were public," Lasko said. "Now everything is programmed." Public space is owned now. Downtown spaces are corporate plazas. What we lose in the process is the collision with the unknown—the very experiences, Lasko said, that make democracy interesting. When we control whom we're with and what we're doing with such precision, we lose the opportunity for spontaneous interaction with perfect strangers—and surprising moments of serendipity.

Lasko recalls an event his group hosted in the Logan Square neighborhood, in northwest Chicago. There, Redmoon set up as a Rube Goldberg–type machine—a ladder that reached up onto a platform, then took a series of turns. At the foot of the contraption, the organizers set up a booth where people could write down any wish they had on a piece of paper and send it along a conveyor ferrying the notes up to the top of the machine through a series of twists and loops. At the top, an actor dressed all in white attached each wish to a white helium balloon and set it free.

"People waited in line for hours to write a note and hand it over to our guys," Lasko said. "And then they waited even longer to watch their note go up in the sky."

MEANINGFUL RITUAL IN THE SECULAR AGE

Large collective rituals like the winter solstice party and the events Redmoon hosts occur throughout the year and across the country, but many of the most meaningful secular rituals are established within the walls of individual homes and are brought to bear in quieter moments of family life. Still half in and half out of religion, many of us craft rituals that contain the elements of the past but are reimagined in new and surprising ways. Deborah Copaken, a writer and artist in New York City, found a way to make a sacred ritual all her own while still keeping the spirit of her Jewish heritage alive.

Deborah was raised Jewish, even teaching Hebrew school for a time. A few years ago, on Rosh Hashanah, instead of standing in line for hours to pay several hundred dollars for tickets for her family to enter the nearby synagogue and worship, Deborah did something new. She had long been bothered by the price of High Holiday services. Certainly, the cost strained her family's budget, but beyond that, paying for religion never sat well with her, and she was troubled by the sexism inherent in the Jewish tradition: She had recently learned that a passage in the Tosefta, a collection of Jewish oral laws, instructs men to wake up every morning and thank God that they weren't born as women. Despite all this, she was raising her kids Jewish, because it was important for her that her children understand who they were, where they came from, and what it means to be Jewish. "I needed them to understand that history," she said.

But she couldn't hew to her religion anymore, and it wasn't just the cost and the inherent sexism. Her relationship to religion changed dramatically when her father was diagnosed with pancreatic cancer just before Yom Kippur in 2008. The cancer was inoperable, and he was given two to six months to live. When Deborah called to tell him she would drive down to the Washington, DC, area to take him, a lifelong practicing Jew, to services, he said it wasn't necessary. He'd given up on religion.

"Fuck Yom Kippur," he said with a laugh. "My fate is sealed. I'm going to the beach."

After her father died, she asked herself what Rosh Hashanah, the Jewish New Year, which she had celebrated at synagogue every year of her life, was really about. "We eat circular bread and we talk about the circle of life, and it's all about circles," she said. "And I thought, 'Okay, let's find some circles in Manhattan.' It was a gorgeous day, so we did this bike ride, the loop of Central Park, and we went on the carousel."

While her husband and eighteen-year-old son went to synagogue (her husband, from whom she has since separated, was more religious than she), she and her two younger children, ages eight and sixteen, used the idea of the circle as a metaphor to frame their discussion that evening: What were their regrets and disappointments that year? What were their hopes for the year ahead?

"The whole idea of a carousel is a metaphor for the year, a metaphor for life, going round and round," she said. "And that's how we marked it." For her, reinterpreting the ritual gave it greater meaning. She said that that year's Rosh Hashanah "felt even more significant than anything we'd ever done in the past."

CREATING FAMILY RITUALS

When it comes time to celebrate family milestones, bringing several generations together to recognize a rite of passage like a birth, the question of ritual can be particularly delicate. Grandparents recall how things were done in their day and may resent the new, looser versions, but parents want to bring their children into the world in a way that expresses their values. When church or mosque no longer feels relevant, many young couples develop an alternative and hope the rest of the family will go along.

Among our friends, one couple, a nonpracticing Catholic woman and culturally Muslim man, chose to forgo any traditional baptism practice and have a DIY welcoming ceremony for their firstborn daughter at their home. A sumptuous brunch of quiches and fresh salads was spread across the dining room table, bubbles and toys were set out for kids in the yard out back, and photos of the smiling baby were lovingly placed around the home. The ceremony itself took place in the living room, where about twenty guests sat in a circle. We each took a small, smooth stone and, as we went around the room sharing our stories, hopes, and dreams for the child, we placed our stone in a keepsake jar meant for her to carry with her throughout her life.

The stories were deeply personal. A babysitter choked back tears as she talked about how special the girl was and how she would no doubt take the world by storm one day. Another woman talked about what great parents our friends were and how she could see their best qualities in the toddler's effervescent smile. Our son, who had just turned ten, took his stone and said, "I don't know what I hope for her, but I do know she is one of the cutest babies I have ever seen." No one mentioned religion, though Jim Morrison was quoted.

Toward the end of the ceremony, both of the girl's grandmothers stood up to speak, each citing her individual faith and reciting a short prayer. When those ancient religious words entered the room, the collective quiet deepened. Those prayers, steeped in the past and spoken through generations, held a gravitas that our personal thoughts spoken around the circle didn't quite have. And yet somehow all of it—old and new—held that space together. The important element was the family, but the heritage was being honored, too, not forgotten. It seemed the perfect way to acknowledge the past while also moving forward. The child was welcomed into a secular fold but also reminded of where she had come from. She didn't have to be anointed as one thing—Catholic or Muslim or even purely secular. She could contain multitudes of identity. In fact, her identity stemmed from the fact that she contained those multitudes.

Later, I asked my friend what her parents had thought about the ceremony. She told me that her father, a lifelong Catholic, had surprised her afterward.

"I said, 'So, Dad, was that okay?' and he said, 'That was more meaningful than any baptism in a church that I've been to.'"

COMING OF AGE IN A SECULAR AGE

Religions have long provided coming-of-age ceremonies marking the transition from adolescence into adulthood. Adolescence is a difficult time, and yet in America today if you don't go through a religious coming-of-age program, transitioning into adulthood consists of getting your driver's license and graduating from high school. We mark this transition by letting young adults drive and continue their studies. Where is the opportunity to state values and commit to something beyond academic achievement and material success? Religions provide structures to acknowledge this passage, but parents who don't want their kids to memorize a creed and profess allegiance to a faith tradition have to create meaning themselves.

As fog lifted off the Pacific coast on an unseasonably cold Mother's Day, sixteen families gathered under the rustic roof of the Green Dragon Temple at the Green Gulch Farm Zen Center in Marin County, California. Incense filled the air, and ritual bells alerted the group that the ceremony—a culmination of nine months of study by a group of teenagers—was about to begin. Sixteen girls and boys would pass from adolescence into adulthood before their mentors and families. Even though the event was being held in a zendo with a statue of the Buddha near the center, the ceremony itself was a secular one. Zen Buddhism is a religion, but a nontheistic one, and many consider it more of a philosophy and practice than a religion. Many of the parents who had signed their kids up for the yearlong program were seeking a meaningful coming-of-age ritual that differed from Christian confirmation or a Jewish bar mitzvah.

Kathryn Guta was sitting beside me on the raised platform along one side of the room. As we waited for the official ceremony to begin, she told me she had been raised Catholic but left and hasn't looked back. When she adopted her daughter, Lakpa, from Nepal, she knew that she wanted her to be grounded in basic morality, and to learn tools to quiet her mind and examine her experience in a nonjudgmental way. She decided to let her choose her framework, so when Lakpa was young, Kathryn took her to all kinds of religious communities, searching for the right fit. At first, Lakpa didn't like any of the groups they tried. Then Kathryn found the Zen center and started attending public lectures there herself. She learned about the coming-of-age program and liked that it was a structured approach and focused on important virtues while being free of religious dogma. Each month the students explored a value, such as listening, persistence, and connection. Through the study of these values, the mentors hoped to help the teens explore what they stood for and what they would seek to give to the world.

Lakpa had been sick that morning and wasn't sure she could make it, but her mother encouraged her to come. She wanted her to see the program through because she wanted to give her daughter something, as her own parents had given her the Catholic faith. "Soon she'll be on her own," Kathryn said. "This is the last chance I have to do something like this for her."

The ceremony began with the students walking in from the back of the room in two lines, one of girls and one of boys. They streamed past the large wooden Buddha set on a platformlike chair and came to sit on cushions in front. Though their hair was neatly combed, no one was formally dressed; they wore plain white shirts and dark pants. Four mentors, two men and two women, sat on the stage area facing them. The mentors took turns asking the girls and boys to rise and tell the group one word that sums up what they stand for and one gift they will give to the world in their lifetime.

The mentors then called up the parents to speak directly about the qualities they most appreciated in the children and their hopes for them. The ceremony was sealed when the mentors gave each student a new name that combined the quality they saw in him or her and their hope for the student in adult life.

When Lakpa stood, her hands tucked into her light-colored hooded sweatshirt, she coughed several times, cleared her throat, and said, "I stand for friendship, and my gift to the world is humor." Kathryn came to the front of the room and spoke about Lakpa's struggles, comparing them to the recent Nepali earthquake and calling her daughter a mountain. "You came from the mountains and you have become a mountain. Your feet are planted in the sweet earth. You have also experienced earthquakes." At this point, both mother and daughter began softly crying. Kathryn closed by saying that, despite all the difficulties, it has been her honor to be Lakpa's mother. The mentors instructed Lakpa to take her gifts into the world as she moves into adulthood and presented her with a card bearing her newly given name: Mountain Humor.

Other students rose and recited what they stood for (change, kindness, compassion) and what gift they offered the world (acceptance, honesty, joy). Their parents walked up and, standing about six feet from their children, told them how profoundly they had touched their lives and what they hoped for them: that you will be happy, that you will be at peace with yourself, that you love yourself as much as we love you. One father told his daughter, "I'm a bow and you're the arrow. As much as I'd like the arrow to go far, I'd like the bow to be stable." He ended by saying, "Thank you for everything you've given us."

The parents' stories were at once unique and universal. They were as different as the kids, each of whom stood and proclaimed an identity and purpose, and alike in their love for their children. The ritual called on them all to put forth their best selves, the ideal of what it is they see in themselves. It was the epitome of the "as-if" world Michael Puett says ritual gives us, that ceremonial situation in which all is aligned so that when we go back out into our chaotic lives, we can remember this touchstone and return as needed to the sense of what is best in us.

The program began about twenty years ago when several parents approached the abbot of the San Francisco Zen Center at the time, Norman Fischer, and asked for his help guiding their sons through adolescence. The parents wanted a Buddhist ceremony similar to the bar mitzvah Fischer had created for his twin sons. Fischer obliged, spending two years meeting regularly with the boys. Over the course of that experience, he developed a program based on nine qualities of maturity, or virtues, that they explored together. Today's program follows that model, which Fischer wrote about in his book *Taking Our Places: The Buddhist Path to Truly Growing Up*.

How do we become who we are meant to be? This is a question religion has long engaged. But just because we lose religion, we don't have to lose the question, or the rituals that help us answer it. Coming of age is a human transition, not a religious one. We all leave childhood for adulthood and take up our places in the world. A program like the one at Green Gulch offers a conscious, structured way to make that transition without asking people to profess something they don't believe.

Before the ceremony, the students and parents attended a dharma talk, a lecture about Buddhism led by a Buddhist teacher. "Today is one of those days that's never happened before," the teacher said by way of opening. He laughed and went on to explain: "It's boundless and unpredictable. What will you do with today?" He said that the Zen tradition is about finding your place. "Can you stand your ground, speak your truth, and honor your gifts?" he asked. He encouraged listeners to seek a life based not on image but on a felt sense, on what we know in our "heart brain." He said material wealth and exploitation would not bring an extraordinary life. In fact, that would be an ordinary one. Instead, "what is extraordinary is to settle down in what is ordinary and bring it alive."

TOWARD A MORE CONSCIOUS SECULAR RITUAL

The year I started thinking about what our Christmas tree meant to me, Michael was out of town on the first night of Hanukkah. Nearly every year Hanukkah would sneak up on us, and we'd scramble to dig out the menorah boxed in the attic and find candles that fit.

Some years we were lucky if we got our act together for the candle lighting by the third or fourth night. That year, I wanted to try to do better. Even though Michael, our main source of Jewish knowledge, wasn't home, I decided to hold the lighting ceremony that night after dinner. I would blend what we had—a dazzling Christmas tree in the corner, a trio of secular kids, and our routine dinner of pasta and chicken nuggets—into some sort of ritual.

That afternoon I found the menorah and placed it in the center of the dining room table. I Googled "Hanukkah candle lighting prayer" and sent the page to the printer. After the kids came home and the older two finished their homework, the four of us ate dinner, and I allowed the two older kids to light the shamash and then the first candle. I watched as they lit the candles reverently. Once the tiny flames were rising, I said, "Great job!" as if that were that, end of story, and I got up to wash the dishes.

"Wait!" my son said. "What about the prayer?"

"Oh. Right," I said. "I left it in the printer." I asked my older daughter if she would go find it for us.

She bolted downstairs and reemerged with the printed page clutched carefully in her hands as if she were bearing a Dead Sea Scroll. She handed it to her brother, who began to read the words in Hebrew, straining to mimic what he took to be the correct inflection. My desire to rush through our nightly routine suddenly changed. I was surprised to find myself fighting back tears. I had put the pieces in place, but my children were the ones who were taking the ritual most seriously. They seemed to crave it, even. As my son read and the other two sat perfectly still, I saw that they were giving the ancient practice new life. I realized how much they wanted this feeling of togetherness within a sacred practice. It's just that no one had ever shown them how.

No great sage of Judaism would have imagined it like this: the four of us sitting around our dining room table, an enormous Christmas tree laden with lights and ornaments just ten feet away, our son botching the Hebrew words that were laser-printed onto a recycled sheet of paper, on the back of which was printed a recipe for corn salsa. We were as clueless as foreigners in a new country.

Our ritual would surely be laughable to many people. And yet it seemed magical to me. There we were, feeling our way as best we could through this thing we didn't really understand but felt compelled to enact. All three children, even our rambunctious two-year-old, fell into deep silence as we listened to the prayer. The air stilled, and for the first time all day, we took a collective breath. I felt closer to my children and my husband and my husband's parents, long deceased. I felt how much I treasured our family's blend of old and new. If I believed in some God-like power, I'm pretty sure I would have felt connected to that, too. This is part of what religious ritual gives people—these structured moments to connect with one another and ourselves.

After he finished the reading, my son turned to me and asked what the blessing meant. I racked my brain. I knew from a children's board book that I'd been reading to the kids for years that we lit the candles to symbolize the eight days and nights the oil lamp of the embattled Jews had remained mysteriously burning in the temple, as if by God's will. But when I told him that I didn't know the literal interpretation of the prayer, he looked like I'd let him down. Here we'd gone to all this trouble and we didn't even know what we were saying?

"Well, I do know something in Hebrew," I told the three of them.

"You do?" they asked, eyeing me suspiciously. "What?"

"I know"—this is where it gets a little embarrassing—"I know 'L'chaim.' It means 'to life.' "

I told them to lift their colored plastic cups and say it with me to close our Hanukkah ceremony. The next night Papa would be home, and he could tell us what the prayer meant because he had learned it as a boy. For now, we would have to do it the only way I knew how. I imagined that what we were doing would be considered blasphemy in the Jewish tradition, and that if my husband's family could see us they would groan at my WASP-y ineptitude. I had a vague feeling that "L'chaim" was generally reserved for wedding toasts or job promotions or birthday parties. I decided I didn't care. Who was to say that the Jewish religion or the Greek Orthodox church across the street knew the only path toward grace? What was sacred was that very moment. I wanted to celebrate the smooth skin of my children's curious faces, the roof over our heads, the rich traditions and great good fortune of being alive here on earth in the first place. I savored the way our voices, however unsteady, lifted as one. If I was going to celebrate anything, it was going to be the crooked, imperfect path of life that I and my part-Christian, part-Jewish, mostly nothing family had found ourselves on together.

"L'chaim," the children and I said in unison, the candles of the menorah washing their faces in soft yellow light as the colored bulbs of our Christmas tree twinkled across the room.

To life.

CHAPTER 12

Facing the Big Unknown

Before you know kindness as the deepest thing inside,
you must know sorrow as the other deepest thing.

*—Naomi Shihab Nye, "*KINDNESS*"*

One night when our older daughter was seven she appeared beside my bed in her pajamas, nearly in tears. For the third night in a row, she was having trouble sleeping. "I know you're going to say I don't have to worry about this yet because it's a long way away," she stammered, "but I keep thinking about my . . . passing away."

And there it was. In every parent's life, there are moments charged with a different kind of energy, moments when we have to drop everything, sit down, and have a talk.

I pulled her into my bed and blustered down a road of explanation that soon turned rocky. I hadn't anticipated the level of detail in her questions: "What happens to the body?" "Does the person still have feelings?" "Are they warm for a little while?"

I soon found myself talking about things like burial, organ donation, and throwing bodies over sides of boats. I was about to explain the rudiments of cremation when I realized my error. My daughter's eyes were wide, and I knew she'd be up half the night, so I quickly wrapped up with soothing talk of cloud-lined heaven and shushed her off to bed. In hindsight, my poor performance reflected my own difficulty in wrestling with thoughts of death.

One reason it was hard to explain death to my daughter was that, without the promise of a soul that continues on in the afterlife, her overwhelming sadness at the thought of herself or anyone she loved dying made perfect sense to me. How sad that we just end. But even more than that: Without a soul that lives on after us, it seemed we were nothing more than stuff even as we lived. If we don't have spirits separate from our bodies, and if there is no afterlife where those spirits end up, the sense of what we are collapses into blood and bones and tissue. Losing that religious conception of a soul sent me straight to the conclusion that every feeling I had was the result of a neurochemical reaction in my brain, and every action I took an unconscious evolutionary adaptation.

Many religious conceptions of existence, on the other hand, say that God's presence infuses everything we do and we are here by his grace. God-given grace bestows on life a feeling of magic through the notions that we are not alone and our actions are not purely biological. Awe and wonder arise from the thought of such a powerful being concocting such a complex, mysterious, beautiful world and guiding us, in mysterious ways, through it.

And religion offers more than the comforting scenario of life after death. Even for those who don't believe in any afterlife, or are unsure about what they believe when it comes to a separate soul that lives on after the body, religious rituals help ground people when they lose a loved one or prepare for their own deaths. More practically, one of the great benefits of religion is that when someone you love dies, you can find solace through the collected wisdom and practices of your faith. Sitting shiva in the Jewish tradition, saying the Catholic rosary, reciting the Muslim funeral prayer—these practices put structure around an experience that so often feels out of control.

One of the most troubling thoughts we can have is to think that our lives or those of our loved ones just end. Imagining our soul going on to heaven, and ritualizing that transition, soothes us. Such rituals are also a way to outwardly demonstrate what we take to be life's sanctity. When people began to bury their dead, it was a sign of the start of civilization. How we approach death says something about who we are while we live.

Every culture prepares for death differently. In some cultures, death is a constant and even welcome presence, such as in Mexico, where people celebrate the dead and create altars to entice them to visit during the Day of the Dead. In the Philippines, the youngest child in a family is passed over the coffin of a deceased grandparent, so that the elder's spirit can live on through the child. In New Orleans, in a combination of French, African American, and West African traditions, funerals are led by a marching band, and mourners dance along. Vajrayana Buddhists in Mongolia and Tibet believe their souls soar above their bodies when they die, and they often have sky burials, in which their corpses are chopped into pieces and placed on a mountaintop, exposing them to the elements and vultures.

In some way, every time I take a yoga class and rest in Shavasana, or corpse pose, at the end, I'm practicing for death. The pose, in which we lie on our backs, close our eyes, and let our arms rest by our sides, is a metaphor for how we should live, ever mindful that we're moving toward final rest. Such awareness gives our lives meaning by reminding us that our time is finite and we should make the most of it before we have to let go.

When people leave religion, they have to weigh the pros and cons of traditional rituals and teachings, or forgo all that and create meaning and rituals themselves. This isn't always easy. Baby-welcoming ceremonies and weddings may be fun to plan out ourselves, but death and funerals are different. In a time of crisis, people may not have the wherewithal to invent rituals or memorial services from scratch. With a nonreligious funeral, there is no script to go by, and mourners have to make it up by themselves during an already stressful time.

DEATH WITHOUT RITUAL

When I was nineteen and my brother was twenty-six, he committed suicide. In the horrible days after, my family turned to the funeral home to make all the arrangements, a friend to give the eulogy, and relatives to bring cakes and trays of cold cuts to my mother's house. My parents, long divorced, had my brother's ashes divided in half. My father had his half buried in a small cemetery near his house in Massachusetts. My mother asked my brother's college friends to take her portion to the top of Pinnacle Mountain in central Arkansas, a place he often went for long walks, and spread them there. I was left to grieve alone, not sure what I believed or where to find condolence.

My brother, whose name was Matthew, was the quintessential older brother, always up for a game of War or Boggle or Monopoly. He was also always ready to take on, unbidden, the neighborhood bully if she was teasing me or to help me make lunch after our parents divorced and our mother started her first job. Matt took me sledding after winter blizzards and gave me rides on his back at our cousins' pool in summertime. He was also a talented artist. I remember him bent over his desk on evenings when we were growing up, his lamp lighting the small space before him as his hand moved across the page.

By his early twenties, he had grown into a 6'2" gentle giant of a man. But he was also increasingly mentally ill. In college, the bipolar disorder that must have lain dormant in him all his life woke up. After years of painful struggle, the illness finally took him. One morning in July he decided he couldn't live anymore. He walked away from his apartment near some woods in Arkansas, climbed up the side of an embankment, and rested his head on a railroad track before an oncoming train. The conductor later told the police that he had bent his head "as if in prayer."

When my father told me what had happened, I'd just returned from a long Sunday drive with a friend. My father stood in the doorway of our house and said, "I have some terrible news. Your brother has gone and killed himself." Stunned, I walked up to my bedroom and sat at the window for hours just watching the cars go by. I had no way to make sense of my brother's death, no belief system to turn to for answers, and no rituals to begin my path through grief. In those first weeks and months, I plucked platitudes and half-thought-through ideas about death from the air. I said things about my brother's "energy" still being there, out in the universe. I imagined him watching and protecting me from above. I dreamed that he came back and that his death had never happened. In those dreams, he'd show up from out of nowhere—a kitchen cabinet, the bathroom door—and act like he had never left.

In the fall after he died, I returned to college and tried to behave as if nothing had happened. I had no container for my grief, no ritual to help me understand and process the loss I felt, and no one to turn to for help. What ritual my family did enact—the separating of Matt's ashes so our parents could commemorate him each in their own way—was more a reflection of our scattered family situation than any grounding tradition we had to fall back on. I almost wished my parents still went to church; at least then we would have had some guidance.

Meghan O'Rourke explores how grief has become increasingly

individualized in the memoir she wrote about struggling through and after her mother's death, *The Long Goodbye*. O'Rourke found herself coming up against what she calls the privatization of grief. Of the experience, she wrote, "I felt the lack of rituals to shape and support my loss. . . . I found myself envying my Jewish friends the practice of saying Kaddish, with its ceremonious designation of time each day devoted to remembering the lost person. As I drifted through the hours, I wondered: What does it mean to grieve when we have so few rituals for observing and externalizing loss?"

The feeling of emptiness so many of us feel after a loved one dies and we have no context through which to grieve reflects again the gap left in the wake of religion. "The enlightened modern age has failed to find a suitable replacement for a religious way of coping with the final *rite de passage* which brings life to a close," writes Peter Watson, author of *The Age of Atheists: How We Have Sought to Live Since the Death of God*. As fewer and fewer people gather with their religious groups to grieve or hold funerals, those in mourning often find themselves alone at a time when they most need other people. Outside the framework of known religious rituals, or the widespread practice of sending flowers or bringing casseroles and other food to families who have suffered a loss, there's no good script in our culture for helping mourners through their grief. Someone posts on Facebook that a parent has died and receives hundreds of Likes or comments, and then everyone moves quickly on, leaving the person to feel even more alone. In the absence of a community with which to ritualize grief, people often have a sense that their grief should be over quickly, like a bad cold.

As we abandon religious practice, we lose the religious structure and belief system built up around helping people traverse life's most difficult terrain. This loss includes the sense of meaning attached to death, be it an afterlife, heaven, or the continuity of reincarnation. It also includes loss of a community in which to die and with whom to grieve. On top of that, we lose the mental preparation for death, the religious practice of confronting its inevitability through religious stories and rituals.

Elizabeth Segel's family story is yet another cautionary tale about the absence of ritual, especially during difficult times. Elizabeth's parents were members of an Ethical Culture Society in New Jersey. Her mother, in particular, was very much against any practice that was even slightly reminiscent of religion. Elizabeth, along with her sister and her brother, grew up in an atheist household where the main tenet was to question everything. "Our lives were infused with that sense of 'Rule? What's a rule? Make up your own,'" she told me when I reached her by phone. "My mother always thought, 'Oh, this is great. Nobody will have to tell us what to do.'"

Elizabeth sometimes sees the shortcomings of the detached secular life. "Where I feel the biggest hole in my life is in these life events where rituals tend to take place," she said. She explained that this was especially true several years ago, when her brother died. It was then that she wished her family had some structure to guide them through memorializing her brother's life and processing their grief.

"There was no community to say, 'Here, we'll take care of you. Here, we'll sit shiva with you. Here, we'll provide this community sense for you,'" she said. When I asked what type of program her family created as a way to memorialize her brother, her answer was succinct: "Nothing." Her brother's friends, many of whom the family hadn't known, surfaced after his death and wanted to do something concrete, but her parents said no. As a result, she felt she and her family never had the opportunity to grieve her brother together as one. "They just were not emotionally ready to share anybody else's emotions about this," she said. "We had no structure with which to do it."

....

SAYING GOOD-BYE WITHOUT GOD

Whether or not you're religious, there seems to be a fundamental human need to gather together after someone dies, to remember the person's life, and to comfort the person's friends and family. It's a time when emotions are high and families are in disarray, with a million things to attend to. It can be a comfort to have someone practiced in death rituals, not just a family friend, to guide mourners through the process. The religious have their leaders, and now there are more and more options for the nonreligious as well.

Segel, O'Rourke, and I might have benefited from some of the resources now popping up for nonreligious people who are grieving or seeking to memorialize a loved one. Online alternatives include rituals that offer comfort, closure, and remembrance when someone dies, without invoking God or religious rites. Funerals, including home burials, are being stripped of all pageantry and finding secular space. Humanist chaplains preside over memorial services, leaving out the religious views on death that make the atheists in the audience cringe. And secular grief support groups offer ways for nonreligious people to experience loss in a community of like-minded people. For many, these additions to the traditional path through burial, commemoration, and grief are welcome changes.

There are also death midwives, or death doulas, who assist people in the dying process and offer emotional and practical support to families afterward, including guidance on burial and cremation, and assistance with a memorial ritual. Similar to the home birth movement, in which women choose to deliver their babies in their own bedrooms aided only by family and perhaps a doula, home death proponents seek to remove the middlemen—funeral homes, religious authority figures, even cemeteries—from the experience of death and memorial. A death midwife comes into the home and helps the family care for the body of the loved one so the family can spend time saying good-bye before burial, which may take place in the backyard of the person's house.

Those seeking to craft a secular memorial can tap an array of sources online, through outlets like the blog *The Inspired Funeral: Creative Ways to Approach the Inevitable,* which includes ideas about shrouds and woolen caskets for green burials, suggestions for family-decorated cremation boxes, and urns that couples can share. Like secular wedding ceremonies, secular memorial services are a grab bag of influences from religious and nonreligious sources. Some people simply ask friends and family to tell stories about the person who has passed away, or share their favorite poems or readings. They may play a favorite song. At one memorial service I attended, friends and family packed an auditorium to hear fifteen people who'd known the man who died speak. The final offering was a video projected on a large screen of the 1970s R&B band the Floaters singing "Float On." What matters most in these DIY memorial services is that the bereaved are surrounded by people who love and support them at a difficult time, and who remember the person they lost.

After moving to Memphis twelve years ago, Liz Hoffmaster, a pediatric nurse, inherited the leadership of the Memphis Atheists Meetup group, organizing get-togethers for godless thirty- and forty-somethings. The group meetings focus mainly on socializing and drinking. On Easter, they hide mini liquor bottles instead of eggs. The group was fun and frivolous, but when Liz lost a loved one, she realized how tight the bonds she'd made really were.

Two years ago, Liz's boyfriend developed cancer and, despite aggressive treatment, died soon after his diagnosis. He was estranged from his family and, like her, wasn't religious. So Liz was left to orchestrate a memorial service for him by herself, a party in a local art gallery. That night, she was still grieving. Her boyfriend had been the love of her life, and it seemed to her doubly unfair that they had had such a short time together. But at one point in the middle of the party, she stopped and looked around the room. She had grown up an Air Force brat and had never really put down roots until moving to Memphis. Now, surveying the people in the room, most of whom she'd met through the atheist group, she realized that she'd built a true tribe. And when the worst thing had happened, its members had made sure she was not alone.

"I looked around the room that night and I couldn't believe it," she said. "I realized I had everything I needed."

SECULAR SERVICES

While some people create memorial services the way Liz Hoffmaster did, others seek an experienced guide through the ceremonial display of their grief. That's where the secular humanist celebrant comes in. Audrey Kingstrom began conducting secular funerals in Minneapolis a few years ago when a friend needed someone to help her with a memorial service. In much the way that there is a cottage industry of nonreligious people who conduct weddings—"mail-order ministers"—there are now those who specialize in leading DIY funerals. They hang out their shingles online or count on people to find them through word of mouth.

When I met Kingstrom at the First Unitarian Society, a humanist congregation whose facility is set on a quiet hill in Minneapolis, she was crafting a secular memorial service for the husband of a woman she'd just met. The woman's husband had died from cancer, and she was seeking a nonreligious officiant for the funeral. The funeral home could connect her only to religious guides, but the woman was an atheist and was relieved when she found Kingstrom from a listing of humanist celebrants on the Internet. Kingstrom told her that she would conduct a service that would be about her husband and his life on earth, not about God or an afterlife.

Kingstrom, who was raised Lutheran in rural Minnesota, grew up loving the ritual and pageantry of the holidays. Christmas Eve would begin with a Swedish meatball and lutefisk dinner, followed by an elaborate gift-giving ritual. Then she and her siblings would create a whole Christmas Eve program, with Swedish songs and traditional Christmas carols, readings from the Bible, and instrumental performances. After their child-led program, the family would head to their church for a late-night candlelight service. "This was very special to me," she said.

After college, she enrolled in seminary, first in Minnesota and later in New York City. One day, she and friends were complaining about the patriarchal structure of the church. Their professor responded, "You can rail all you want, and you can tear down the church. But unless you have something to replace it with, it will continue."

"I remember being mad at her when she said that," Kingstrom told me, laughing. "I mulled that over for years." While she was mulling it over, she was also losing her faith during a ten-year period she calls her "great depression." As she emerged from that dark time, her interest in something to replace religion grew, and she now describes herself as a secular humanist. At the First Unitarian Society, with its strong humanistic bent, she observed the congregation's enthusiasm around a winter solstice party that an intern put together one year. The following year, the intern moved on, and Kingstrom took over the celebration and found her calling. Now the winter solstice celebration is the group's largest ritual event.

In her work as a humanist celebrant, Kingstrom looks closely at death as it's experienced in the United States. She encourages people to make plans for how they would like to die—at home? in hospice?—and how they would like to be memorialized. She sees the way we celebrate and memorialize people who have died as an opportunity for those who have left religious institutions to reclaim their social nature and embrace a philosophy of life. "Dealing with death is partly about finding a community and partly about understanding that we have one life to live," she said.

Kingstrom sees her role as providing a completely nonreligious ceremony that walks the bereaved through the ritual process of letting go; the first step is remembering what the person's life was all about. The only problem is, because she's not a leader of any congregation, she doesn't always know the person who has died; it can be hard for her to grasp a whole life story in a short time and craft a eulogy that would speak to who the person was. So she guides the family in crafting a eulogy themselves, then draws on comforting words from naturalist and humanist philosophies, along with secular readings and poems.

Kingstrom often hears complaints that religious ceremonies barely mention the person who has passed. "It's like 'fill in the blank,'" she said. "It's as if we're just ushering the person from this life to the next." She said the value of a secular life celebration is that it connects with people on a very human level; in fact, very religious people often come up to her after a service and tell her how meaningful the program was. "We don't need the God talk," she said. "If you just reach people at the level of shared human experience, you can touch them very deeply."

SECULAR GRIEF

Losing the "God talk" in grief groups has become one of Rebecca Hensler's life missions. Hensler started an online group called Grief Beyond Belief after her three-month-old baby boy died in her arms of a rare genetic disease. A counselor at a public middle school in San Francisco, Hensler wears glasses and has neatly cropped auburn hair, which she pushes behind her ears. When we met, she spoke in a clear, no-nonsense way, as if considering each word with extreme care. Her black tank top revealed the tattoo on her left shoulder that commemorates her son's life. The name "Jude" is wrapped in twin sprays of flowers, one red and one blue, with a dormouse beneath. The dormouse is from the poem "The Dormouse and the Doctor," from A. A. Milne's *When We Were Very Young.* It was a poem she read to her son every day in the hospital.

Hensler's tattoo was a kind of secular ritual to remember her son. Her son's life was so brief that she did not see the need for a full-blown memorial service. Instead, she, family, and friends met at home and talked about the baby, read from books they had read to him, and comforted each other.

After he died, she sought comfort in her grief through an online parental bereavement forum called The Compassionate Friends, which provided resources and connections to other grieving parents. It was a great help during a terrible time. "Grieving parents feel like an alien species; the only people who get you are other grieving parents," she said.

Even in The Compassionate Friends, however, it was hard for Hensler to find people who could support her without resorting to spiritual language and religious philosophizing. Some people expressed their religious beliefs, saying that "everything happens for a reason" and "your baby is with God now." The in-person parental grief support groups she found in the San Francisco area where she lives were often laced with New Age-y spiritual talk she dubs "woo." Someone would say she saw a butterfly and knew it was her child coming back to check on her; others said their children came to them in dreams. "At some point, I realized this wasn't working for me," she said. "I wished I could have the same kind of support without all the religion and all the woo."

About two years after her son died, she created a Facebook page for secular grief. It was so popular that she expanded her resources and community on the larger Grief Beyond Belief website, which offers links to writings, videos, and podcasts on secular grieving, as well as articles from the fields of psychology and philosophy. With the site's popularity, in the world of organized secular groups, Hensler has become what she calls "the Grief Lady." People approach her for help in person, over e-mail, and on the online forum.

After she was profiled in *USA Today*, the number of hits to her website shot up. In the past, visitors to the site usually found their way to it through atheist bloggers, but this wave of newcomers was made up of people with no connection to organized atheism or secularism. She saw this as a result of increased awareness about the nonreligious, "people all over the country who had not really given a name to what they are." She said that it's important to her that Grief Beyond Belief is serving those people as well.

Hensler has been an atheist as long as she can remember. Though she was raised Jewish and attended Hebrew school, she convinced her parents not to bother with a bat mitzvah for her when she announced that it would only be for the party and the presents anyway. For a while she believed the woo she now jokes about, which she characterizes as "belief in human soul-energy connecting us all—that whole thing." She thinks a lot of people end up with that because it's hard to say it's natural that we simply return to the earth. As she learned more and more about atheism, she realized she was ready to "be a grown-up."

Often she hears that nonreligious people like herself can't possibly find meaning without God or belief in the afterlife. But, she said, "to say you need the afterlife to have meaning is the bleakest form of insanity." In her own life, she created profound meaning from her son's seemingly senseless death by reaching out to others like her who were grieving but had no community or rituals that fit them.

"Grief Beyond Belief is my son's legacy," Hensler said. "This is the way that this tiny little person who lived for only ninety days is touching the lives of thousands of people."

....

DEATH AND COFFEE

Beyond death midwives, humanist celebrants, and secular grief support communities, a new movement of people who are trying to change the way we think about death has popped up. Death Cafes, starting up all over the world, are part of this growing movement of people who are intent on wresting death back from the throes of religion—and from our own solitary worry zones—by bringing it into our everyday consciousness in the hopes of enriching our lives. Death Cafes are held in various places, from senior centers to coffee shops and even cemeteries. They are salons for death talk that allow people to discuss openly what they often keep hidden, even from themselves. The point is to demystify death, so we can accept and even embrace it.

One of the advantages of religion is that we consider death every time we sit in a pew; death is a presence in every church, synagogue, or mosque. Without a religious community and framework, many people avoid thinking about death at all because it's so uncomfortable. Yet it's also essential that we as human beings are able to somehow come to terms with the inevitable. Anyone can go to deathcafe.com and find a nearby Death Cafe. Here's the announcement I found for one in Evanston, Illinois:

> *We are starting a MONTHLY Death Cafe because we want people to have the opportunity to discuss death, without anyone saying "Let's change the subject and talk about something else more positive." But death can indeed be positive, serving as a persistent reminder to live our lives to the fullest, with whatever time we do have left. Many of us are scared of death; medical professionals see it as a failure; and society tends to deny it and discourage us from talking about it. Yet, there are still many of us out there who really want to talk about it! So at Evanston Death*

> *Cafe we will come together and openly discuss our feelings, beliefs, attitudes, and fears about death. Hopefully, we will gain a sense of peacefulness and freedom in our sharing with each other, as well as a renewed inspiration for living! Please join us. Refreshments served, and is free-of-charge. This is solely a discussion group and is not suitable or appropriate for the newly bereaved or those seeking a grief support group.*

I decided to visit. In a quiet room in a modern senior center on a gray day, I joined ten people assembled to talk about death—openly, without fear, and without reference to religion or spirituality.

We began with blueberry cake served on white foam plates as we introduced ourselves around the circle. Our facilitator, Eric Jacobson, began the session by reading *Duck, Death and the Tulip,* a children's book by Wolf Erlbruch, which shows death as a skeleton that accompanies the duck wherever he goes. Jacobson used the children's story as an example of what Death Cafes do. "This is not a bereavement group and not a therapy group," he said. Instead, the group is part of a larger movement to normalize talk about death without religion. The point, Jacobson said, is to be more honest and forthright about death in our culture. "Religion has hijacked certain precincts of our life," he said. "If someone dies, we call a priest. But it doesn't have to be that way."

For the next two hours, we sat in a circle and did something so simple and yet so rare: We shared our thoughts on death, a topic not often broached in polite company. The facilitator guided the conversation to ensure that it didn't devolve into therapy or a grief session. Because we were at a senior citizens center, many in the group were elderly and intimately aware of death, having lost many close friends and relatives. One older woman, slightly hunched in her chair, said, "Everybody's going to die sooner or later."

"Yeah," the man in suspenders and a green turtleneck sitting next to her shot back. "But we want it to be later!"

A woman named Rose told the group that she lost her two best friends in the last year. She was raised Jewish but became agnostic when her daughter was in fourth grade, when the rabbi said that even he didn't believe in heaven and hell but rather in good works on earth. In the group, she was able to talk about some of the emotions she'd gone through when she experienced two losses so close together, and others in the group were able to give her support and empathy.

The simple act of talking with strangers that day made death feel a little bit more normal, less to be feared and denied. As I sat in the room amid those people, most of them much older, I felt for the first time that I didn't have to fear dying so much that I never talked about it. I also realized how rarely I spent time with the elderly, and that another benefit of religious belonging is a greater opportunity for intergenerational relationships and awareness. There, with a group of people so close to death themselves, the greatest gift we had for one another was the openness to discuss something often left off the table. Ironically, that elevated awareness of death made the fear of it subside.

Despite the growth of the death acceptance movement and the many resources for secular grieving, I still felt there was no good way to explain death to a child, just as there had been no explanation that had made sense to me when my brother died. I needed to keep searching for a way to think about life's end that wasn't so upsetting. But I knew, at least, that the first time any of my kids encountered death, whether of a beloved pet or a cherished grandparent, we would create a ritual where they would be free to cry, to grieve, to wonder, and they would know that they were embraced by those who loved them and understood their loss.

....

ONE SUNDAY MORNING, we were sprawled out in the living room, still in our pajamas, with toys everywhere. Our younger daughter was holding her favorite plaything, a twelve-inch-high painted wooden horse, which for some reason she'd dubbed Hello Kitty. She asked me where the horse had come from, and I said, "That was Papa's grandmother's. When she died, we took it from her apartment."

Staring squarely at the horse's painted saddle, she asked, "Is dying when you don't live anymore and you go in the water, with the river?"

I thought for a minute, staring at her as she stared at the wooden horse. I wanted to tell her that I was pretty sure, though not certain, that this life right now is the river, and that after we die, we leave the river. I didn't want to scare her with the concept of our eventual oblivion, though, and the image she presented didn't seem too far off. Our bodies decompose, falling back into the earth, merging with all the other matter that makes up our planet. In the future, our decomposed bodies might provide nutrients to the trees. Someone might hang a swing from one of those trees or sit beneath the shade of its leafy branches or make a painted horse from its wood.

I watched my daughter with raised awareness, knowing that she and I and everyone we knew would one day die, and that that was in some way what connected us.

"Yes," I finally said. "It's just like that."

CHAPTER 13

The Wonder of the Natural World

The true mystery of the world is the visible,
not the invisible.

—*Oscar Wilde,* THE PICTURE OF DORIAN GRAY

On spring break, Michael and I took our kids to Arizona for several days to see the Grand Canyon. One morning on our drive up, we stopped off at a smaller canyon just north of Sedona, the New Age mecca known for its energy vortexes and shops hawking crystal tchotchkes. The path from the parking lot led us to the river-bed of a red-rock canyon whose walls shot up all around us. Entering the dramatic space, our son yelled, "Oh my God!" as we all stood staring up and around. His voice echoed up and down the canyon: "Oh my God! Oh my God! Oh my God!" Here he was, a child who'd been raised without religion, standing in a stunning natural setting, shouting the best response he had: God.

The next day, up at the Grand Canyon, the five of us walked to-gether from the parking lot to the South Rim, the popular tourist point where people from all over the world first view the canyon. Leaving the car, we agreed to cast our eyes downward until we got to the rim, and then look up all at once so we would see the panorama for the first time together. When we reached the spot, our arms entwined, I counted "one . . . two . . . three!" and we all looked up at the same time. The view—the enormous expanse of layered gray and brown rock stretched across the whole horizon—rendered us silent. It was as if the air had been knocked out of us. We couldn't move. And the hundreds of fellow tourists around us were hushed as well. Instead of gabbing and jostling for position, a kind of quiet reverence came over all of us, the kind that falls over a city after a big snow or a congregation during communion.

I was awed by the Grand Canyon, but something was bothering me, a feeling that always troubled me in stunning natural settings. I wanted there to be some explanation behind it all that went beyond geology and evolution and natural forces. I yearned for the sense of meaning that came from belief that God had created everything, including us. I wanted everything I saw to mean more than just what I was seeing. I wished I could perceive in the view before me the hidden hand of God.

The day before, the only way my son had been able to articulate such vastness was through the word "God." I didn't have a much better expression myself. Taking in the enormity of the canyon made me feel like there had to be something bigger than scientific explanations and natural laws, but I had no idea what. How can you explain the beauty and mysteries of the universe without religion?

It turns out that awe-inspiring sights like the Grand Canyon may actually make people more religious. Piercarlo Valdesolo, a psychologist at Claremont McKenna College in Claremont, California, was curious about whether dramatic vistas were enough to change a person's belief in God. He noted that many historical accounts of people experiencing religious epiphanies involved being awe-struck by the presence of a divine being. That led him to wonder: Is it the belief in the presence of a divine being or the supernatural that elicits a sense of awe, or is it awe that elicits the perception of the presence of the supernatural? In other words, does the Grand Canyon make you believe in God?

In his study, subjects who were shown videos of awe-inspiring sights were much more likely to change their minds about whether they believed in God than those who watched other kinds of videos. One group saw a video clip of a dramatic scene from the BBC's *Planet Earth*, another viewed a *60 Minutes* news interview, and the last group watched a comedy clip. The subjects then took a survey that measured their belief in God, their belief "that the universe is controlled by God or supernatural forces, such as karma," and their feelings of awe while watching the video clip. Subjects who saw the *Planet Earth* video experienced the most awe and, at least while they were in that state, a greater belief in both God and supernatural control.

"The irony in this is that gazing upon things that we know to be formed by natural causes, such as the jaw-dropping expanse of the Grand Canyon, pushes us to explain them as the product of supernatural causes," Valdesolo told reporters after the study was published. That irony led to another of the study's findings: Atheists responded to the scenes of awe with feelings of discomfort—and a strong desire to seek out explanations for the unknown through science.

How do those of us who don't center our lives on religion explain the awe and wonder we often feel? My quest for a full life without religion was, at heart, a search for an answer to this question, for an alternative to God-given meaning. If we, our planet, the birds and trees, and everything around us are just material without souls, matter without prospect of an afterlife, what makes us feel awe and wonder?

....

WHAT IS AWE AND WHY DO WE FEEL IT?

Awe has been described as a mix of wonder, reverence, and fear, and we've all felt it, that sudden awareness that there is something larger than ourselves. But what causes us to feel it? And is the religious experience of it, felt in a spiritual building, through a sacred communal ritual, or in contemplation of a supernatural being, different or somehow better than the nonreligious experience of awe, felt in nature, in considering the vastness of the universe, in deep connection to other people or animals? I wanted to know if the ways I sometimes felt awe, whether in nature, appreciation of art, or simply a heightened awareness of my own sentience—a child's touch, the taste of ripe fruit, the smell of ocean air—gave me the same quality of experience that the religious say they feel.

In recent years, researchers have begun to look more closely at awe, both what it is and why we feel it. In 2007, Dacher Keltner, a professor of psychology and author of the book *Born to Be Good: The Science of a Meaningful Life,* conducted an experiment to show what awe does for us. He found that the feeling of awe arises when we sense vastness, which makes us feel like a part of a greater whole.

Keltner showed this by asking people to write twenty statements about themselves. Half of the subjects wrote their statements while seated in front of a full-sized replica of a *Tyrannosaurus rex* in the life sciences building on campus. The other half sat in a hallway. Those who wrote their statements while sitting in front of the *T. rex* were three times more likely to give answers that suggested they felt like part of some larger whole. Such answers included phrases like "I am an organic form" and "I am part of the human species." Those who wrote their statements seated in the hallway showed a narrower vision of themselves as individual units. They wrote things like "I am a soccer player" or "I am a sorority member."

The feeling of awe didn't just make people feel small; it made them feel connected to something larger. Keltner supposes that the human propensity for feeling awe may have evolved for a purpose—to bind people into groups instead of remaining individual and alone. Work led by Keltner has revealed that images inspiring awe cause the same parts of the brain to light up that light up when we connect to others. Physically, awe leads to a reduction in activity in the sympathetic nervous system and is physiologically soothing, which is the opposite effect of fight-or-flight mode. Awe makes us feel rooted and slows us down. People who experience awe seek to memorize their surroundings and freeze the experience.

Experiencing awe can also prompt us to act more benevolently toward others. When we are not stressed, perhaps in a moment of seeing the big picture rather than the details, we're more able to help others. In five different studies, Paul Piff of the University of California at Irvine and his colleagues found that subjects who were exposed first to awe-inspiring videos were more likely to display positive behaviors such as compassion and generosity in games and tests, meaning they were more likely to be generous and ethical. The researchers concluded, "Awe, although often fleeting and hard to describe, serves a vital social function. By diminishing the emphasis on the individual self, awe may encourage people to forgo strict self-interest to improve the welfare of others."

Awe also makes us step back and find new answers. One reason awe-filled experiences can be so powerful is that they expand our thinking quickly, allowing us to bypass our normal filtering. Awe forces us to accommodate new information so rapidly that we can't filter it through preexisting heuristics. It is through the process of being awed that we are able to change and develop our beliefs. In colloquial terms, awe blows our minds.

"Awe experiences knock us back into our baby state," Michelle

Shiota, an associate professor of psychology at Arizona State University who studies awe, told me when I reached her by phone. Babies and children, she said, are awe experts. This is because everything is so new to them that everything blows their minds. They are constantly updating what they know about the world.

As we age, it becomes harder for us to experience awe, which is perhaps why it feels so special when we do experience it. We also experience less awe when we are busy or stressed and don't give ourselves the time and space to be surprised and moved by the world around us. To some degree, our capacity to experience awe is thus a choice, Shiota explained.

I told her I felt something I thought was awe at times that didn't seem all that grand—rubbing my daughter's back at night as I put her to sleep or reading a beautiful passage in a book. She said these were perfect venues for awe, and that I was in fact experiencing vastness, which didn't have to mean a trip to the Grand Canyon. The sense of vastness could come from any experience in which we feel profound connection to others, to nature, to the universe. It doesn't have to be physically huge or overpowering. To Shiota, the experience of connecting to such vastness, however we found it, was what the word "spirituality" meant.

I'd always shied away from the term because it has come to encompass so much for so many that it seems hopelessly vague. It also suggests a belief in some supernatural force pulling the strings, a watered-down version of traditional religious belief in God. But Shiota said it didn't have to be that way. To her, spirituality was this sense of connection I described feeling as I put my daughter to sleep. It was one she had felt through her years training in dance and theater. It was what many felt in nature. Spirituality, she explained, simply meant feeling part of a vast and complex web, the web of life.

....

WHERE DO ATHEISTS COME FROM?

Why are some people more likely to believe in religious explanations for the wonders of the universe than scientific ones? So much about religion seems to be wired in us, and yet there are substantial numbers of atheists on the planet. Is there a religious gene, or an atheist one? To find out I attended a lecture about differences in the religious and atheist mind-sets.

I took my seat in a folding chair among about forty secular humanists who had gathered for their monthly meeting in a community room at the Unitarian Universalist First Parish in Concord, Massachusetts. The presenter, Catherine Caldwell-Harris, an associate professor of psychology at Boston University, was passionate about her topic: the differences between secular and religious minds.

Caldwell-Harris was lecturing on the research showing that there is a spectrum of belief that corresponds with the spectrum of how the brain organizes information. Toward one end of the spectrum are the systemizers, or people who prefer studying parts of a whole to see how a given system operates. They like to break things down to understand how they work. I thought of my son, who loves math, and his early Thomas the Tank Engine fixation, which led to Lego and, later, to Minecraft. At the far end of the systemizing group are people with Asperger's syndrome or autism, but many people, engineers and scientists in particular, fall toward the systemizer end of the cognitive spectrum. These are people who use reason, logic, and evidence to draw their conclusions.

On the other side of the spectrum are those whom researchers call mentalizers. These people are less concerned with pulling apart the pieces to understand how something works. Instead, they use their strong proclivity for imagining what's going on in other people's minds to make assumptions. Educators call this skill "theory of mind," and my older daughter has it in spades. She readily imagines herself into other people's situations—the children of slaves she reads history books about, American women before they could vote, the homeless people we see in our neighborhood, you name it. Simply put, mentalizers excel at placing themselves in another person's shoes and imagining what that person is feeling. They also are more likely to see hidden agency behind any action, even if that action is simply a limb falling from a tree. When reasoning about problems, mentalizers also often go by their "gut," while systemizers prefer to use logical analysis.

Each one of us falls somewhere on this cognitive spectrum. Interestingly our position is somewhat predictive of whether or not we believe in God. It turns out that the mentalizers, those who focus on understanding people by imagining their likely mental states, are more likely to imagine hidden agency in the world and believe in God at higher rates than the systemizers. The systemizers, who use evidence to reach their conclusions, are less likely to believe in God. Some theorists say this is because their focus is on analyzing the natural world, rather than people's mental states. If we are looking for the God gene, that biological component that makes some of us believers and some of us nonbelievers, such research may lead us to it.

Caldwell-Harris believes these cognitive differences may even explain the gender gap in religious belief. Women are more likely to be mentalizers and also more likely to be religious than men. Men are more likely to be systemizers and to be atheists and agnostics. Caldwell-Harris stresses that we are all on a continuum when it comes to these different ways of thinking, and that each of us has what she calls a "cognitive comfort zone" corresponding to our preferred reasoning style; this reasoning style is part of the explanation for individual differences in religiosity.

Toward the end of the session, a fifty-something, graying man in a plain shirt raised his hand. "Since we're in Concord," he said, referencing the town's history as home to Ralph Waldo Emerson, Henry

David Thoreau, and other Transcendentalists, "I wonder if I might bring a Transcendental perspective into the conversation." He said that when his children were babies and he would hold them on his lap, they would look above his head, seeming to gaze at something he couldn't see. He said he thought maybe we are all born with the ability to see invisible forces. I was intrigued by the question, but then a woman raised her hand and dismissed him, asking what the proof might be.

It seemed a mentalizer and a systemizer had butted into one another. What was lost in the tension before Caldwell-Harris called on another person with a raised hand was that they were both there at the meeting searching for an understanding of how the world works. Strip away our different cognitive settings, the positions we start from when we seek our understanding of the world, and aren't we all reaching for the same thing?

Whether we call it science or religion, we're all after a framework for understanding the mysteries inherent in being alive and the wonder we experience when we start to grasp them. In fact, both worldviews—both sides of the spectrum—offer their own existential comfort.

THE COMFORTS OF SCIENCE

We know that religion offers people answers for the meaning of life, comfort in the face of difficult, inescapable ideas like mortality, and beliefs that help them fend off dread and hopelessness. But is there something people who aren't religious can believe in that will offer the same kinds of comfort for the difficulties of life and explanations for its wonders?

No other human endeavor has played as important a role in removing God from our lives as science. In the Renaissance, Copernicus declared that the sun doesn't revolve around the earth. Darwin's theory of evolution went against the biblical story of Genesis, in which the world is said to have been created in seven days. The more scientists have learned about the universe, the harder it has become to see it as anything but uncaring. Religious stories of creation no longer make sense as literal interpretations of the way the world came to be. Natural laws challenge the concept of divine plans as spelled out in sacred texts, causing many to abandon ideas about God-given meaning and purpose.

Yet two hundred years on from the Enlightenment, with science and technology ever more powerful in all spheres of our lives, researchers have shown through a clever experiment that science may be able to give the nonreligious the same kinds of existential solace that religion gives the faithful.

Miguel Farias, a lecturer on psychology at the University of Oxford, wanted to know if religion was the only belief system that provided existential consolation. Was it belief in religion or just belief in something that made people feel better? He and his team developed a scale for measuring belief in science, which, as one might expect, was inversely correlated with religiosity. Then they ran two experiments in which they manipulated the levels of stress and existential anxiety that participants confronted.

The first study, of one hundred rowers, compared forty-eight who were about to do a normal training session with fifty-two who were under more stress because they were about to compete in a regatta. The ones who were about to compete scored higher on tests of scientific belief than those who were just training. Under pressure, they wanted something to believe in.

In the second experiment, sixty people were randomly assigned to one of two groups. Those in the first group were asked to write about the feelings aroused by thinking about their own death, while the other group was asked to write about dental pain. The participants who had been asked to think about their death scored higher in the scale of belief in science.

The researchers suggested that a belief in science may offer comfort and reassurance to nonreligious people who are under stress or experiencing an existential crisis, just as researchers know religion does. There seems to be some basic human motivation to believe—whether it is in God or science.

"It's not just believing in God that is important for gaining these psychological benefits, it is belief in general," Farias reported. "It may be that we as humans are just prone to have belief, and even atheists will hold nonsupernatural beliefs that are reassuring and comforting." Nonreligious people, in other words, may use science for the comfort others find through faith.

SCIENTIFIC WONDER

I was curious as to how scientists themselves address awe, faith, and meaning in the world. More specifically, how might one of the world's most outspoken atheists, one who studies cosmology, explain how he finds meaning in a godless universe?

When I arrived to meet Lawrence Krauss, a professor of theoretical physics at Arizona State University, he was running late. He hurried into his office to clear away some pornographic images that had been planted by an online troll on the website for his movie *The Unbelievers,* in which he and his friend Richard Dawkins travel the world talking about the implausibility of God and the dangers of organized religion. When Krauss finally came to rest amid the books and papers that cluttered his office, his frazzled energy was slow to subside. He was dead serious but also surrounded by silliness. On either side of the table were propped two life-size cardboard cutouts, one of Mr. Spock and the other of Captain Kirk. Krauss wore a red

T-shirt bearing the image of the Cat in the Hat corralling Thing One and Thing Two and the words TEACHER OF ALL THINGS.

Krauss is indeed a teacher of many things, not just of physics to his students at ASU but also of atheism, which he explains and defends at engagements around the world. He was taking time to meet with me during his busy week in part out of his eagerness to spread the gospel of science to a world he finds frustratingly attached to its religious myths. I wanted to know how he finds wonder and awe in a world without God, and he was happy to oblige.

Krauss's first inkling that he might choose science as his profession came in elementary school when he read a book about Galileo that his teacher had given him. The book told the story of the seventeenth-century astronomer's quest to confirm heliocentrism, that the sun is the center of the universe, rather than the earth (which gained him nearly nine years of house arrest at the end of his life). Galileo's story struck Krauss as the most exciting kind of work he could imagine. "It seemed courageous to try and understand how the universe worked," he said. "It was very romantic."

Around the same time, Krauss left the religious world in which his parents had raised him. Leaving it, he said, was just a matter of growing up. "I realized these are clearly silly stories created by people who just didn't know any better," he said. "These miracles don't happen in the world that I live in." His world now is one of theoretical physics, a discipline that uses mathematical models and abstract concepts to explain natural phenomena. In his book *A Universe from Nothing*, Krauss applies his learning to the question of how the universe we live in sprang from nothing, with no help from a creator or intelligent design.

I asked him why we were here in the first place. What's the purpose or meaning of the universe? He clasped his hands behind his head and looked up at the ceiling.

"Every bit of evidence from four hundred years of physics, particularly the last hundred years, is that really, there is no purpose to the universe," he said. "There's no evidence of planning or design." Instead, he said, the universe may have arisen from a quantum vacuum, without a creator, that exploded 13.72 billion years ago and has been expanding ever since.

After that settled in, I asked him if this explanation renders our own lives meaningless, devoid of awe and wonder. He said that it's actually quite the opposite. Living in a world with no built-in meaning is far from a bad thing. "If you think about it right," he said, "it's much better."

That's because, he said, the belief that God put us here and pulls the strings makes us nothing more than puppets. It's infantilizing to see ourselves with so little control. In fact, belief in God is what renders life meaningless, he said. To him, the godless life has the potential for more awe and wonder, not less.

As a scientist, Krauss is trained to look at the world to uncover the mechanisms of its natural processes. Doing so forces him to engage his sense of wonder. Krauss claimed he experiences more wonder each day than someone who sees the world through the lens of religious belief. This is because he doesn't have the answers. He never knows what he's going to discover, and he works from a position of constantly wanting to know more.

"Until you have science," he said, "everything's a miracle." When the answer is that God created the universe and that's the way it is, he said, we have no incentive to explore. Science shifts the focus from whatever it was that gave rise to the universe, the question of *why?*, to natural processes all around us, the question of *how?* The first question cannot be answered, except by faith. The second can, and it contains an unending series of mysteries to be solved: Why are no two snowflakes alike? When did animals first walk on land? Why do human bodies contain the same elements as stars? To Krauss, each day is a new opportunity to work along the frontier between what is known and unknown about the universe. In that space, the world explodes with questions, possibilities, and wonder. The key to wonder is in not knowing the answers ahead of time.

But what about that nagging sense that without God, we are all just matter? After leaving religion, I couldn't shake the dark idea that I was no more than skin and bones and the neurological firings in my brain. I asked Krauss what we should replace God with to gain a sense of meaning and purpose. He said we have two choices: We can think that we are special because God created us or we can think that we are special because our very existence is so rare and unlikely. In fact, Krauss says, the universe is trying to kill us. Life on our planet is the result of such unusual events and natural processes over such a long period of time that the existence of any one person is an extreme statistical anomaly.

"What you have to do is get yourself in the mind frame that you weren't created for a purpose, but you happen to have the opportunity to have one," he said, gazing at me steadily. "This remarkable accident, which may be very, very rare in the universe, is something you're part of."

We may be just matter, but it is extraordinary that the matter making us up even exists—much less that it can walk and talk and think and love. In fact, life in the universe makes up just one millionth of one billionth of all matter. Not only that: Every bit of our own human matter is connected not just to all life on earth but to the very stars in the sky. That's because life on earth is composed of nitrogen, oxygen, iron, and carbon—but the only elements that were made in the Big Bang were hydrogen, helium, and a little bit of lithium. That means that the elements in our bodies didn't exist in the universe at the time of the Big Bang. They had to have been created in the nuclear reactions in the cores of stars. If stars hadn't exploded, Krauss says, we wouldn't exist.

"Since those elements are in your body and they once were in the stars, that means every atom in your body experienced the most violent explosion in the universe, a supernova. Literally, every atom, essentially, in your body must have come from a star, so you must be stardust because those elements just didn't exist anywhere else in the universe except inside stars." It is, he says, the most poetic thing he knows about physics.

The path to wonder is in paying attention to what is right in front of us, he said, not making up something we can't see. The idea that our very existence is so unlikely, that we have this little blip of life on a fingernail shred of time that by all accounts should never have happened in the first place, infuses life with a new and higher meaning. I left Krauss's office wondering how I could cultivate such wonder, as he does with science, more deliberately in my own life.

CHAPTER 14

The God of Here and Now

There is no need for divine election.
Perception is itself a form of grace.

—*Diane Ackerman,* A Natural History of the Senses

If you drive east out of Santa Fe, New Mexico, leaving the picturesque downtown streets lined with southwestern rug shops and jewelry stores, eventually you will find a dirt road that runs between clusters of modest homes, set close together. Somewhere along that road a playground backs up to a parking lot, and from the parking lot, a path opens up. Take the path down a gentle hill and you will enter the Upaya Zen Center. If it's lunchtime, large bowls of bread, lentils, rice, and salad will be set out on long rustic tables in the main lodge. Throngs of people will be lined up for food served by the handful of year-round residents, mostly young, handsome men with shaved heads and dark uniforms that mimic taekwondo doboks.

I had come to Upaya to join seventy or so others for a weekend retreat to explore an intriguing alternative to religion: secular Buddhism. Upaya is a place rich in religious symbolism and ritualistic practice, but it doesn't bear traces of the Catholicism, Episcopalianism, or evangelical Protestantism that many who've come here have left behind. Upaya was founded on one of the oldest religious traditions in the world—Zen Buddhism—and it supplies a rich, symbolic experience within the frame of an ethics-based philosophy based on ancient wisdom. But to me it felt brand new.

I chose Upaya because the leader of the weekend workshop, Stephen Batchelor, has written about an idea that resonates with many who've left religion. In his book *Buddhism Without Beliefs: A Contemporary Guide to Awakening*, published in 1997, Batchelor presents his ideas about the applicability of secular Buddhism, which provides a framework for leading an ethical, contemplative, and philosophical life. Batchelor reinterprets what we think of as Buddhism, saying that the Buddha's original teachings were altered by later followers who laced a very practical, secular practice with supernatural beliefs. Batchelor wants to wrest Buddhism from those mystical beliefs, including those of karma and reincarnation, and return the Buddha's teaching to its secular space.

In fact, he prefers not to call his subject Buddhism at all, because that "-ism" implies religion and he thinks the term is an effort to wedge the Buddha's teachings into a Western frame. He is after something else, even replacing the term "Four Noble Truths"—the essential Buddhist teachings—with "dharma practice." This is because, like many who leave religion, Batchelor wants to move discussion away from any notion that there is an absolute truth to be found. His practice focuses on human experience, governed by our brains, bodies, and animalistic urges we shouldn't deny. He believes enlightenment comes not in one big blaze of light but in the most mundane experiences here on earth—holding a child's hand, planting a garden, taking a photograph, or listening to music. The title of the retreat reflected his practical approach to awakening. He called it "Being Completely Human."

How do we become completely human in an overly charged world? We start with the most essential thing we have: our breath.

After lunch at Upaya, the group dispersed to rest for an hour before meeting outside the zendo. There, we removed our shoes, placed the palms of our hands together, and bowed as we walked into the zendo, a rustic space edged in dark, rough-hewn logs and filled with natural light from high windows. Black cushions, mats, and folding chairs were set in a wide arc facing a statue of an Eastern goddess. Outside, a resident rhythmically hit a gong; as the start of the meeting approached, the gonging got faster, then stopped. A young woman rang a small chime, and all seventy of us stopped talking or moving and closed our eyes. For the next fifteen minutes the only sound in the room was an occasional cough or rustling of clothes. The hum of energy you might encounter in a room full of seventy people condensed into thick silence.

Another chime sounded, and we opened our eyes. Stephen Batchelor, bushy-browed, bespectacled, and wearing a white button-down oxford shirt and black pants, cut a surprisingly professorial figure sitting beside a statue of the Buddhist goddess Manjushri, who was holding a sword that symbolized discerning wisdom. In his calm British accent, Batchelor told us that the meditation practice is not meant to make us feel comfortable. "Its purpose is to serve as a mirror to ourselves." He said that there's no rulebook up in the sky. We learn to be ethical people through the practice of life. And it starts by cultivating our awareness and self-knowledge through meditation. According to Batchelor, in the Pali Canon, an early collection of Buddhist texts, the Buddha refers to himself as a bodhisattva, or one who aspires to awakening. The phrase Batchelor uses for such awakening is "completely human" (hence the name of the retreat).

Batchelor said he doesn't want to let go of that rich source at the heart of dharma practice. He says we must hold tight to what is essential and foundational. What he does want to do is reframe the practice, which he says has been altered through the ages by mystics who got hold of the Buddha's teachings and changed their original intent. He introduced us to an easy-to-remember acronym, ELSA, which sounded almost laughable as I thought of my younger daughter's obsession with Disney princesses. Why not, he said, think of the Four Noble Truths with a handy acronym that's easy to remember as we go about our days and face crisis, doubts, hurt feelings—all the components of dukkha, or suffering. ELSA stands for Embracing all of life, Letting go of habitual reactivity, Seeing the letting go, and Acting. Taking these four steps allows us to transcend the inevitable pain of living and move toward awakening, or being completely human.

Batchelor's own journey, which he recounts in his memoir *Confession of a Buddhist Atheist,* began with more traditional Buddhism. At the age of nineteen, Batchelor traveled to India and soon after became a Buddhist monk. But he found himself increasingly full of doubts about the metaphysical teachings that were part of traditional Buddhism. He didn't believe in a supernatural realm and refused to think of himself as spiritual. After eleven years as a monk, he disrobed. "I am trying to bring the Buddha back down to earth, to bring the Buddha back into his human form," he told us. He said the Buddhist tradition gave primary emphasis to the practice and cultivation of doubt and uncertainty rather than knowing all the answers. "I came back to the question 'What is this? What is it to be fully human?' "

He realized there was no absolute truth, but there was a practice that would allow him to live with greater psychic ease. Inherent in this practice is knowing that we don't really know. In fact, he said, "all our theories are a highly elaborate screen to persuade ourselves that we've got it figured out." We don't know, and the dharma practice as he sees it is about pulling "that particular rug from beneath one's feet."

We do this is by opening ourselves up to not knowing, to seeing the gray areas not as a cop-out but as an opening to wonder. The key is not to flee ambiguity, shutting the door because we can't answer the questions of why we're here. Instead, we consider *how* we are here, how we exist in the world. We do this by embracing the messiness, the poignancy, and the knowledge that life will end.

THE MINDFULNESS MOMENT

Americans are growing intrigued by Eastern practices. Practices like yoga and meditation are now so mainstream in the United States that you can find venues for them anywhere in the country. They appeal to the spiritual-but-not-religious set because they offer seekers a complete package, an alternative worldview as well as a framework for how to live.

Mindfulness meditation, in particular, is having a heyday. Educators claim it helps their students focus. Corporate titans say it gives them a competitive edge by, strangely, removing their edge. There are mindfulness apps and meditation franchises, and the practice itself made the cover of *Time*. In an increasingly busy, connected world that leaves many of us overwhelmed and overstimulated, meditation offers a secular alternative to prayer. It works like this: We find a comfortable seat, alone or with others, close our eyes, and observe whatever thoughts arise, silently and without judgment, for some length of time. Some people practice for five minutes every morning, while others have a more extensive practice.

The documented benefits of meditation are increasing. Neuroscientists have observed that the practice reduces stress and inflammation, cultivates a sense of calm acceptance, and makes people happier. But it doesn't just help us find our personal bliss. Research has shown that people who practiced mindfulness meditation over the course of just six weeks were kinder and more compassionate toward others. Some researchers suspect that by enhancing our capacity for attention by concentrating on our breath, we increase the chances of noticing what others are going through. It may also help us to mentally diminish barriers between groups through the practice of being nonjudgmental. With meditation, perhaps we start to see how we're all connected. It also helps us let go of our own habitual reactive patterns.

Unlike religions, with their creation myths, Batchelor's secular Buddhism doesn't venture beyond the human mind. A dharma practice doesn't demand faith in supernatural entities. In fact, Buddhist ideas about mindfulness, for example, are backed up by modern neuroscience and psychology. Much of contemporary cognitive behavioral therapy is in sync with dharma practice. But Buddhism also addresses questions of meaning and connection that science can't approach. It offers both a science-based understanding of the world and a way of life that anyone can practice.

It's also similar to the concept of flow put forth by Mihaly Csikszentmihalyi, a professor of psychology and management at Claremont Graduate University in Claremont, California. Csikszentmihalyi wanted to know why some people thrive in their lives and others don't, so he studied those who flourish. What he found was that they achieved what he calls flow, a psychological state during which people are optimally engaged and challenged in work that gives them a profound sense of purpose. Flow is not unlike the Buddhist awareness achieved through a practice of mindfulness meditation, because it requires complete, focused attention.

"The most important step in emancipating oneself from social controls is the ability to find rewards in the events of each moment," writes Csikszentmihalyi in his book *Flow: The Psychology of Optimal*

Experience. "If a person learns to find meaning in the ongoing stream of experience, in the process of living itself, the burden of social controls automatically falls from one's shoulders. Power returns to the person when rewards are no longer relegated to outside forces."

SECULAR SEEKERS

Mindfulness works for people with all kinds of priorities and backgrounds. The retreat participants came from diverse places, but all were in search of emotional and spiritual sustenance that their often-difficult work lives did not provide. They were not navel-gazers. Many were nurses, social workers, and prison and hospital chaplains—people whose jobs put them on the front lines of human suffering. Over meals and in between lectures, they told me that their meditation practice rooted them to a core of calmness and strength, which allowed them to bear the suffering of others they worked with. In their jobs, they often have to lend their nervous systems to the people around them to calm and console them. Through mindfulness, they developed the capacity to stay calm even in stressful moments by focusing on the dharma practices of embrace and acceptance.

There were also many who had come to Buddhism to cope with pain that religion had failed to relieve and, in some cases, caused. William LaRue lives in Santa Fe. A slight, soft-spoken man with refined facial features framed by a bushy auburn beard, LaRue told me that after high school he was searching to live a life of meaning and ended up in the US Army's 3rd Ranger Battalion. We were sitting in the bright sun on a wooden bench on the grounds of Upaya after lunch as he explained how he found secular Buddhism. After fighting in the Panama invasion, where he was wounded, and being discharged, he came home and attended college, including classes in evolutionary biology. He'd been raised in a strict Methodist household and was very much involved with the church community, mentoring kids in the arts program and helping in the nursery. But he was losing his faith. On a church retreat, the group he was with had set up a schedule of twenty-four hours of continuous prayer. LaRue had the 3:00 AM time slot.

"I woke up and absolutely and profoundly did not believe in God," he said. He told himself that he would go back to sleep after the hour of prayer and when he woke up he'd believe again. "But I woke up and said, 'It's done. I'm not a Christian anymore.'" For four more years, he continued to go to church and pretended to believe, but he'd skip saying a prayer here or singing a song there. Sometimes the kids would ask him questions about his beliefs, which he'd dodge with jokes. When he finally came out, like so many other people I had met from strict backgrounds, he lost his community, and eighteen years later, his parents are still upset.

It wasn't just the intentional community he missed. He started to experience symptoms of post-traumatic stress disorder related to his time in combat. (He thinks being in a spiritual community might have kept the symptoms of PTSD at bay.) Through the Department of Veterans Affairs he started psychotherapy. His therapist introduced him to meditation, one day suggesting that he try a few minutes of the simple Zen style, noticing his own breath moving in and out. After one or two breaths he said to his therapist, "I just felt a little spark of joy!"

Meditation helped him manage his PTSD and the flashbacks from his time in combat. His brain couldn't differentiate between having a rifle in his hand and his vivid memories of it, but if he focused on his own sensations in the moment, he could turn down the volume on those images. He now has a daily practice of focusing his attention on the moment and visits Upaya regularly.

Another participant I met, Greg Rice, also felt that mindfulness meditation had turned his life around, in a less dramatic way. Rice, a tanned, muscular fisherman from Alaska who has been coming to Upaya for several years, said that before discovering Buddhism, he felt trapped in his life. "It wasn't a bad life," he said, "but you're just doing your thing." Then he and his wife separated. Because he's a fisherman, he has winters off from work. "If you're lucky like me and have time to say, 'The way that I am in the world just isn't working,' you can come to a place like Upaya." He now comes every year in the off-season. "The process of change is slow—like growing hair," he said—but he knows something has changed in him. "I pay attention more to how other people see me. I'm opening myself up and having deeper connections. I don't even direct the conversations I have with people, but they move to important things in the heart."

Part of what resonated with Rice about Stephen Batchelor's work was his embrace of humanity's messiness. We are animals, Batchelor says, and as such we are programmed to be reactive. Dharma practice doesn't deny that. It doesn't reject human nature. But it shows people how to work with it. "We train ourselves to disown ourselves, to reject parts of ourselves," Rice said. "But we don't have to do that. We can find and love the parts of ourselves we were taught to reject." The benefits for him have been revelatory. For years he struggled to find peace of mind. But since coming to this practice, he said, "I feel so at home in the world."

THE NEED FOR NORMS

One of the risks of bringing Eastern practices to the West is that they then detach from their original roots. Yoga turns into exercise, for example, or Buddhism becomes a bumper sticker. This is why Batchelor believes so strongly in holding on to the original teachings of the

Buddha. During the retreat, Batchelor and I met in a small side room called the Wayring Temple's Dokusan Room. Like the Zendo, the small room was a ritual space, saturated with meaning. We sat cross-legged on pillows. Batchelor told me he thinks our modern impulse away from rituals and sacred spaces is a problem, and that's why dharma practice grounded in ancient wisdom and practices could be helpful to people like me. Rituals are important because they make explicit our implicit values. Sacred spaces bring us together to celebrate our values. We leave religion, but we still seek meaningful communal experience and the wisdom of the ages.

He believes that what's missing in secular life is a public place for contemplative community rituals. "When we leave religion, we leave the physical edifice of the church," he said. "We leave gathering together on Sunday mornings." We also leave rituals that publicly connect us to strangers.

"The trouble is that these religious rituals are so encoded in doctrine that they put people off." And yet starting from scratch makes these new attempts at secular community feel contrived. "We don't feel at ease," he said. "We have to get over that initial feeling of 'we're making this up as we go along.' "

He told me that sometimes he attends Mass in the thirteenth-century church in the small town in the southwest of France, where he lives. "Every six weeks or so they have a Mass and I go," he said. He's not going for the message in the Mass but for the ritual. "I mean, they're talking gobbledy-gook," he said, "but it's a powerful communal confirmation of values."

He wishes that secular people had such spaces in which to gather and convey their implicit values in an explicit way. For Batchelor, the beauty of the dharma practice is that it offers a secular practice tied to ancient norms and wisdom—a framework that was born thousands of years ago but holds up even today.

"Dharma is a norm, it means literally a law," he told me. "The

Buddha understood his dharma as providing a normative framework for living." It's that framework that is so needed in our individualistic culture. It pulls people back together yet lets them experience meaning on their own. "Secular dharma would be a life that is entirely committed to flourishing on this earth with no expectation or longing for anything after death," he said. "So in that sense it's very much of this world, but it's governed by norms derived from traditional dharma."

THE ONGOING PATH

Batchelor used the last day of the four-day retreat to discuss the path we are all on, which is both familiar and novel. We travel where others have walked in the past. We have their norms and wisdom to guide us. But we also walk the path ourselves, ensuring that it continues for those who come after us. The dharma practice gives us the kind of vertical stake in the ground that is so hard to find in a secular age, where we don't often experience time beyond the one we live in. On the path, we are connected through time to those who've come before us and those who'll come after. The path itself, not heaven or God or reincarnation, is our consolation.

"One dimension of walking on a path is that as long as you are on it you are never alone," Batchelor said. "It is still something that has been opened up and traveled by others. It's only from having been walked upon by others that it exists at all. And it is your walking on the path that keeps it open for others to walk on in the future. It's an experience of being part of a community or a society—an emotional indebtedness and at the same time an act of responsibility."

As I listened to his words, I thought of all that had come before me—my family's deep religious past—and what might come after.

Surely we were leaving a worthy path for our children, that they might feel connection through time to something larger one day, too.

As more and more people abandon their religious affiliations—the labels and precepts, the texts and practices—many of them replace religious practice with a spiritual practice and belief. We can still find connection to something larger than self and the something doesn't have to be supernatural. It is possible to be both an atheist and a deeply spiritual person.

Spending time in nature is one way people do this. In nature we come closer to what's big and extraordinary about the world and to the sense of our connection to the vast tableaux around us. But to be in nature and sense not just the here and now but our collective history is to be aware of the path that others have walked, our indebtedness to them, and our hope for the future. That is when we might feel not just awe but something deeper, the peace that comes from being part of a larger, lasting whole.

In August my family visited Maine for vacation, and one day we drove to Thunder Hole in Acadia National Park. There, along the Atlantic coast, we walked over bald, lichen-mottled rock and through pygmy pine forest in the blazing end-of-summer sun. One narrow path took us to an inlet filled with round gray rocks the size of large bowling balls that had been washed smooth by the sea. Amid and atop the rocks were about a hundred cairns of all sizes that visitors had made—stacks of stones normally used to mark a hiking trail when no other signs are there to show the way. Here the cairns, made into arches and obelisks, were more decorative than useful. At water's edge, we were at the end of the trail and needed no further direction. But there was something purposeful about these cairns nonetheless.

All those human-made creations, rocks set atop rocks, were emblems of human life, testimonies to those who'd come through this place and wanted to leave something behind to show they'd been there. There was something generous and industrious about building and leaving behind these offerings. How often in life we hold tight to things; here all was let go. Surely the cairns would be demolished by strong waves later when the tide came in. But the people who made them had made them anyway. Why do we create anything—make art, devise scientific theories, form religions—if not to make a path for ourselves and others, and to leave some little bit of ourselves behind? We need to show that we were here and that our lives mattered.

Our kids ran ahead and fanned out, each finding a spot to build a cairn. Our son accidentally tipped over a tall cairn made of heavy oval rocks. Our younger daughter wobbled across the rocks in her too-big pink Crocs. And our older daughter raced toward the sea, where she crouched and let the water lap her feet as she plucked her rocks and set them in place. Each of them started making a cairn, without thought or discussion.

Michael and I made them too, setting stone upon stone until we had built our own little monuments. As I placed the rocks on top of each other, trying not to unbalance them and make them fall, I thought about how much life surrounded me, in this far reach of nature, with the people I loved most, and the traditions we were creating every day on our own. The cairn-making by the sea was its own kind of ritual, not led by anyone yet still influenced by history. I sensed a connection to an ancient past as I placed the rocks in rough configurations.

After all my searching, I still didn't know what the meaning of life was. I sensed that I never would. Still, I felt a new fullness every day. I was learning to embrace the life we were making, not regret the one we hadn't chosen. Even if all we were was contained in the blood beating through our very hearts and limbs, it was, suddenly and resoundingly, enough. Though religion promises something beyond all that we can see and feel and touch, standing at that spot with my family at the edge of the sea, I wondered how I could have ever longed for anything more than this.

As we walked back to our car, I turned to try to find the cairns we'd erected. They were already indecipherable amid all the others. I pressed my younger daughter's hand in mine and helped her over the rocks jutting along our path. *This,* I thought as we walked together, her hair blowing in a wind that would never blow in exactly the same way again, our feet walking over stones that had been there for ages. *This is grace.*

CONCLUSION

Make Your Own Sunday

> Shall she not find in comforts of the sun,
> In pungent fruit and bright, green wings, or else
> In any balm or beauty of the earth,
> Things to be cherished like the thought of heaven?
>
> —*Wallace Stevens, "Sunday Morning"*

From my many trips to learn about people who'd left religion and were creating new secular communities, one couple in particular stays in my mind. I met Allen and Brenda Glendenning, a couple in their fifties, at the American Atheists National Convention. Allen and Brenda live in Great Bend, Kansas, and were once active members of the Church of the Nazarene. They were sitting a few seats down from me in a session on secular grief when Allen raised his hand and shared that he was starting to worry about what he and Brenda would do when one of them died now that they didn't have a religious community to fall back on. It was something I thought about, too, and after the session I asked him if he'd tell me his story.

We sat in upholstered chairs on the balcony overlooking the hotel lobby. Allen wore a crisp suit and square-framed glasses, and Brenda kept her hair in neat waves. They had met in third grade and were both raised in the church. Allen's father was a pastor in the Church of the Nazarene, and Allen attended a Nazarene university. He and Brenda said that their upbringings were very strict, with their parents training their thoughts on not upsetting God through evils such as social dancing. But Brenda said that her family had always been a bit more open-minded, more welcoming, and less judgmental compared to others in their very conservative religion.

After losing their faith, Allen and Brenda left the church and began to find fellowship on the road, at conventions like the one where I met them. They remained friends with another couple who had also left the church when they did, and they all got together on weekends and sometimes even took trips together. But they said they missed the larger community bonds they'd grown up with, and the music at the church. For a moment as Allen described how much he enjoyed singing in the choir, I sensed a touch of nostalgia. But then he looked me directly in the eye and said something I'll never forget: "I wish I had been raised the way you're raising your kids. And I wish I could have raised my kids that way."

He said that if he had it to do all over again, he would spend his Sundays differently. Instead of going to church, where the kids went into one room for Sunday school and the parents went into another for the main services, and instead of obeying the strict religious culture all around him, he would spend that time with his kids one-on-one, pursuing the things he and his family really enjoyed, not what they were told they had to do. At the end of our interview, before getting up to go, he added, "I wish I could have all those Sundays back."

IT HAS BEEN four years since my son asked me what we were, and I'd come up short. We have not gone out and joined a church or a synagogue. We haven't prayed to the four directions or donned Buddhist robes. I don't make my kids meditate or prostrate themselves on prayer rugs or study the Torah. Nevertheless, everything in our lives has changed in ways both imperceptible and profound.

In our new neighborhood in Chicago, where we moved over a year ago, we are connected to our past in a way that gives us a true sense of belonging. We live a block away from where Michael grew up, and our children attend the school he and his brother went to. Our son plays basketball at the same Neighborhood Club where Michael and his brother once played, and our daughters take gymnastics there. The older two kids walk home from school each day past the brick apartment building where their great-grandparents lived after coming to the United States from Germany in the 1930s to escape the Holocaust. They also see their cousins regularly for sleepovers and the kind of hearty family meals I envied in my Catholic friends' homes growing up. Even here, in a new place, our son never says he feels homesick.

Our children continue to try to find their places in the world, both real and imagined. Our youngest has a clutch of invisible friends who keep her company wherever she goes. When I ask her where they are, she looks at me as if I'm blind and says, "Can't you see them?" Our older daughter recently told me that she has three religions: Judaism, Christianity, and gymnastics. Our son finds the Greek gods and goddesses fascinating, plays basketball, and loves math. This year he joined the school choir, and sometimes I hear him singing the religious songs he's learned in class. The sweet notes remind me of the boys choir at the Episcopal church on the New Haven Green that I loved so much as a child. Detached from religion, yet somehow still connected to it, they waft through our house and are even more beautiful to me now.

At night when I tuck the kids into bed, we share two things from the day that we are thankful for and one story they want to hear about my childhood—or Michael's when he tucks them in. They love these stories of their parents as kids, of our families, of who we were and what we did.

This year I joined the board of the Neighborhood Club, and I work to raise money so kids and their families can benefit from the club's many programs. Our kids like to give, too. On warm weekends they often run a lemonade stand and donate the money they earn to an animal shelter, the Ronald McDonald House, or another worthy cause. We participate in school-led volunteer activities as well, recently packing hundreds of bag lunches for a homeless shelter and cleaning up a community center in an underserved area of our city. Our children seem to be soaking up the values modeled in our tight-knit community, where service, diversity, and giving are prized.

Occasionally, I take myself to church. There's a United Church of Christ a block from our house, and on the first Friday of each month it holds a Taizé service, based on a form of worship created in a French monastery during World War II as a way to bring Catholics and Protestants together. The ecumenical service lasts an hour and consists of singing simple, repetitive hymns while holding lit candles in the dimmed light of the cavernous church. There are usually only about fifteen of us there, and we sit scattered as pairs and singles through the pews. Beneath the vaulted ceiling, only the sound of our voices lifting up, I feel at once infinitesimal and valuable beyond measure.

We continue to celebrate the Jewish and Christian holidays in our secular way, but with renewed interest in the history of the traditions. This year, on the final night of Hanukkah, Michael's brother and his family, along with old friends of Michael's parents and a dear high school friend of his, joined us for brisket, latkes, and kugel. Surrounded by our loved ones, the children took turns lighting the candles and later opened Hanukkah gifts around the Christmas tree.

Though our lives bear all the traces of the modern American family's trademark busyness—work and school, errands and activities—we create pockets of togetherness, in nature, at home, in our neighborhood. As we make our way forward without religion, I still don't have answers to all the big questions. But I'm starting to see that becoming more comfortable holding the questions is the only way that makes sense to me. I turn the questions over and over again until they are like smooth, solid stones.

THE NOVELIST MARILYNNE ROBINSON speaks of grace as a form of reverence for life. Her understanding of grace is based in Christian theology, but I believe I can find that same sort of grace, too. I know that's what I found one morning when our younger daughter, then four, had risen before dawn and wrangled herself into her glittering blue-and-white princess outfit. The dress had a satiny bodice and a gauzy skirt that puffed out from her waist. A size too big, it hung to her ankles. She wanted to go out to the driveway and get the newspaper, her favorite errand. It was 5:30 AM, and, though I was in my rumpled pajamas and my head was still in its pre-coffee fog, I opened the front door and stood at the top of the steps as she floated down them. With her feet hidden beneath the fabric of her skirt, her movements gave the impression of a fairy-tale figure descending on air, her blond tangle of hair bouncing slightly as she went down the steps.

There was no sound in the neighborhood except for a bird chirping in a nearby neighbor's yard. I froze, suddenly awake. She was a shiny blue jewel rendered all the more brilliant because of the green and brown tones of the trees and yard surrounding her.

As I watched her bend to pick up the newspaper and turn back to face me, the flash of her crystal-blue eyes showing her pride and excitement, I didn't need her to mean anything more to me than what she was before me. I didn't need our lives to be part of a divine, unfolding plan. I didn't need to believe that God's hand would guide us through that morning and ever after. Meaning came from the intense awareness of the moment itself, from my reverence for her, for this life we were joined in as family. I simply needed to remain still enough to notice.

EPILOGUE

A Letter to My Children

What is the meaning of life? . . . a simple question; one that tended to close in on one with years. The great revelation had never come. The great revelation perhaps never did come. Instead, there were little daily miracles, illuminations, matches struck unexpectedly in the dark . . .

—*Virginia Woolf*, *To the Lighthouse*

Dear William, Jessica, and Anne,

For years you've been asking me the big questions. Like miniature Greek philosophers, Catholic theologians, or Buddhist monks, you walk up to me as I wash dishes or unpack groceries or sit paying bills and toss out one of your big questions: *What is God? Who named everything? Who were the parents of the first people? What happens when we die? What's the meaning of life? Why are we here?*

I take a deep breath and narrow my gaze. There's so much to say, and I fear I know so little. Then I tell you to go brush your teeth, read a book, or get ready for bed. And I promise we will talk about it all later when we have more time. This letter is that "later."

All these years, I've been listening to your questions more closely than you can possibly imagine. They are my questions, too. Like you, I have been asking them all my life. Every time I've given you that confused look or shunted you off to some chore or activity, I've been buying myself time to come up with better answers. But I think that's been the problem all along: trying to convince myself that I could find the answers and share them with you. I can't. The truth is that I will never have clear answers for you about life's big mysteries.

What I have instead—after nearly five decades on this planet, untold hours pondering these questions, and several years actively researching and writing this book—are some ideas about life and how to live it. They are influenced by religion, humanism, science, literature, culture, society, the experiences I've had, and the people I've met. They are the silt caught in the sieve, the bits of wisdom I most want to share with you. I hope you will use them as a starting point along your own search for meaning.

1. **Your life is a privilege.** Live it well and seek to help others live well, too.
2. **Find your people.** Find friends who share your values, though not necessarily your beliefs. Welcome people of all faiths and no faith at all into your life. Grace comes in many forms, colors, and creeds, with and without God, and connecting with others is one of our greatest sources of meaning.
3. **Learn the religious stories.** You don't have to believe them, but they are a part of your heritage and history, whether you embrace religion or not. Be curious about them. Figure out what they may

have meant to your ancestors and what they mean to people today. See if the values they embody apply to your life in some way.

4. **Study the rich history of nonbelief**. Learn about the doubters and atheists and secular humanists who have likewise shaped our world, often at their peril. They, too, are part of your heritage.
5. **Mark time with ritual**. Celebrate Passover and Hanukkah, Christmas and Easter, Kwanzaa or Eid, or all of them. These rituals help us feel connected through time to those who've come before us and those who will come after. Create new holidays—solstice parties, harvest festivals, weddings, baby-namings—that speak to who you are and who you want to be.
6. **Open yourself to awe and wonder.** Visit art museums, walk through nature, read great poetry. Pay attention to the mundane: Notice the cracks in the sidewalk, the green of the leaves. Marvel at the full harvest moon low in the autumn sky, the two-week-old baby in her mother's arms, the bursts of playground laughter piercing the air across the street. Don't get so busy that you forget we are all living in a mystery.
7. **Never stop seeking more knowledge.** Science discovers new things about the world every day. Artists and writers create works that inspire us. Learning is one of life's greatest pleasures. You can never know everything, but adding any new dimension of knowledge makes our lives more complete. Challenge yourself to think about issues from all angles. Treat your own skepticism with curiosity. Learn more about the very things you are most apt to dismiss.
8. **Connect to a larger purpose through work that is bigger than you**. The documentary film you are making in high school is really about good versus evil. That novel you are reading teaches you how to connect to others. Someday you will choose a career. Pursue not just what you love and are good at but also something that has a bigger message, that matters to the wider world.

9. **Contemplate death.** We don't know why we are here, but we do know we will die. We all have a finite time on this earth. Don't be afraid of death. Instead, realize that it gives life urgency and makes each moment matter more. We can soothe our fear of death, through acknowledgment and acceptance, through our own rituals, and through knowing that our mortality is what makes life sweet.
10. **Create your own grace**. Christians believe that God grants us grace, but I believe we create it for ourselves, through persistence, awareness, connection, and reflection. Grace comes from knowing that to be alive and conscious in this world is a rare gift. If we are open to it, we can see that there is grace all around us, with or without God.

Chicago, Illinois
December 2015

ACKNOWLEDGMENTS

Writing this book has been the biggest act of faith I've ever committed, a journey that required a belief in the unseen as I waded through moments of self-doubt, fear, joy, and unexpected grace. This project also involved, from the very start, a people. The work, dedication, and skill of those listed here, as well as the many I don't have space to name, appear on every page. Without such a committed tribe, this book would not exist.

There is no finer agent than Gillian MacKenzie, whose initial bid of confidence launched me on my way and whose ready support throughout the process kept me going.

At Harper Wave, Karen Rinaldi believed in the bigness of this book before I saw it and guided this project through every turn with her signature wisdom and toughness. I was lucky to have my manuscript land on the desk of Sarah Murphy, who edited the text with skill, smarts, and grace. Hannah Robinson had answers to all my questions. And Victoria Comella and Brian Perrin brought their incredible talent and knowledge to the marketing and publicity efforts.

Christine Gross-Loh was with me on every step of this journey, whether sharing a desk as we worked alongside each other at the Cambridge Public Library or, after I moved to Chicago, via daily texts and emails.

Laura Fraser has been a friend and mentor for many years, but she showed up like never before to help me find the true shape and storyline of this book. I can never thank her enough.

David Dreyer and Eric London, of TSD Communications, never wavered in their faith in this project, even as they read through many barely-held-together drafts to offer outstanding advice on how to make them better.

Many generous people read early drafts and helped me shape the ideas and words herein more thoughtfully than I ever could have alone. For their sharp insights and sensitive feedback, I will be forever grateful to these talented writers and editors: Michael Blanding, Samuel Douglas, Don Harrell, Jennifer Margulis, Alexandria Marzano-Lesnevich, and Barbara Spindel.

Jack Cassidy provided thorough fact-checking, and I also received early (and late) research assistance from Melissa Chianta, Megan Koehnen, and Laura Simeon.

John Wolfson, former editor of *Boston* magazine, green-lit my grain of an idea to write about nonreligious parenting, and Toby Lester edited the piece that gave rise to this book.

Tracy Mayor, Robin Schoenthaler, and Amy Yellin never blanched as I slid my terrible first drafts across a small wooden table at Porter Square Books at the start of each of our writing group meetings. Each time they slid them back with suggestions that made the book, and me, clearer and stronger.

Through the years, Boston's Grub Street Writers and San Francisco's Writers' Grotto have made writing a lot less lonely and a lot more fun, and I'm thankful to the people who gave those organizations life and make them run today. In addition, Katrin Schumann, Lynne Griffin, and the participants of Grub Street's

Launch Lab program taught me how to joyfully launch a book into the world.

It is not lost on me that a story that began in isolation propelled me out of my own small world and into the welcoming arms of strangers I now call friends. My reporting led me into the homes, offices, and community meetings of scores of generous people across the country. To all of you who took the time to share your stories, thank you. Your examples are the heart and soul of this book.

Many experts and community leaders contributed their time and expertise as I sought to untangle this complicated topic. Special thanks to: Raymond Arnold, Stephen Batchelor, Peter Blake, Joshua Boetigger, Adam Chalom, Catherine Caldwell-Harris, Greg Epstein, Marshall Ganz, Dan Gilbert, Cynthia Hager, Rebecca Hensler, Mary Johnson, Deb Kelemen, Sean Kelly, Audrey Kingstrom, Lawrence Krauss, Jim Lasko, Jeremy Levie, Dale McGowan, Michael Puett, Robert Putnam, Graham Robinson, Pamela Shepherd, Mark Shibley, Michelle Shiota, Buddy Stallings, Chris Stedman, David Voas, Rick Weissbourd, Mark Yaconelli, and Phil Zuckerman.

I am (secularly) blessed to have the most wonderful friends and family in the world. A big shout-out to my high school book club, the members of which were with me the night I sold the book and the night I turned in my final draft. And to my college roommates, who were my first, and ever steadfast, tribe away from home.

Special thanks to my immediate family for always asking me about the book even when they were probably sick of hearing about it: Dan and Heidi, Jim and Ruth, Jody and Sadie, Amanda, Emma, and Andrea. And for my beloved brother Matthew, who would have asked the toughest questions: I miss you every day.

My father has inspired me all my life with his diligence and hard work. And my mother nurtured my creativity as a child with the many arts and crafts projects she sprawled across our dining room table. From them I learned to think, to create, and to love.

My children, William, Jessica, and Anne, set me on this journey with their constant inquiries about life's most essential matters. They put up with my many absences as I traveled to conduct research and spent untold hours writing and rewriting. But mostly they taught me how to find beauty and wonder in every moment of each day. I thank them for their love, for their patience, and for reminding me of what really matters. (P.S. We can get the dog now.)

Finally and most importantly, this book would never have been written without the unending love and support of my husband, Michael. I know of no better example of the true power, reach, and impact of a human life than his, and I count myself lucky beyond measure that I get to share my life with someone so wonderful.

RESOURCES FOR READERS

Charting Your Own Path to Grace Without God

You've read about my journey, and the journeys of many others, to find grace without God. Now it's your turn. On the pages that follow, as well as on my website (www.katherineozment.com), I offer you some tools to set out on your own secular-spiritual exploration. Anyone can go on a quest toward a more meaningful, reflective, and connected life. We can all think more deeply and make the concrete changes necessary to actively find what religion has long given. All this project requires is honest awareness as you assess where you've come from, examine where you are, and commit to who and where you want to be.

It helps to have friends and family involved in your journey. Consider forming your own Grace Without God group or joining a local organization such as a secular humanist group, Sunday Assembly, or Ethical Culture. Parents, especially, might come together to clarify their values and create new ways to pass those values on to their children. Twentysomethings, at the outset of their careers, could gather to talk about how to find meaning through work and make a difference in the world. Grandparents could discuss what it means to them that their grandchildren aren't being baptized or bar mitzvahed. When we come together in open and respectful discussion, we learn and grow.

The journey includes four stages: Reflection, Declaration of Values, Action, and Deepening and Commitment.

PHASE ONE: REFLECTION

Take time to reflect on your own spiritual-secular biography. Consider how you were raised, what your family's belief system meant to you, and how your connection to religious and family traditions has evolved over time. Do you miss aspects of your religious heritage? If so, how can you recapture those religious traditions in secular ways? These questions are just starting points. Keep a journal, start a blog, or share ideas with trusted friends in a private Facebook group. Writing down your reflections can help you better understand your past and clarify what elements of religion you may wish to carry forward. Here are more questions, arranged by theme, to guide both your own personal reflections and a group discussion.

Community and Belonging

What groups have you belonged to in the past, and where do you feel the greatest sense of belonging now?

What binds you? What do you and the people you're closest to hold sacred? How do you outwardly express those values?

What does it mean to belong to a people? Where does true belonging come from?

How do you find people you feel connected to? What ways have worked in the past, and how can you learn from the ways that failed?

Who most accepts you as you are, in all your individuality? Can you come together with these fellow seekers and create a community?

You don't have to have one people; you likely have many. How can you deepen and expand your connections within and among your groups?

Rituals

What have been the most meaningful rituals, religious or secular, in your life? What made them so?

How has ritual helped you through difficult times?

How has ritual helped you celebrate your life's transitional moments?

Which rituals have called on you to be your best self? Where and when could you create more such rituals to increase the feeling of meaning in your life?

In your opinion, what are the most important transitions or milestones to mark? Why? How can you mark them in ways that feel meaningful?

Where do you go to feel a sense of stopped time or relief from the pressures of everyday life?

Meaning and Purpose

What experiences have given your life the most meaning?

When and where have you felt the most alive?

What do you see as the purpose of your life? What is the story you tell yourself about who you are and why you are here?

How has helping others, even in small ways, increased your sense of meaning and purpose? Can you build helping others into each day?

Where and when do you feel the greatest sense of wonder about the world?

How would you describe awe, and under what circumstances have you felt it most?

Identity

What is your story? How is it part of a larger story of a larger people?

Who do you identify with, and what does that relationship reveal about the values you hold dear?

What makes us who we are, and how does one's sense of self change over a lifetime?

How do we define and identify ourselves in a secular age when the old labels don't always apply?

Morality and Values

What were you taught about being a good person when you were growing up? What lessons stick in your mind?

Where do morals come from? How has your understanding of morality shifted as you've gotten older?

What values make someone a good person?

What does it mean to raise good kids? What values do you want your children to hold most dear?

Who are your "saints" or heroes, people who have lived or are living in a manner you'd like to emulate? How do or did they live their values in concrete ways?

PHASE TWO: DECLARATION OF VALUES

Once you've reflected on what faith has and hasn't given you and how you want to enhance certain areas of your life, create your own declaration of values: the beliefs and values on which you strive to base your life. Think of your declaration of values as a kind of secular Ten Commandments that conveys those ideals you hold sacred and inviolable. My values are written in the form of a letter to my children, the epilogue of this book, and you can also structure yours that way. Or you could write them on cards and choose one to focus on each day or week. Whichever form you choose, explore the following: What are your own absolutes (one may be that you have no absolutes)? What are the values that you hold most sacred? If you were someone else's moral role model, what would that person admire most about you?

PHASE THREE: ACTION

The next step is to formalize these values so they become a conscious part of your everyday life. This is the stage where you think about how to enact your values in concrete ways. Research shows that when we write down our intentions, we're more likely to follow through on them. Pair actions, big and small, with the values you've declared. Here are some examples of the types of commitments you can make:

- To improve your sense of connectedness to others, practice gratitude. People who practice gratitude have stronger relationships, are quicker to forgive, and are more compassionate and altruistic. Keep a gratitude journal. Before getting out of bed, consider five things you're thankful for. Ask your partner or children to share what they're thankful for each night at dinner or just before bed.
- To create more meaning in your life, give to others. Research shows we reap a wealth of benefits, physical and mental, when we give, and charitable acts also benefit the common good. Find a volunteer activ-

ity or cause in your area that you can devote even a small amount of time and energy to each week or month. You may find, as researchers have, that giving is contagious.

- To celebrate meaningful family moments (a child's entrance into adolescence, a wedding, a birth), create a secular ritual, invite your friends, and ask them to participate. For a coming-of-age ceremony, ask people to share the most important lessons they've learned in life and make those lessons into a book for your child to keep. For a wedding, people can send scraps of fabrics to be woven into a canopy. At a baby-naming ceremony, have guests state a hope for the child; ritualize that offering by having each person place a stone in a jar as he or she states that hope.

If you're stuck, why not steal some of the great ideas from religion and reframe them to reflect your own beliefs and values? Here are some ideas:

- ***Tikkun Olam*:** The Jewish concept of *tikkun olam* states that the world is broken and it is our job to repair it. Use this concept, minus the religion, as your own secular call to arms. Where can you lend a hand, and how can you use your own life to make a difference?
- **The Golden Rule:** The Golden Rule reminds us to "do to others as you would have others do to you." How do you interact with other people? Consider a straightforward statement of values to remind yourself how to treat others.
- **Zakat:** One of the Five Pillars of Islam is zakat ("alms"), the practice of giving at least 2.5 percent of one's savings each year to a cause of your choice. Tap the charitable practice found in this and other religions, find a group that needs your help, and commit to giving on a regular basis.
- **Rosh Hashanah/Nowruz/Eid:** Many religions hold symbolic annual feasts to commemorate an important part of history, welcome the harvest, or mark the end of a time of atonement or sacrifice. How can you illustrate your own values and history through a ritual feast and gathering of friends and family? In what ways can we use food and fellowship to demonstrate what we're grateful for, what we celebrate, and what life means to us?

- **Atonement, Confession:** In most religions, there are rituals asking people to consider their own behavior and how they might improve. How can you use rituals of reflection and accountability at various times of the year to push yourself to be a better person? What areas of your life could benefit from clear-eyed examination, and how can you build rituals into your year to remind yourself to practice it?
- **Lent, Ramadan:** Giving up something of value is part of many religious traditions. Practice giving up something you enjoy to remind yourself how much you have and make you more aware of the needs of others.
- **Communal Singing:** Collective group ritual is one of the most powerful transcendent experiences of all religions. Science shows that collective rituals like singing bring us together in meaningful ways. Find community groups at your local farmers' market, carolers, or others who enjoy music and lend your voice.
- **Sunday School:** Most religions have youth programs through which the beliefs and values of the group are transmitted. How can you create sacred family time during which you detach from pressures of work, school, and extracurriculars, not to mention digital distractions, to teach and reflect on values such as kindness and peace?
- **Sabbath:** The Christian and Jewish faiths practice a sabbath, or day of rest, each week. Few people, religious or otherwise, have time for a whole day of rest, but where can you find more balance in your life, carving out quiet time to stop and reflect on who you are and why you are here? Can you build in mini secular sabbaths on the weekends or even at recurring times throughout the week?
- **Solstice Celebrations:** Many early religious traditions created rituals synchronized with the earth's movements, notably winter and summer solstice. Return to the ancient rituals to bring community from all backgrounds together to celebrate the cycles of our planet.

PHASE FOUR: DEEPENING AND COMMITMENT

Once you've set up your structure, experiment with committing fully to enacting your values in meaningful ways. You might form a group that meets once a month to check in on your goal of doing volunteer work in your neighborhood. Or create a book group for kids focused on values you cherish. Whatever you choose, think about how you can draw others in, to hold you accountable, offer guidance, and share in the process.

The journey continues online. If you or your group would like to deepen and sustain your experience, visit my website (www.katherineozment.com) to learn more about how to chart your own path toward grace without God.

SUGGESTIONS FOR FURTHER READING

While researching this book, I read everything from dense, scholarly texts to brief, intimate memoirs. The following list is by no means definitive, but these are the books about religious loss and transformation that I found the most helpful, by some of my favorite thinkers and writers.

SECULAR-SPIRITUAL MEMOIRS

Barnes, Julian. *Nothing to Be Frightened Of.* New York: Random House Vintage, 2009.

Batchelor, Stephen. *Confession of a Buddhist Atheist.* New York: Spiegel & Grau, 2011.

Butler, Katy. *Knocking on Heaven's Door: The Path to a Better Way of Death.* New York: Scribner, 2014.

Crittenden, Lindsey. *The Water Will Hold You: A Skeptic Learns to Pray.* New York: Harmony Books, 2007.

Ehrenreich, Barbara. *Living with a Wild God: A Nonbeliever's Search for the Truth About Everything.* New York: Twelve, 2015.

Gilbert, Elizabeth. *Eat, Pray, Love: One Woman's Search for Everything Across Italy, India and Indonesia.* New York: Viking Penguin, 2007.

Hitchens, Christopher. *Mortality.* New York: Twelve, 2014.

Johnson, Mary. *An Unquenchable Thirst: A Memoir.* New York: Spiegel & Grau, 2013.

Krasny, Michael. *Spiritual Envy: An Agnostic's Quest.* Novato, CA: New World Library, 2012.

O'Rourke, Meghan. *The Long Goodbye: A Memoir.* New York: Riverhead Books, 2012.

Scheeres, Julia. *Jesus Land: A Memoir.* Berkeley, CA: Counterpoint, 2012.
Shapiro, Dani. *Devotion: A Memoir.* New York: HarperCollins, 2011.
Stedman, Chris. *Faitheist: How an Atheist Found Common Ground with the Religious.* Boston: Beacon Press, 2013.
Walker, Rebecca. *Black, White, and Jewish: Autobiography of a Shifting Self.* New York: Riverhead Books: 2002.

GUIDES FOR PARENTS

Coles, Robert. *The Spiritual Life of Children.* Boston: Houghton Mifflin, 1990.
Gopnik, Alison. *The Philosophical Baby: What Children's Minds Tell Us About Truth, Love, and the Meaning of Life.* New York: Farrar, Straus & Giroux, 2010.
Kasl, Charlotte. *If the Buddha Had Kids: Raising Children to Create a More Peaceful World.* New York: Penguin, 2012.
Kabat-Zinn, Jon, and Myla Kabat-Zinn. *Everyday Blessings: The Inner Work of Mindful Parenting.* New York: Hachette Book Group, 2014.
Manning, Christel J. *Losing Our Religion: How Unaffiliated Parents Are Raising Their Children.* New York: New York University Press, 2015.
McGowan, Dale, Molleen Matsumura, Amanda Metskas, and Jan Devor. *Raising Freethinkers: A Practical Guide for Parenting Beyond Belief.* New York: American Management Association, 2009.
———, ed. *Parenting Beyond Belief: On Raising Ethical, Caring Kids Without Religion.* New York: American Management Association, 2007.
Miller, Lisa J. *The Spiritual Child: The New Science on Parenting for Health and Lifelong Thriving.* New York: St. Martin's Press, 2015.
Mitchell, Deborah. *Growing Up Godless: A Parent's Guide to Raising Kids Without Religion.* New York: Sterling Ethos, 2014.
Russell, Wendy Thomas. *Relax, It's Just God: How and Why to Talk to Your Kids About Religion When You're Not Religious.* Long Beach, CA: Brown Paper Press, 2015.
Weissbourd, Richard. *The Parents We Mean to Be: How Well-Intentioned Adults Undermine Children's Moral and Emotional Development.* New York: Mariner Books, 2010.

BOOKS FOR INTERFAITH, NO-FAITH, AND EVERYTHING-IN-BETWEEN COUPLES

Cox, Harvey. *Common Prayers: Faith, Family, and a Christian's Journey Through the Jewish Year.* New York: Houghton Mifflin, 2002.

Kasl, Charlotte. *If the Buddha Married: Creating Enduring Relationships on a Spiritual Path.* New York: Penguin Compass, 2001.

McGowan, Dale. *In Faith and in Doubt: How Religious Believers and Nonbelievers Can Create Strong Marriages and Loving Families.* New York: American Management Association, 2014.

Miller, Susan Katz. *Being Both: Embracing Two Religions in One Interfaith Family.* Boston: Beacon Press, 2014.

Riley, Naomi Schaefer. *'Til Faith Do Us Part: How Interfaith Marriage Is Transforming America.* New York: Oxford University Press, 2013.

BOOKS FOR SMALL PEOPLE WITH BIG QUESTIONS

Ages 0–5

Dr. Seuss. *The Sneetches and Other Stories.* New York: Random House, 1961.

Fox, Mem. *Whoever You Are.* New York: Houghton Mifflin Harcourt, 2006.

Global Fund for Children. *Global Babies* board book. Watertown, MA: Charlesbridge, 2007.

Karst, Patrice. *The Invisible String.* Camarillo, CA: DeVorss, 2000.

Mellonie, Bryan. *Lifetimes: The Beautiful Way to Explain Death to Children.* New York: Bantam Books, 1983.

Mochel, Kelly. *One World, Many Beliefs: A Family Book for Nonbelievers & Their Children.* N.p.: Kelly Mochel, 2012.

Pearson, Emily. *Ordinary Mary's Extraordinary Deed.* Layton, UT: Gibbs Smith, 2002.

Ages 6–9

Barker, Dan. *Maybe Right, Maybe Wrong: A Guide for Young Thinkers.* Amherst, MA: Prometheus Books, 1992.

———. *Maybe Yes, Maybe No: A Guide for Young Skeptics.* Amherst, MA: Prometheus Books, 1990.

Bunting, Eve. *One Green Apple*. New York: Clarion Books, 2006.

Corwin, Judith Hoffman. *Harvest Festivals Around the World*. Parsippany, NJ: Julian Messner, 1995.

Erlbruch, Wolf. *Duck, Death and the Tulip*. Wellington, N. Z.: Gecko Press, 2011.

Fox, Karen C. *Older Than the Stars*. Watertown, MA: Charlesbridge, 2011.

Hanh, Thich Nhat. *Is Nothing Something? Kids' Questions and Zen Answers About Life, Death, Family, Friendship, and Everything In Between*. Berkeley, CA: Plum Blossom Books, 2014.

Harris, Annaka. *I Wonder*. N.p.: Four Elephants Press, 2013.

Hosford, Kate. *Infinity and Me*. Minneapolis: Carolrhoda Picture Books, 2012.

Kelsey, Elin. *Wild Ideas: Let Nature Inspire Your Thinking*. Toronto: Owlkids Books, 2015.

———. *You Are Stardust*. Toronto: Owlkids Books, 2012.

Kindersley, Anabel, and Barnabas Kindersley. *Children Just Like Me: A Unique Celebration of Children Around the World*. New York: DK Publishing, 1995.

London, Jonathan. *Giving Thanks*. Somerville, MA: Candlewick, 2011.

McCloud, Carol. *Have You Filled a Bucket Today? A Guide to Daily Happiness for Kids*. Brighton, MI: Bucket Fillers, 2015.

Muth, Jon J. *Zen Shorts*. New York: Scholastic Press, 2005.

Nagaraja, Dharmachari. *Buddha at Bedtime: Tales of Love and Wisdom for You to Read with Your Child to Enchant, Enlighten and Inspire*. London: Watkins Publishing, 2008.

Peters, Lisa Westberg. *Our Family Tree: An Evolution Story*. Orlando, FL: Harcourt Books, 2003.

Pfeffer, Wendy. *The Longest Day: Celebrating the Summer Solstice*. New York: Puffin Books, 2015.

———. *The Shortest Day: Celebrating the Winter Solstice*. New York: Penguin, 2003.

Shragg, Karen. *A Solstice Tree for Jenny (Search for the Future)*. Amherst, MA: Prometheus Books, 2001.

Snel, Eline. *Sitting Still Like a Frog: Mindfulness Exercises for Kids (and Their Parents)*. Boston: Shambhala Publications, 2013.

Viorst, Judith. *The Tenth Good Thing About Barney.* New York: Aladdin, 1988.

Wood, Douglas. *The Secret of Saying Thanks.* New York: Simon & Schuster Books for Young Readers, 2005.

Woodson, Jacqueline. *Each Kindness.* New York: Nancy Paulsen Books, 2012.

Ages 10–14

Bennett, Helen. *Humanism, What's That? A Book for Curious Kids.* Amherst, MA: Prometheus Books, 2005.

Boritzer, Etan. *What Is God?* Buffalo: Firefly Books, 1990.

Ganda, Martin, and Caitlin Alifrenka. *I Will Always Write Back: How One Letter Changed Two Lives.* New York: Little, Brown Books for Young Readers, 2015.

Lewis, Barbara. *What Do You Stand For? For Kids: A Guide to Building Character.* Minneapolis: Free Spirit Publishing, 2005.

Metcalf, Franz. *Buddha in Your Backpack: Everyday Buddhism for Teens.* Berkeley, CA: Ulysses Press, 2003.

Schwiebert, Pat, and Chuck DeKlyen. *Tear Soup: A Recipe for Healing After Loss.* Portland, OR: Grief Watch, 2005.

Star, Fleur, ed. *What Do You Believe? Religion and Faith in the World Today.* New York: DK Children, 2015.

Stock, Gregory. *The Kids' Book of Questions.* New York: Workman Publishing, 2015.

Winston, Diana. *Wide Awake: A Buddhist Guide for Teens.* New York: TarcherPerigree, 2003.

GUIDES TO AND EXPLORATIONS OF RITUAL

Marriage

Searl, Edward, ed. *We Pledge Our Hearts: A Treasury of Poems, Quotations and Readings to Celebrate Love and Marriage.* Boston: Skinner House Books, 2006.

Birth

Costanzo, Charlene. *The Twelve Gifts of Birth.* New York: HarperCollins, 2001.

Seaburg, Carl, ed. *Great Occasions: Readings for the Celebration of Birth, Coming-of-Age, Marriage, and Death*. Boston: Skinner House Books, 2003.

Searl, Edward, ed. *Bless This Child: A Treasury of Poems, Quotations and Readings to Celebrate Birth*. Boston: Skinner House Books, 2005.

Coming of Age

Fischer, Norman. *Taking Our Places: The Buddhist Path to Truly Growing Up*. New York: HarperCollins, 2004.

Searl, Edward, ed. *Coming of Age: A Treasury of Poems, Quotations and Readings on Growing Up*. Boston: Skinner House Books, 2006.

Death

Bennett, Amanda, and Terence Foley. *In Memoriam: A Practical Guide to Planning a Memorial Service*. New York: Fireside, 1997.

Lang, Virginia, and Louise Nayer. *How to Bury a Goldfish and Other Ceremonies and Celebrations for Everyday Life*. Boston: Skinner House Books, 2007.

Searl, Edward, ed. *Beyond Absence: A Treasury of Poems, Quotations and Readings on Death and Remembrance*. Boston: Skinner House Books, 2005.

In Memoriam: A Guide to Modern Funeral and Memorial Services. Boston: Skinner House Books, 2000.

Willson, Jane Wynne. *Funerals Without God: A Practical Guide to Non-religious Funerals*. Amherst, MA: Prometheus Books, 1990.

York, Sarah. *Remembering Well: Rituals for Celebrating Life and Mourning Death*. Fairview, NC: Apollo Ranch Institute Press, 2012.

Holidays

Cox, Meg. *The Book of New Family Traditions: How to Create Great Rituals for Holidays and Everyday*. Philadelphia: Running Press Book Publishers, 2012.

Edwards, Carolyn McVickar. *The Return of the Light: Twelve Tales from Around the World for the Winter Solstice*. Boston: Da Capo Press, 2005.

McKibben, Bill. *Hundred Dollar Holiday: The Case for a More Joyful Christmas*. New York: Simon & Schuster, 2013.

Montley, Patricia. *In Nature's Honor: Myths and Rituals Celebrating the Earth*. Boston: Skinner House Books, 2005.

Robinson, Jo, and Jean Coppock Staeheli. *Unplug the Christmas Machine: A Complete Guide to Putting Love and Joy Back into the Season*. New York: William Morrow, 1991.

Wall, Kathleen, and Gary Ferguson. *Rites of Passage: Celebrating Life's Changes*. Hillsboro, OR: Beyond Words Publishing, 1998.

Making Space

Heller, Rick. *Secular Meditation: 32 Practices for Cultivating Inner Peace, Compassion, and Joy*. Novato, CA: New World Library, 2015.

Heschel, Abraham Joshua. *The Sabbath*. New York: Farrar, Straus & Giroux, 2005.

Iyer, Pico. *The Art of Stillness: Adventures in Going Nowhere*. New York: TED Books, 2014.

Ryan, M. J., ed. *A Grateful Heart: Daily Blessings for the Evening Meal from Buddha to the Beatles*. San Francisco: Conari Press, 2002.

Shulevitz, Judith. *The Sabbath World: Glimpses of a Different Order of Time*. New York: Random House, 2011.

BOOKS ABOUT MORALITY

Bloom, Paul. *Just Babies: The Origins of Good and Evil*. New York: Broadway Books, 2014.

Epstein, Greg. *Good Without God: What a Billion Nonreligious People Do Believe*. New York: HarperCollins, 2010.

Grayling, A. C. *Meditations for the Humanist: Ethics for a Secular Age*. New York: Oxford University Press, 2003.

Haidt, Jonathan. *The Righteous Mind: Why Good People Are Divided by Politics and Religion*. New York: Vintage Books, 2013.

Keltner, Dacher. *Born to Be Good: The Science of a Meaningful Life*. New York: Norton, 2009.

Keltner, Dacher, Jason Marsh, and Jeremy Adam Smith, eds. *The Compassionate Instinct: The Science of Human Goodness*. New York: Norton, 2010.

Pinker, Steven. *The Better Angels of Our Nature: Why Violence Has Declined*. New York: Penguin, 2012.

BOOKS ABOUT THE SECULAR AGE

Aronson, Ronald. *Living Without God: New Directions for Atheists, Agnostics, Secularists, and the Undecided*. Berkeley, CA: Counterpoint Press, 2009.

Bass, Diana Butler. *Christianity After Religion: The End of Church and the Birth of a New Spiritual Awakening*. New York: HarperCollins, 2013.

———. *Grounded: Finding God in the World—A Spiritual Revolution*. New York: HarperCollins, 2015.

Brewster, Melanie E., ed. *Athiests in America*. New York: Columbia University Press, 2014.

De Botton, Alain. *Religion for Atheists: A Non-believer's Guide to the Uses of Religion*. New York: Vintage Books, 2013.

Comte-Sponville, André. *The Little Book of Atheist Spirituality*. New York: Viking Penguin, 2008.

Drescher, Elizabeth. *Choosing Our Religion: The Spiritual Lives of America's Nones*. New York: Oxford University Press, 2016.

Dreyfus, Hubert, and Sean Dorrance Kelly. *All Things Shining: Reading the Western Classics to Find Meaning in a Secular Age*. New York: Free Press, 2011.

Dworkin, Ronald. *Religion Without God*. Cambridge, MA: Harvard University Press, 2013.

Hecht, Jennifer Michael. *Doubt: A History: The Great Doubters and Their Legacy of Innovation from Socrates and Jesus to Thomas Jefferson and Emily Dickinson*. New York: HarperCollins, 2004.

Jacoby, Susan. *Freethinkers: A History of American Secularism*. New York: Metropolitan Books, 2004.

Levine, George, ed. *The Joy of Secularism*. Princeton, NJ: Princeton University Press, 2011.

Niose, David. *Nonbeliever Nation: The Rise of Secular Americans*. New York: St. Martin's Press, 2012.

Oppenheimer, Mark. *Knocking on Heaven's Door: American Religion in the Age of Counterculture*. New Haven, CT: Yale University Press, 2003.

Putnam, Robert D. *Bowling Alone: The Collapse and Revival of American Community*. New York: Simon & Schuster, 2001.

Sharlet, Jeff. *Sweet Heaven When I Die: Faith, Faithlessness, and the Country In Between*. New York: Norton, 2012.

Solomon, Robert C. *Spirituality for the Skeptic: The Thoughtful Love of Life*. New York: Oxford University Press, 2006.
Stephens, Mitchell. *Imagine There's No Heaven: How Atheism Helped Create the Modern World*. New York: St. Martin's Press, 2014.
Taylor, Charles. *A Secular Age*. Cambridge, MA: Harvard University Press, 2007.
Zuckerman, Phil. *Faith No More: Why People Reject Religion*. New York: Oxford University Press, 2015.
———. *Living the Secular Life: New Answers to Old Questions*. New York: Penguin, 2015.

ATHEISM'S GREATEST HITS

Dawkins, Richard. *The God Delusion*. Boston: Houghton Mifflin, 2008.
Dennett, Daniel. *Breaking the Spell: Religion as a Natural Phenomenon*. New York: Viking Penguin, 2007.
Harris, Sam. *The End of Faith: Religion, Terror, and the Future of Reason*. New York: Norton, 2005.
Hitchens, Christopher. *God Is Not Great: How Religion Poisons Everything*. Toronto: Twelve, 2009.

RELIGION: PAST, PRESENT, AND FUTURE

Armstrong, Karen. *A History of God: The 4000-Year Quest of Judaism, Christianity, and Islam*. New York: Random House, 2011.
Eliade, Mircea. *The Sacred and the Profane: The Nature of Religion*. New York: Harcourt Brace Jovanovich, 1987.
James, William. *The Varieties of Religious Experience: A Study in Human Nature*. New York: Bedford/St. Martin's, 2012.
Monda, Antonio. *Do You Believe? Conversations on God and Religion*. New York: Vintage Books, 2007.
Norenzayan, Ara. *Big Gods: How Religion Transformed Cooperation and Conflict*. Princeton, NJ: Princeton University Press, 2013.
Putnam, Robert D., and David E. Campbell. *American Grace: How Religion Divides and Unites Us*. New York: Simon & Schuster, 2012.
Smith, Huston. *The World's Religions*. New York: HarperCollins, 2009.
Tickle, Phyllis. *Emergence Christianity: What It Is, Where It Is Going, and Why It Matters*. Grand Rapids, MI: Baker Books, 2012.

Wuthnow, Robert. *After the Baby Boomers: How Twenty- and Thirty-Somethings Are Shaping the Future of American Religion*. Princeton, NJ: Princeton University Press, 2010.

RELIGIOUS LITERACY AND INTERFAITH DIALOGUE

Boorstein, Sylvia. *That's Funny, You Don't Look Buddhist: On Being a Faithful Jew and a Passionate Buddhist*. New York: HarperCollins, 1998.

Knitter, Paul F. *Without Buddha I Could Not Be a Christian*. London: Oneworld Publications, 2013.

Patel, Eboo. *Sacred Ground: Pluralism, Prejudice, and the Promise of America*. Boston: Beacon Press, 2013.

Prothero, Stephen. *Religious Literacy: What Every American Needs to Know—and Doesn't*. New York: HarperCollins, 2008.

Spong, John Shelby. *Jesus for the Non-religious*. New York: HarperCollins, 2008.

Wertheimer, Linda K. *Faith Ed: Teaching About Religion in an Age of Intolerance*. Boston: Beacon Press, 2015.

PHILOSOPHY AND MEANING

Batchelor, Stephen. *Buddhism Without Beliefs: A Contemporary Guide to Awakening*. New York: Penguin, 1998.

Csikszentmihalyi, Mihaly. *Flow: The Psychology of Optimal Experience*. New York: Harper Perennial, 2008.

Eagleton, Terry. *The Meaning of Life: A Very Short Introduction*. New York: Oxford University Press, 2008.

Ferry, Luc. *A Brief History of Thought: A Philosophical Guide to Living*. New York: HarperCollins, 2011.

Gottschall, Jonathan. *The Storytelling Animal: How Stories Make Us Human*. New York: Mariner Books, 2013.

Holt, Jim. *Why Does the World Exist? An Existential Detective Story*. New York: Liveright, 2013.

Wilson, Edward O. *The Meaning of Human Existence*. New York: Liveright, 2015.

SCIENCE AND THE BIG QUESTIONS

Frank, Adam. *The Constant Fire: Beyond the Science vs. Religion Debate.* Oakland: University of California Press, 2010.

Krauss, Lawrence. *A Universe from Nothing: Why There Is Something Rather Than Nothing.* New York: Atria Books, 2012.

Lightman, Alan. *The Accidental Universe: The World You Thought You Knew.* New York: Vintage Books, 2014.

Musolino, Julien. *The Soul Fallacy: What Science Shows We Gain from Letting Go of Our Soul Beliefs.* Amherst, MA: Prometheus Books, 2015.

Sagan, Carl. *The Varieties of Scientific Experience: A Personal View of the Search for God.* New York: Penguin, 2007.

Shubin, Neil. *Your Inner Fish: A Journey into the 3.5-Billion-Year History of the Human Body.* New York: Vintage Books, 2009.

———. *The Universe Within: The Deep History of the Human Body.* New York: Pantheon Books, 2013.

ONLINE RESOURCES AND ORGANIZATIONS

Whether you're an atheist, an agnostic, a humanist, a freethinker, a spiritual-but-not-religious-type, or simply a curious seeker looking for resources and community, here are the online resources I found most helpful as I researched this book.

Resources for Families and Students

Camp Quest

A sleepaway summer camp for children that teaches secular and humanist values, with sites around the country. Promotes scientific thinking and reason.
www.camp-quest.org

Doing Good Together

A Minneapolis-based national nonprofit that works to make volunteering and service, along with daily kindness, easy for families.
www.doinggoodtogether.org

Big-Hearted Families

An online resource with suggested readings, ideas for service projects, and empathy-building tools for families, operated through Doing Good Together.

www.doinggoodtogether.org/bigheartedfamilies

Interfaith Youth Core

IFYC promotes interfaith dialogue and understanding through its campus-based leadership institutes and programs.

www.ifyc.org

Secular Student Alliance

This umbrella organization for secular high school and college students provides community and resources.

www.secularstudents.org

Resources for People Leaving Religion

Apostasy Project

A website sponsored by *New Humanist*, a British quarterly journal, for people separating from their religion.

https://newhumanist.org.uk/series/apostasy-project

The Clergy Project

A protected, anonymous online support network for religious professionals who no longer consider themselves believers.

www.clergyproject.org

Freedom from Religion Foundation

The largest free-thought organization in North America, FFRF focuses on protecting the separation of church and state. Resources include a debaptism certificate. This group also presents the Atheist in Foxhole Award.

www.ffrf.org

Recovering from Religion

Recovering from Religion provides resources and community to those who've recently left religious communities they no longer wish to be a part of.

http://www.recoveringfromreligion.org

National Advocacy Groups

American Atheists

A vocal advocacy group for civil rights for atheists, American Atheists promotes the absolute separation of church and state.
www.atheists.org

American Humanist Association

A national advocacy organization whose goal is to raise awareness about issues facing humanists, atheists, freethinkers, and other nonbelievers. The group's website offers a list of local humanist chapters and resources for parents.
http://americanhumanist.org/

Center for Inquiry

Founded to foster a secular society and promote rational, science-based reason over religious belief in the public sphere. The website offers podcasts, research, legal advocacy, and secular parenting tools. The Center for Inquiry also runs www.secularhumanism.org, with thought-provoking articles and further links to resources.
www.centerforinquiry.net

Secular Coalition for America

Serves as the voice for secular Americans in Washington, DC, and coordinates activities and resources for various state chapters.
www.secular.org

The Skeptics Society

Focuses on the dissemination of scientific information pertaining to controversial questions; publishes *Skeptic* magazine.
www.skeptic.com

Secular Community Groups

American Ethical Union

The hub for the Ethical Culture movement. The website contains extensive resources for children, parents, and educators, as well as information on local Ethical Societies.
http://aeu.org/

Black Nonbelievers

Provides resources specifically for African Americans searching for nonreligious community and fellowship, trying to leave religion, or wishing to do charitable work outside of religion.
www.blacknonbelievers.org

Ex-Muslims of North America

Dedicated to supporting those who have left or are leaving their Muslim faith. Holds private gatherings through local chapters.
www.exmna.org

Foundation Beyond Belief

Focuses on organizing community members to perform charitable work and support charitable causes outside of religious avenues.
www.foundationbeyondbelief.org

The Humanist Institute

Offers a certificate program and training for those wishing to become humanist leaders, as well as lessons and activities for children.
www.humanistinstitute.org

The Society for Humanistic Judaism

Helps people celebrate cultural Judaism without the religious aspects by espousing a humanistic philosophy and connecting people to like-minded community and causes. The site offers resources for youth education (the program is playfully called HuJews), humanistic rites of passage, and links to local organizations.
www.shj.org

Sunday Assembly

The Sunday Assembly movement began in London as a secular answer to church. Local Sunday Assemblies seek to build community through regular gatherings and community service.
www.sundayassembly.com

Unitarian Universalist Association

Provides a directory of Unitarian Universalist communities and information about the value of religious diversity.
www.uua.org

Unitarian Universalist Humanist Association

Provides community for people who identify both as Unitarian Universalist and humanist.
www.huumanists.org

Meditation, Buddhism, and Zen

Esalen Institute

A famed destination for the spiritual but not religious, this nonprofit retreat center in Big Sur, California, offers workshops, internships, and extended study programs in humanistic alternative education.
www.esalen.org

Green Gulch Farm Zen Center

Just north of San Francisco, Green Gulch is a Soto Zen practice center that offers public classes, retreats, and family programs for people wishing to engage with Buddhist Zen practice, with an emphasis on gardening and organic farming.
www.sfzc.org/green-gulch

Kripalu Center for Yoga and Health

This nonprofit, located in western Massachusetts, offers training on the philosophy and practice of yoga, meditation, holistic health, and self-discovery.
www.kripalu.org

Omega Institute of Holistic Studies

Set in New York's Hudson Valley, this educational center brings together multiple philosophies and practices for holistic living. Resources range from family and relationship counseling to healthy living advice to opportunities for creative expression.
www.eomega.org

Shambhala Mountain Center

This Colorado Rockies–based retreat center, with eight miles of surrounding hiking trails, is rooted in the idea of human goodness. Shambala offers activities meant to heighten awareness via meditation and mindfulness.
www.shambhalamountain.org

Spirit Rock Meditation Center

North of San Francisco, Spirit Rock offers classes, training, and retreats that focus on the teachings of the Buddha through the vipassana tradition. Instructors guide students in Insight Meditation, the practice of mindful awareness.
www.spiritrock.org

Upaya Zen Center

This Buddhist center in Sante Fe, New Mexico, offers daily Zen meditation, weekly dharma talks, and programs on how Buddhist teachings apply to modern life. Upaya offers long-term residencies as well as professional training in end-of-life care.
www.upaya.org

Secular Death and Memorial Support

Grief Beyond Belief

An online support network for those dealing with grief and loss without faith.
www.griefbeyondbelief.org

Death Cafe

Provides a geographical listing of upcoming Death Cafes, pop-up events in which people come together to discuss death. Discussions are undirected and focus on death as a philosophical exploration as opposed to grief support.
www.deathcafe.com

The Inspired Funeral: Creative Ways to Approach the Inevitable

Gives ideas for how to craft a meaningful funeral or memorial service without religion.
https://amyacunningham.wordpress.com

Modern Loss

Essays, resources, and advice for those mourning the loss of a loved one.
www.modernloss.com

The Humanist Society

Offers a directory of humanist celebrants, resources for people who'd like to become humanist celebrants, and sample secular services and invocations.

www.thehumanistsociety.org

Center for Inquiry Celebrant Program

Trains individuals to perform secular milestones-of-life ceremonies such as weddings and memorials.

www.centerforinquiry.net/education/secular_celebrants

Online Directories of Resources

Atheism United

Comprehensive listing of national and regional atheist groups.

www.atheismunited.com/wiki/Huge_list_of_atheist_agnostic_skeptic_humanist_websites

Congress of Secular Jewish Organizations

Provides a list of organizations that promote cultural Jewishness independent of religion.

www.csjo.org

Secular Seasons

Offers a comprehensive list of secular holidays, alternative ceremonies, and events.

www.secularseasons.org

United Coalition of Reason

Provides a directory of atheist organizations and promotes candidates who run for political office on atheist platforms.

www.unitedcor.org

Thought-Provoking Podcasts and Websites

Beliefnet

Take the Belief-O-Matic quiz to find out what spiritual or nonspiritual tradition best defines you, and then search copious resources for all types of traditions.

www.beliefnet.com

Greater Good Science Center

A website brimming with news of the latest research into well-being, with a focus on awe, gratitude, and compassion.
www.greatergood.berkeley.edu

How to Be a Stoic, with Massimo Pigliucci

Resources and inspiration for people who'd like to learn more about the Greek philosophy of Stoicism.
www.howtobeastoic.wordpress.com/massimo-on-stoicism

Life After God

Ryan Bell, author of *A Year Without God*, interviews a range of big thinkers.
www.podcastchart.com/podcasts/life-after-god

On Being, with Krista Tippett

The popular radio host probes the topic of spirituality in the modern day with a fascinating roster of top-name guests.
www.onbeing.org

Rationally Speaking

The official podcast of the New York City Skeptics; explores science, pseudo-science, and everything in between.
www.rationallyspeakingpodcast.org

The School of Life

Run by Alain de Botton, author of *Religion for Atheists*, this London-based venue offers ideas, books, and workshops on how to live a meaningful life.
www.theschooloflife.com/london

NOTES

PROLOGUE

4 People from every faith, racial background, ethnic group: "A Closer Look at America's Rapidly Growing Religious 'Nones,'" *Pew Research Center,* May 13, 2015, accessed January 25, 2016, http://www.pewresearch.org/fact-tank/2015/05/13/a-closer-look-at-americas-rapidly-growing-religious-nones/.

4 Never before had so many Americans: Michael Hout and Claude S. Fischer, "Explaining Why More Americans Have No Religious Preference: Political Backlash and Generational Succession, 1987–2012," *Sociological Science* 1 (2014): 423–447, https://www.sociologicalscience.com/download/volume%201/october/SocSci_v1_423to447.pdf.

CHAPTER 1: Losing My Religion

9 first woman to run for public office: "Susan Hampton Newton Pryor (1900–1984)," *The Encyclopedia of Arkansas History and Culture,* June 9, 2010, accessed January 17, 2016, http://www.encyclopediaofarkansas.net/encyclopedia/entry-detail.aspx?entryID=1743.

10 "It was the moment I knew what it meant to be a survivor.": Don Harrell, "Moms Are Back in Style," *Arkansan* 1, no. 2 (May 1979): 21.

11 Catholic nun who is said to have escaped her convent: Steven Ozment. *Protestants: Birth of a Revolution.* (New York: Doubleday, 1992), 154.

11 attendance at mainline Protestant churches: David E. Campbell and Robert D. Putnam. *American Grace: How Religion Divides and Unites Us* (New York: Simon & Schuster, 2012), 282.

18 a more authentic expression of what the couple held dear: Dan Cox, "Millennials Aren't Going to the Chapel When They Get Married," *Yahoo,* October 21, 2015, accessed January 24, 2016, https://news.yahoo.com/millennials-aren-t-going-to-the-chapel-when-they-get-married-162532118.html.

CHAPTER 2: How Did We Get Here?

23 Nearly 50 million Americans: "Nones on the Rise," *Pew Research Center,* October 9, 2012, accessed January 17, 2016, http://www.pewforum.org/2012/10/09/nones-on-the-rise/.

23 Nearly one-fourth of Americans: "U.S. Public Becoming Less Religious," *Pew Research Center,* November 3, 2015, accessed January 17, 2016, http://www.pewforum.org/2015/11/03/u-s-public-becoming-less-religious/.

23 Some researchers describe this as a kind of "slippery pole": David Voas and Mark

Chaves, "Is the United States a Counterexample to the Secularization Thesis?" *American Journal of Sociology* 121, no. 5 (March 2016): 1–40.

23 The percentage of people who never attend: Mark Chaves, "The Decline of American Religion?" *The Association of Religion Data Archives*, accessed January 17, 2016, http://www.thearda.com/rrh/papers/guidingpapers/chaves.pdf.

24 99 percent of Americans professed belief in God: Frank Newport, "More Than Nine in Ten Americans Continue to Believe in God," *Gallup*, June 3, 2011, accessed January 20, 2016, http://www.gallup.com/poll/147887/americans-continue-believe-god.aspx.

24 Americans' increasing distaste for institutions: "Millennials in Adulthood: Detached from Institutions, Networked with Friends," *Pew Research Center*, March 7, 2014, http://www.pewsocialtrends.org/2014/03/07/millennials-in-adulthood/.

24 President Obama regularly gives a nod to nonbelievers: Cathy Lynn Grossman, "An Inaugural First: Obama Acknowledges 'Non-believers,'" *USA Today*, January 22, 2009, accessed January 20, 2016, http://usatoday30.usatoday.com/news/religion/2009-01-20-obama-non-believers_N.htm.

24 slow uptick in the "acceptability" of being an atheist: Jeffrey M. Jones, "Atheists, Muslims See Most Bias as Presidential Candidates," *Gallup*, June 21, 2012, accessed January 21, 2016, http://www.gallup.com/poll/155285/Atheists-Muslims-Bias-Presidential-Candidates.aspx.

25 He answered right back and suggested a meeting: Robert Putnam interview with the author, November 1, 2012.

26 one-third of adults under the age of thirty: "Religious Landscape Study: Age Distribution," *Pew Research Center*, accessed January 20, 2016, http://www.pewforum.org/religious-landscape-study/age-distribution/.

26 While 5 percent of baby boomers were raised: Daniel Cox, "Born and Raised: More Americans Are Being Raised Without Religion and Choosing to Stay that Way," *Huffington Post*, last updated September 30, 2013, accessed January 20, 2016, http://www.huffingtonpost.com/daniel-cox/born-and-raised-more-amer_b_3682847.html, and Daniel Cox, Research Director, Public Religion Research Institute, e-mail message to the author, December 4, 2015.

28 self-identified atheists make up just a little over a tenth: Michael Lipka, "A Closer Look at America's Rapidly Growing Religious 'Nones'," *Pew Research Center*, May 13, 2015, accessed January 20, 2016, http://www.pewresearch.org/fact-tank/2015/05/13/a-closer-look-at-americas-rapidly-growing-religious-nones/.

29 when two people of different backgrounds marry: David McClendon, "CCF Civil Rights Symposium: Interfaith Marriage and Romantic Unions in the United States," *Council on Contemporary Families*, February 4, 2014, accessed January 24, 2016, https://contemporaryfamilies.org/interfaith-marriage-in-the-us/.

29 With today's age of first marriage: D'Vera Cohn et al., "Barely Half of U.S. Adults Are Married—A Record Low," *Pew Research Center*, December 14, 2011, accessed January 20, 2016, http://www.pewsocialtrends.org/2011/12/14/barely-half-of-u-s-adults-are-married-a-record-low/.

29 married to someone of a different religion: Caryle Murphy, "Interfaith Marriage Is Common in U.S., Particularly Among the Recently Wed," *Pew Research Center*, June 2, 2015, accessed January 20, 2016, http://www.pewresearch.org/fact-tank/2015/06/02/interfaith-marriage/.

29 If you include Catholic-Protestant unions: Naomi Schaefer Riley, *'Til Faith Do Us Part: How Interfaith Marriage Is Transforming America* (New York: Oxford University Press, 2013), xiii.

29 Thirty-five percent of marriages: "Interfaith Marriage Is Common in U.S." For more on interfaith marriage, see also: Schaefer Riley, *'Til Faith Do Us Part.*

29 children raised in interfaith households: Schaefer Riley, *'Til Faith Do Us Part,* 80.

29 "It has the potential for just eliminating religion": Putnam interview. While Pew's projections suggest that the US will continue to see a rise in the number of Nones, it's unlikely religion will be eliminated. Putnam is right that big changes are afoot, but perhaps not as far and as fast as his casual quote might suggest. "The Future of World Religions: Population Growth Projections, 2010–2050: Why Muslims Are Rising Fastest and the Unaffiliated Are Shrinking as a Share of the World's Population," *Pew Research Center,* April 2, 2015, accessed January 23, 2016, http://www.pewforum.org/2015/04/02/religious-projections-2010-2050/.

30 Erin O'Connor still calls herself a Catholic: Erin O'Connor, interview with the author, March 13, 2015.

CHAPTER 3: Religion Tries to Stay Relevant

35 ongoing dialogue with the past: Alasdair MacIntyre, *After Virtue: A Study in Moral Theory* (New York: Bloomsbury Academic, 2013), 258.

35 church leaders began to embrace the very people: "Our Story," *Glide,* accessed January 21, 2016, http://glide.org/story.

35 A charismatic Cecil Williams: Nathan Aaseng, *African-American Religious Leaders: A–Z of African Americans* (New York: Facts On File, 2003), 238–40.

36 Glide found its soul: "The Controversial, Yet Popular, Reverend Cecil Williams," *NPR Faith Matters,* last modified April 8, 2013, accessed January 20, 2016, http://www.npr.org/2013/04/05/176341818/-the-controversial-yet-popular-reverend-cecil-williams.

38 At Christ Episcopal Church in Slidell, Louisiana: Bob Warren, "'Ashes to Go' Draws Numerous Motorists to Slidell Church on Ash Wednesday," *The Times-Picayune,* March 5, 2014, accessed January 24, 2016, http://www.nola.com/religion/index.ssf/2014/03/ashes_to_go_draws_numerous_mot.html.

38 a group called Mass Mob chooses an old, struggling Catholic church: Anne Neville, "Mass Mob Packs the Pews at Corpus Christi," *The Buffalo News,* August 24, 2015, accessed January 24, 2015, http://www.buffalonews.com/city-region/east-side/mass-mob-packs-the-pews-at-corpus-christi-20150823.

38 your own personal drive-through prayer: Dan Adams, "Scituate Lutheran Church Offers Drive-Through Prayers," *The Boston Globe,* October 12, 2013, accessed January 22, 2016, https://www.bostonglobe.com/metro/2013/10/12/scituate-lutheran-church-offers-drive-through-prayers/cf6SqQCupXa30XLNH4UgFM/story.html.

38 Graham Robinson, a Presbyterian minister in Aston: Graham Robinson, interview with and e-mail message to the author, October 14, 2014, and September 23, 2015.

39 "I can't help myself from rooting for the 76ers": Graham Robinson, "Pastor Graham Robinson: Welcome to Aston Presbyterian Church!" *Aston Presbyterian Church,* 2014, accessed January 21, 2016, http://www.astonpresbyterianchurch.org/our-minister/.

39 every five hundred years, religion goes through a major upheaval: Phyllis Tickle, *Emergence Christianity: What It Is, Where It Is Going, and Why It Matters* (Grand Rapids, MI: Baker Books, 2012), 17–18.

40 Muslim and Hindu populations in the United States are expected to grow: "America's Changing Religious Landscape: Christians Decline Sharply as Share of Population; Unaffiliated and Other Faiths Continue to Grow," *Pew Research Center*, May 12, 2015, accessed January 20, 2016, http://www.pewforum.org/2015/05/12/americas-changing-religious-landscape/.

40 7.5 million people reported having left the religion: "Frequently Requested Church Statistics," *Center for Applied Research in the Apostolate*, 2015, accessed January 22, 2016, http://cara.georgetown.edu/caraservices/requestedchurchstats.html.

40 In Evangelical Lutheran churches across the country: Nicole Radziszewski, "The Shrinking Church: Congregations Look for Solutions as They Face Declines in Membership, Attendance," *The Lutheran*, January 2013, accessed, January 22, 2016, http://www.thelutheran.org/article/article.cfm?article_id=11186.

40 Episcopalians closed 45 parishes in 2013: Jonathan Pitts, "Episcopal Leader in Spotlight After Bishop Charged in Baltimore Hit-and-Run," *The Baltimore Sun*, March 7, 2015, accessed January 24, 2016, http://www.baltimoresun.com/news/bs-md-cook-and-tec-20150303-story.html.

41 22 percent of Jewish American adults: Jonah Lowenfeld, "1 in 5 U.S. Jews: No Religion," *Jewish Journal*, October 2, 2013, accessed January 21, 2016, http://www.jewishjournal.com/religion/article/1_in_5_u.s._jews_no_religion, and "A Portrait of Jewish Americans," *Pew Research Center*, October 1, 2013, accessed January 21, 2016, http://www.pewforum.org/2013/10/01/jewish-american-beliefs-attitudes-culture-survey/.

41 the number of child baptisms has dropped rapidly: Maureen Fiedler, "Keeping an Eye on the Falling Baptism Rate," *National Catholic Reporter*, October 24, 2013, accessed January 20, 2016, http://ncronline.org/blogs/ncr-today/keeping-eye-falling-baptism-rate.

41 In her book *Searching for Sunday*: Rachel Held Evans, *Searching for Sunday: Loving, Leaving, and Finding the Church* (Nashville: Nelson Books, 2015), xiv.

42 "If someone is gay and he searches for the Lord": Lizzy Davies, "Pope Francis Signals Openness Towards Gay Priests," *The Guardian*, July 29, 2013, accessed January 21, 2016, http://www.theguardian.com/world/2013/jul/29/pope-francis-openness-gay-priests.

43 The current program began under Pope Benedict: "Georgetown Hosts Conference with Vatican Office for Culture, Washington Archdiocese," *Georgetown University*, April 14, 2014, accessed January 21, 2016, http://www.georgetown.edu/news/faith-culture-common-good-event-announcement.html.

45 pay attention to "the beat of this age": Lizzy Davies, "Catholic Church Must Listen to Beat of This Age, Pope Francis Tells Bishops," *The Guardian*, October 5, 2014, accessed January 21, 2016, http://www.theguardian.com/world/2014/oct/05/catholic-church-listen-pope-francis.

45 Francis maintains that the "door is closed" on women being ordained: Tracy Connor, "Renegade Female Priests Hold Peaceful Protest Amid Pope Francis' Visit," *NBC News*, September 23, 2015, accessed January 21, 2016, http://www.nbc-

news.com/storyline/pope-francis-visits-america/renegade-female-priests-hold-peaceful-protest-amid-pope-francis-visit-n432371.

45 areas that boast large Latino populations: Michael Lipka, "A Closer Look at Catholic America," *Pew Research Center*, September 14, 2015, accessed January 21, 2016, http://www.pewresearch.org/fact-tank/2015/09/14/a-closer-look-at-catholic-america/.

45 being turned into restaurants and condos: Kathy McCabe, "Empty Churches Open Doors to Development." *Boston Globe*, July 27, 2008.

45 has turned many Catholics away: Laurie Goodstein, "Pope Francis to Find a Church in Upheaval," *The New York Times*, September 21, 2015, accessed January 21, 2016, http://www.nytimes.com/2015/09/22/us/pope-francis-to-find-a-church-in-upheaval.html.

46 Pamela Shepherd, the Senior minister of the United Church of Christ: Pamela Shepherd interview with the author, July 30, 2014.

CHAPTER 4: The Big Picture

53 84 percent of the people around the globe still describe themselves as religious: "The Global Religious Landscape," *Pew Research Center*, December 18, 2012, accessed January 22, 2016, http://www.pewforum.org/2012/12/18/global-religious-landscape-exec/.

54 Deb Kelemen, a professor of psychology: Deb Kelemen interview with the author, May 31, 2013.

55 they tend to think that both living and nonliving things: Deborah Kelemen, Rebecca Seston, and Laure Saint Georges, "The Designing Mind: Children's Reasoning About Intended Function and Artifact Structure." *Journal of Cognition and Development* 13, no. 4 (2012): 439–453, http://www.bu.edu/cdl/files/2013/08/2012_KelemenSestonStGeorges.pdf.

56 choose teleological reasons when they can't come up with another answer: Deborah Kelemen, Joshua Rottman, and Rebecca Seston. "Professional Physical Scientists Display Tenacious Teleological Tendencies: Purpose-Based Reasoning as a Cognitive Default." *Journal of Experimental Psychology: General* 142, no. 4 (2013): 1074.

57 "Sympathy . . . will have been increased through natural selection": Charles Darwin, *The Descent of Man, and Selection in Relation to Sex* (London: John Murray, 1871), 130.

57 I met Sean Kelly in his office: Sean Kelly interview with and e-mail message to the author, March 11, 2014, and January 7, 2015.

59 "If God is dead, everything is permitted": Hubert Dreyfus and Sean Dorrance Kelly. *All Things Shining: Reading the Western Classics to Find Meaning in a Secular Age* (New York: Free Press, 2011), 46.

60 Dan Gilbert, the famed happiness researcher: Dan Gilbert interview with the author, May 27, 2014.

62 A study of 132 countries: Shigehiro Oishi and Ed Diener, "Residents of Poor Nations Have a Greater Sense of Meaning in Life Than Residents of Wealthy Nations," *Psychological Science* 25, no. 2 (February 2014): 422–30.

63 found that the religious do have a deeper sense of purpose: Stephen Cranney, "Do People Who Believe in God Report More Meaning in Their Lives? The Existential Effects of Belief," *Journal for the Study of Religion* 52, no. 3 (September 2013): 638–46.

63 "How we spend our days": Annie Dillard, *The Writing Life* (New York: Harper Perennial, 2013), 32.

CHAPTER 5: Moral Authority

66 social constructs that bound individuals together into protective groups: Ara Norenzayan, *Big Gods: How Religion Transformed Cooperation and Conflict* (Princeton: Princeton University Press, 2015), 5–8.

67 these systems emerged as ways for individuals to manage: Karen Armstrong, *The Great Transformation: The Beginning of Our Religious Traditions* (New York: Alfred A.Knopf, 2006), xi–xviii.

67 a single, watchful God who monitors behavior and inflicts punishment: Norenzayan, *Big Gods*, 13–54.

68 "Religions exist primarily for people to achieve together": David Wilson, *Darwin's Cathedral: Evolution, Religion, and the Nature of Society* (Chicago: University of Chicago Press, 2003), 59.

68 churchgoers give more of their money, time, and energy: David E. Campbell and Robert D. Putnam. *American Grace: How Religion Divides and Unites Us* (New York: Simon & Schuster, 2012), 445–53.

68 32 percent of all such contributions: Robert Frank, "Americans Gave a Record $358 Billion to Charity in 2014," *CNBC*, June 16, 2015, accessed January 22, 2016, http://www.cnbc.com/2015/06/16/americans-gave-a-record-358-billion-to-charity-in-2014.html.

69 33 percent of volunteer work: "Volunteering in the United States, 2014," *Bureau of Labor Statistics*, February 25, 2015, accessed January 22, 2016, http://www.bls.gov/news.release/volun.nr0.htm.

69 "Active membership in a church or synagogue": Eric M. Uslaner, "Religion and Civic Engagement in Canada and the United States," *Journal of the Scientific Study of Religion* 41, no. 2 (2002): 239–54, http://www.academia.edu/841046/Religion_and_civic_engagement_in_Canada_and_the_United_States.

69 people who help others have a greater sense of meaning: Daryl R. Van Tongeren et al., "Prosociality Enhances Meaning in Life," *The Journal of Positive Psychology* 11, no. 3 (2016): 225–36, http://www.tandfonline.com/doi/abs/10.1080/17439760.2015.1048814?journalCode=rpos20&.

70 "children have some of the foundations of morality": Alison Gopnik, *The Philosophical Baby: What Children's Minds Tell Us About Truth, Love, and the Meaning of Life* (New York: Picador, 2010), 203–4.

72 students have become dramatically *less* empathic: Sara H.Konrath, Edward H. O'Brien, and Courtney Hsing. "Changes in Dispositional Empathy in American College Students over Time: A Meta-Analysis." *Personality and Social Psychology Review* 15, no. 2 (2010): 180–98, http://psr.sagepub.com/content/15/2/180.

72 getting rich is an important goal: Ibid.

72 children develop narcissistic tendencies: Eddie Brummelman et al., "Origins of Narcissism in Children." *Proceedings of the National Academy of Sciences* 112, no. 12 (2015): 3659–62, http://www.pnas.org/content/112/12/3659.full.

72 it's more important to pursue their own personal happiness: Richard Weissbourd,

The Parents We Mean to Be: How Well-Intentioned Adults Undermine Children's Moral and Emotional Development (New York: Mariner Books, 2010), 41.

72 Richard Weissbourd, a lecturer at the Harvard Graduate School of Education: Richard Weissbourd interview with the author, September 7, 2011.

74 fathers spent an average of five more hours: Garey Ramey and Valerie A. Ramey, "The Rug Rat Race," *Brookings Papers on Economic Activity, Economic Studies Program, The Brookings Institution* 41, no. 1 (Spring 2010): 129–99, http://www.nber.org/papers/w15284.

74 "I'm not a big fan of heaven and hell as moral orientation": Richard Weissbourd, "Sunday Program: Raising Moral Kids," (panel discussion, Humanist Community at Harvard, Cambridge, MA, May 18, 2014).

75 Marshall Ganz, a senior lecturer at Harvard's Kennedy School of Government: Marshall Ganz interview with the author, October 6, 2014.

78 In the text of one of his speeches: Marshall Ganz, "Some Reflections on Faith and Politics," *Marshall Ganz*, accessed February 27, 2016, http://marshallganz.usmblogs.com/files/2012/08/Faith-and-Politics.pdf.

CHAPTER 6: Religious Literacy

80 "Massive unlearning is taking place": Charles Taylor, *A Secular Age* (Cambridge, MA: The Belknap Press, 2007), 727.

81 "Religion is the ultimate expression of story's dominion over our minds": Jonathan Gottschall, *The Storytelling Animal: How Stories Make Us Human*, (New York: Mariner Books, 2013), 138.

82 the Pew Foundation conducted a poll of Americans: "U.S. Religious Knowledge Survey: Executive Summary," *Pew Research Center* September 28, 2010, accessed January 22, 2016, http://www.pewforum.org/2010/09/28/u-s-religious-knowledge-survey/.

82 "the ability to understand and use the religious terms": Stephen Prothero, *Religious Literacy: What Every American Needs to Know—and Doesn't* (New York: HarperCollins, 2008), 13.

82 students couldn't grasp basic religious references: "Religious Literacy: What Every American Should Know," *Pew Research Center*, December 3, 2007, accessed January 22, 2016, http://www.pewforum.org/2007/12/03/religious-literacy-what-every-american-should-know/.

86 I had to credit my regular yoga practice: You can test your own religious literacy (or lack thereof) by following this link: "U.S. Religious Knowledge Quiz," *Pew Research Center*, accessed January 22, 2016, http://features.pewforum.org/quiz/us-religious-knowledge/.

86 Americans conflate the ban on school prayer: For more information on Engel v. Vitale and Abington School District v. Schempp see: "Similar Cases—Engel v. Vitale," *United States Courts*, accessed January 22, 2016, http://www.uscourts.gov/educational-resources/educational-activities/similar-cases-engel-v-vitale.

86 only 36 percent of respondents knew the difference between the two: "U.S. Religious Knowledge Survey," *Pew Research Center*.

86 "The history of man is inseparable from the history of religion": Neal Devins and Louis Fisher, *The Democratic Constitution* (New York: Oxford University Press, 2004), 201.

87 "One's education is not complete without a study of comparative religion": "Abington v. Schempp," *Digital History,* accessed January 22, 2016, http://www.digitalhistory.uh.edu/disp_textbook.cfm?smtID=3&psid=4087.

87 One proponent of mandating religion as a cultural study: Dan Dennett, "Let's teach religion—all religion—in schools," *TED,* February 2006, accessed February 27, 2016, https://www.ted.com/talks/dan_dennett_s_response_to_rick_warren?language=en.

88 In Modesto, California, ninth-graders have to take a nine-week survey course in world religions: Linda K. Wertheimer, *Faith Ed: Teaching About Religion in an Age of Intolerance* (Boston: Beacon Press, 2015), 160–62.

88 created by Janet Cardiff called *The Forty Part Motet*: "Janet Cardiff: The Forty Part Motet," *The Metropolitan Museum of Art,* accessed February 27, 2016, http://www.metmuseum.org/exhibitions/listings/2013/janet-cardiff.

CHAPTER 7: A Sense of Belonging

92 Communitas is a group bound by the shared quest for values, purpose, and meaning: Victor Turner, *The Ritual Process: Structure and Anti-Structure* (Chicago: Aldine Publishing, 1969), 94–113, 125–30.

94 the difference between life and death: "Psychologist John Cacioppo Explains Why Loneliness Is Bad for Your Health," *Institute for Genomics & Systems Biology,* January 25, 2011, accessed January 22, 2016, http://www.igsb.org/news/psychologist-john-cacioppo-explains-why-loneliness-is-bad-for-your-health.

94 "Congregating physically may actually play a role": John T. Cacioppo and William Patrick, *Loneliness: Human Nature and the Need for Social Connection* (New York: Norton, 2008), 258.

94 Citing a study by Lynda H. Powell: Lynda H. Powell, Leila Shahabi, and Carl E. Thoresen. "Religion and Spirituality: Linkages to Physical Health." *American Psychologist* 58, no. 1 (2003): 36.

94 "Weekly attendance at the Rotary Club may also be good for you": Cacioppo and Patrick. *Loneliness,* 259.

95 "fosters feelings of self-worth and control while reducing feelings of depression": Ibid.

95 created the greatest sense of meaning: Roy F. Baumeister, "The Meaning of Life," Aeon, September 16, 2013, accessed January 24, 2016, https://aeon.co/essays/what-is-better-a-happy-life-or-a-meaningful-one.

96 the highest rates of perceived meaning in their lives: Nathaniel M. Lambert et al., "To Belong Is to Matter Sense of Belonging Enhances Meaning in Life." *Personality and Social Psychology Bulletin* (November 2013): 0146167213499186, http://psp.sagepub.com/content/39/11/1418.

96 Once people have that sense of belonging: Ibid.

97 The religious groups, on the other hand: Richard Sosis, "Religion and Intragroup Cooperation: Preliminary Results of a Comparative Analysis of Utopian Communities," *Cross-Cultural Research* 34, no. 1 (2000): 70-87, http://ccr.sagepub.com/content/34/1/70.abstract.

97 a study of a religious fire-walking ritual in Spain: Ivana Konvalinka et al., "Synchronized Arousal Between Performers and Related Spectators in a Fire-Walking Ritual." *Proceedings of the National Academy of Sciences* 108, no. 20 (2011): 8514–19, http://www.pnas.org/content/108/20/8514.full.

98 the group experiences an elevated sense of collective purpose: Richard Sosis and Eric R. Bressler, "Cooperation and Commune Longevity: A Test of the Costly Signaling Theory of Religion," *Cross-Cultural Research* 37, no. 2 (May 2003): 211–39, http://citeseerx.ist.psu.edu/viewdoc/download?doi=10.1.1.500.5715&rep=rep1&type=pdf.

98 the popular rector there at the time, Buddy Stallings: Buddy Stallings interview with the author, April 25, 2014.

101 Neil Carter, who lost everything when he left his religion: Neil Carter interview with the author, April 2, 2015.

102 Like Lightyear, Neil fell to earth: Neil Carter, "How Toy Story Illustrates When I Lost My Faith," *Patheos,* August 13, 2014, accessed January 22, 2016, http://www.patheos.com/blogs/godlessindixie/2014/08/13/how-toy-story-illustrates-losing-the-faith/.

103 Marci Olsen also knows the pain of leaving a faith: Marci Olsen interview with the author, April 28, 2015.

106 Mohamed Abdelziz remembers the moment he left Islam: Mohamed Abdelziz interview with the author, April 14, 2015.

CHAPTER 8: Morality Without a Map

113 the least trusted group in the United States is atheists: "How Americans Feel About Religious Groups: Jews, Catholics & Evangelicals Rated Warmly, Atheists and Muslims More Coldly," *Pew Research Center* July 16, 2014, accessed January 23, 2016, http://www.pewforum.org/2014/07/16/how-americans-feel-about-religious-groups/.

113 Americans rate atheists as the group least likely to care: Penny Edgel, Joseph Gerteis, and Douglas Hartmann. "Atheists as 'Other'": Moral Boundaries and Cultural Membership in American Society." *American Sociological Review* 71, no. 2 (2006): 211–34.

114 the more religious a family was, regardless of which religion, the less generous the child was: Jean Decety et al., "The Negative Association Between Religiousness and Children's Altruism Across the World." *Current Biology* 25, no. 22 (2015): 2951–55.

115 a result of more complex reasoning: Jason M. Cowell and Jean Decety. "Precursors to Morality in Development as a Complex Interplay Between Neural, Socioenvironmental, and Behavioral Facets." *Proceedings of the National Academy of Sciences* 112, no. 41 (2015): 12657–662, http://www.pnas.org/content/112/41/12657.abstract.

117 Sarah Aadland was raised in a predominantly Lutheran town: Sarah Aadland interviews with the author, March 17, 2015, and April 10, 2015.

120 Hang a poster of two eyes on the wall in his bedroom: Sander Van der Linden, "How the Illusion of Being Observed Can Make You a Better Person," *Scientific American,* May 3, 2011, accessed January 23, 2016, http://www.scientificamerican.com/article/how-the-illusion-of-being-observed-can-make-you-better-person/.

120 Places like Norway and Finland: Ara Norenzayan, *The Mind Report,* video, 50:45, February 16, 2013, http://bloggingheads.tv/videos/15334.

122 Marcie Griffiths, the adviser to the youth program: Marcie Griffiths interview with the author, October 17, 2012.

CHAPTER 9: Do-It-Yourself Religion

128 Sheilaism suggested the breakdown of that unifying power of religion: Robert N. Bellah, "Habits of the Heart: Implications for Religion" (lecture, St. Mark's Catholic Church, Isla Vista, California February 21, 1986), http://www.robertbellah.com/lectures_5.htm.

129 create their own DIY religion: "Many Americans Mix Multiple Faiths," December 9, 2009, accessed January 23, 2016, http://www.pewforum.org/2009/12/09/many-americans-mix-multiple-faiths/.

130 the level of happiness that religiously affiliated people felt: Chaeyoon Lim and Robert D. Putnam. "Religion, Social Networks, and Life Satisfaction," *American Sociological Review* 75, no. 6 (December 2010): 914–33.

131 there are 68 affiliate Sunday Assemblies around the world: "Our Story," *The Sunday Assembly,* accessed January 23, 2016, https://www.sundayassembly.com/story.

134 I met group leaders James and Anjali Murphy: James and Anjali Murphy, interview with the author, March 29, 2014.

137 Kimberly is a no-nonsense mother of two: Kimberly Hansen, interview with the author, March 29, 2014.

139 sociologists have dubbed the region the "None Zone": Patricia O'Connell Killen and Mark Silk, eds., *Religion and Public Life in the Pacific Northwest: The None Zone* (Walnut Creek, CA: AltaMira Press, 2004), 28–29.

140 I met a woman named Maddy DiRienzo: Maddy DiRienzo interview with the author, February 12, 2014.

140 I asked Yaconelli why he started the Hearth: Mark Yaconelli interviews with the author, January 10, 2014, and February 13, 2014.

141 modeled the storytelling ritual on religious structures: Testimony of this sort is primarily used in evangelical and Anabaptist traditions. For a chapter on the history and use of testimony, see: Dorothy Bass, *Practicing Our Faith: A Way of Life for a Searching People* (San Francisco: Jossey-Bass, 2010), 99–101.

142 Joshua Boettiger, the rabbi at Temple Emek Shalom: Joshua Boettiger interview with the author, May 9, 2014.

144 have been welcoming atheists and agnostics: "Unitarian Universalist Origins: Our Historic Faith," *Unitarian Universalist Association,* accessed January 23, 2016, http://www.uua.org/beliefs/history/our-historic-faith.

144 Humanistic Judaism, started in 1963: "Rabbi Sherwin T. Wine," *Society for 146 Judaism,* accessed January 23, 2016, http://www.shj.org/humanistic-judaism/rabbi-sherwin-t-wine/.

144 Ethical Societies have provided an alternative to religion: "History," *American Ethical Union,* accessed January 23, 2016, http://aeu.org/who-we-are/history/.

144 The group prides itself on "deed before creed": "Ethical Humanism," *American Ethical Union,* accessed January 23, 2016, http://aeu.org/who-we-are/ethical-humanism/.

144 the Brooklyn Society for Ethical Culture: "Building Rentals," *Brooklyn Society for Ethical Culture,* accessed January 23, 2016, http://www.bsec.org/#!rentals/c14wm.

146 After that night, I e-mailed Helen Zuman: Helen Zuman interview with the author, March 12, 2015.

148 "Can there be a church of the Nones?" Robert Putnam interview with the author, November 1, 2012.

CHAPTER 10: Almost Church

150 I found a smorgasbord of faiths: You can take the quiz yourself here: Belief-O-Matic, *Beliefnet*, accessed January 23, 2016, http://www.beliefnet.com/Entertainment/Quizzes/BeliefOMatic.aspx.

151 I called Phil Zuckerman, the secular studies professor: Phil Zuckerman interview with the author, October 31, 2012.

153 I went to visit Greg Epstein, the Humanist Chaplain at Harvard: Greg Epstein interview with the author, August 28, 2012.

155 saw the number of its chapters rise from 59 to 180: "AHA Affiliates and Chapters," *American Humanist Association*, accessed January 18, 2016, http://americanhumanist.org/What_We_Do/Local_Groups/AHA_Groups, and Maggie Ardiente, Director of Development and Communications, American Humanist Association, email message to the author, December 8, 2015.

155 now registered with the national Secular Student Alliance: Tori Rehr, Administrative Associate, Secular Student Alliance, e-mail message to the author, November 17, 2015.

156 Mark, a thirty-five-year-old biologist at a Boston university: Mark DeSanto interview with the author, November 18, 2013.

161 before leaving the convent and eventually losing her faith: Mary Johnson, *An Unquenchable Thirst: A Memoir.* (New York: Spiegel & Grau, 2011), 522.

CHAPTER 11: Ritual Without Religion

168 whether they believed in the power of the ritual: Michael I. Norton and Francesca Gino. "Rituals Alleviate Grieving for Loved Ones, Lovers, and Lotteries." *Journal of Experimental Psychology: General* 143, no. 1 (2014): 266.

169 Puett was the keynote speaker: Michael James Puett, "Ritual as a Category of Religious Experience" (presentation, Ways of Knowing: Graduate Conference on Religion, Cambridge, MA, October 25–26, 2013).

171 Raymond Arnold had organized the event: Raymond Arnold interview with the author, September 20, 2013.

174 Jim Lasko is a rugged-looking Chicagoan: Jim Lasko interview with the author, March 10, 2015. Nine months after our conversation, Redmoon Theater closed down due to financial problems. Stephanie Lulay, "Redmoon Theater Permanently Closing After Fire Fest Debacle, Financial Woes," *DNAinfo*, December 21, 2015, accessed January 23, 2016, http://www.dnainfo.com/chicago/20151221/pilsen/redmoon-theater-permanently-closing-after-fire-fest-debacle-financial-woes.

176 Deborah Copaken, a writer and artist in New York City: Deborah Copaken interview with the author, September, 15, 2013.

180 Kathryn Guta was sitting beside me on the raised platform: Kathryn Guta: interview with the author, May 10, 2015.

CHAPTER 12: Facing the Big Unknown

192 "What does it mean to grieve": Meghan O'Rourke, *The Long Goodbye: A Memoir* (New York: Riverhead Books, 2012), 13.

192 "The enlightened modern age has failed to find": Peter Watson, *The Age of Atheists: How We Have Sought to Live Since the Death of God* (New York: Simon & Schuster, 2014), 2.

193 Elizabeth Segel's family story is yet another cautionary tale: Elizabeth Segel interview with the author, September 27, 2013.

195 Liz Hoffmaster, a pediatric nurse, inherited the leadership of the Memphis Atheists Meetup: Liz Hoffmeister interview with the author, April 2, 2015.

196 Audrey Kingstrom began conducting secular funerals: Audrey Kingstrom interview with the author, April 9, 2015.

198 one of Rebecca Hensler's life missions: Rebecca Hensler interview with the author, Arpil 2, 2015.

CHAPTER 13: The Wonder of the Natural World

207 subjects who were shown: Piercarlo Valdesolo and Jesse Graham, "Awe, Uncertainty, and Agency Detection," *Psychological Science* 25, no.1 (2014): 170–78, http://pss.sagepub.com/content/25/1/170.

207 "gazing upon things that we know to be formed by natural causes": Piercarlo Valdesolo and Jesse Graham, "Awe, Uncertainty, and Agency Detection," *Psychological Science* (2013): 0956797613501884, http://www.psychologicalscience.org/index.php/news/releases/experiencing-awe-increases-belief-in-the-supernatural.html.

208 that the feeling of awe arises: Michelle N. Shiota, Dacher Keltner, and Amanda Mossman. "The Nature of Awe: Elicitors, Appraisals, and Effects on Self-Concept." *Cognition and Emotion* 21, no. 5 (2007): 944–63, http://greatergood.berkeley.edu/dacherkeltner/docs/shiota.2007.pdf.

208 answers that suggested they felt like part of some larger whole: Ibid.

209 People who experience awe: Dacher Keltner, *Born to Be Good: The Science of a Meaningful Life* (New York: W.W. Norton & Company, 2009), 263.

209 "awe may encourage people to forgo strict self-interest": Paul Piff et al., "Awe, the Small Self, and Prosocial Behavior," *Journal of Personality and Social Psychology* 108, no. 6 (2015): 883–99, http://media.wix.com/ugd/80ea24_0ca3eda3711d4fbc958a77bb74cef73a.pdf.

209 "Awe experiences knock us back to our baby state": Michelle Shiota interview with the author, May 6, 2015.

211 the differences between secular and religious minds: Catherine Caldwell-Harris, "Wednesday Dialogue: Differences Between the Secular and Religious Minds," (presentation, Concord Area Humanists, Concord, MA, April 2, 2014).

213 Caldwell-Harris was lecturing on the research showing that there is a spectrum: Catherine L. Caldwell-Harris et al., "Exploring the Atheist Personality: Well-being, Awe, and Magical Thinking in Atheists, Buddhists, and Christians," *Mental Health, Religion & Culture* 14, no. 7 (2011): 659–72 and Catherine L. Caldwell-Harris, "Understanding Atheism/Non-belief as an Expected Individual-Differences Variable," *Religion, Brain & Behavior* 2, no. 1 (2012): 4–23.

212 these cognitive differences may even explain the gender gap: Patrick Rosenkranz and Bruce G. Charlton, "Individual Differences in Existential Orientation: Empathizing and Systemizing Explain the Sex Difference in Religious Orientation and Science Acceptance," *Archive for the Psychology of Religion* 35, no. 1 (2013): 119–46.

215 "even atheists will hold nonsupernatural beliefs": Miguel Farias et al., "Scientific Faith: Belief in Science Increases in the Face of Stress and Existential Anxiety," *Journal of Experimental Psychology* 49, no. 6 (November 2013): 1210–13, http://www.ncbi.nlm.nih.gov/pmc/articles/PMC3807800/.

215 Lawrence Krauss, a professor of theoretical physics: Lawrence Krauss interview with the author, March 25, 2015.

218 one millionth of one billionth of all matter: Alan Lightman, *The Accidental Universe: The World You Thought You Knew* (New York: Pantheon, 2014), 101.

CHAPTER 14: The God of Here and Now

221 Stephen Batchelor, has written about an idea: Stephen Batchelor interview with the author, March 28, 2015.

224 the practice itself made the cover of *Time*: "The Science of Meditation," *Time*, August 4, 2003, accessed January 23, 2016, http://content.time.com/time/magazine/0,9263,7601030804,00.html.

224 The documented benefits of meditation: Stefan G. Hofmann, Paul Grossman, and Devon E. Hinton, "Loving-Kindness and Compassion Meditation: Potential for Psychological Interventions," *Clinical Psychology Review* 31, no. 7 (November 2011): 1126–32, http://www.ncbi.nlm.nih.gov/pmc/articles/PMC3176989/.

224 the practice reduces stress and inflammation: Seth Zuihô Segall, "Book Review of Owen Flanagan's "The Bodhisattva's Brain: Buddhism Naturalized," *The Existential Buddhist* (blog), October 30, 2011, http://www.existentialbuddhist.com/tag/owen-flanagan/.

225 perhaps we start to see how we're all connected: Paul Condon et al., "Meditation Increases Compassionate Responses to Suffering." *Psychological Science* 24, no. 10 (2013): 2125–27.

225 "The most important step in emancipating oneself": Mihaly Csikszentmihalyi, *Flow: The Psychology of Optimal Experience* (New York: Harper Perennial, 2008), 19.

227 But he was losing his faith: William LaRue interview with the author, March 27, 2015.

228 For years he struggled to find peace of mind: Greg Rice interview with the author, April 14, 2015.

229 "Dharma is a norm, it means literally a law": Stephen Batchelor interview with the author, March 28, 2015.

CONCLUSION

235 I met Allen and Brenda Glendenning: Allen and Brenda Glendenning interview with the author, April 2, 2015.

239 The novelist Marilynne Robinson: Marilynne Robinson, interview by Tom Ashbrook, "Marilynne Robinson on Hope in a Time of Fear," *On Point*, 90.9 WBUR FM, November 25, 2015, accessed January 24, 2016, http://onpoint.wbur.org/2015/11/25/marilynne-robinson-gilead-hope-fear-faith.

RESOURCES FOR READERS

252 have stronger relationships, are quicker to forgive, and are more compassionate: "What Is Gratitude?," *Greater Good*, accessed January 23, 2016, http://greatergood.berkeley.edu/topic/gratitude/definition#what_is.

252 Research shows we reap a wealth of benefits: Jill Suttie and Jason Marsh, "5 Ways Giving Is Good for You," *Greater Good*, December 13, 2010, accessed January 23, 2016, http://greatergood.berkeley.edu/article/item/5_ways_giving_is_good_for_you.

253 giving is contagious: James H. Fowler and Nicholas A. Christakis. "Cooperative Behavior Cascades in Human Social Networks." *Proceedings of the National Academy of Sciences* 107, no. 12 (2010): 5334–38.

254 collective rituals like singing bring us together: Jacques Launay and Eiluned Pearce, "The New Science of Singing Together," *Greater Good*, December 4, 2015, accessed January 23, 2016, http://greatergood.berkeley.edu/article/item/science_of_singing, and Eiluned Pearce, Jacques Launay, and Robin IM Dunbar. "The Ice-Breaker Effect: Singing Mediates Fast Social Bonding." *Royal Society Open Science* 2, no. 10 (2015): 150221,http://rsos.royalsocietypublishing.org/content/2/10/150221.

INDEX

NOTE: Pages numbers followed by an *n* indicate an endnote.

ABOUT THE AUTHOR

Katherine Ozment is an award-winning journalist and former senior editor at *National Geographic.* Her essays and articles have been widely published in such venues as the *New York Times, National Geographic,* and *Salon.* She lives in Chicago with her husband and three children.